GREEN WOOD STOOLS

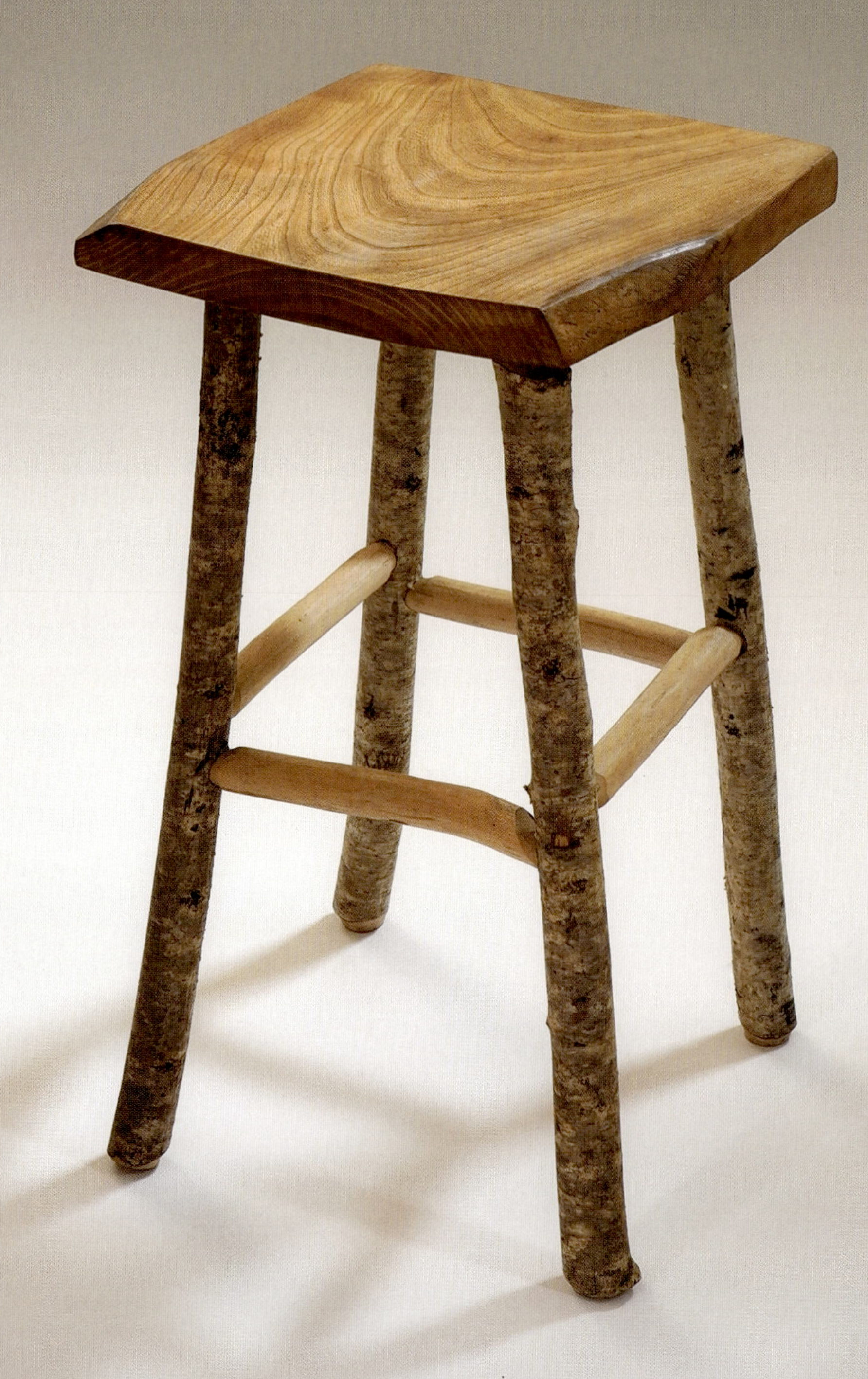

Green Wood Stools

Alison Ospina

Stobart Davies

British Library Cataloguing in Publication Data.

A catalogue record of this book is available from the British Library.

ISBN 978-0-85442-147-3

Published 2017 by
Stobart Davies Limited
Stobart House, Pontyclerc,
Penybanc Road, Ammanford,
Carmarthenshire SA18 3HP, UK
www.stobartdavies.com

Layout and design Stobart Davies Ltd

Cover photograph: Moon Gate by Michael Stephens courtesy of Ann Hurley

Photography by Ben Russell, Michael Stephens, Kate Bean, Roland Paschhoff and Emma Jervis

Illustrations by Ana Lucia Ospina

Printed by Akcent Media Ltd

Page 2: Tall kitchen stool, hazel with elm top
page 6: Woolly footstool, birch frame with upholstered sheepskin top

Contents

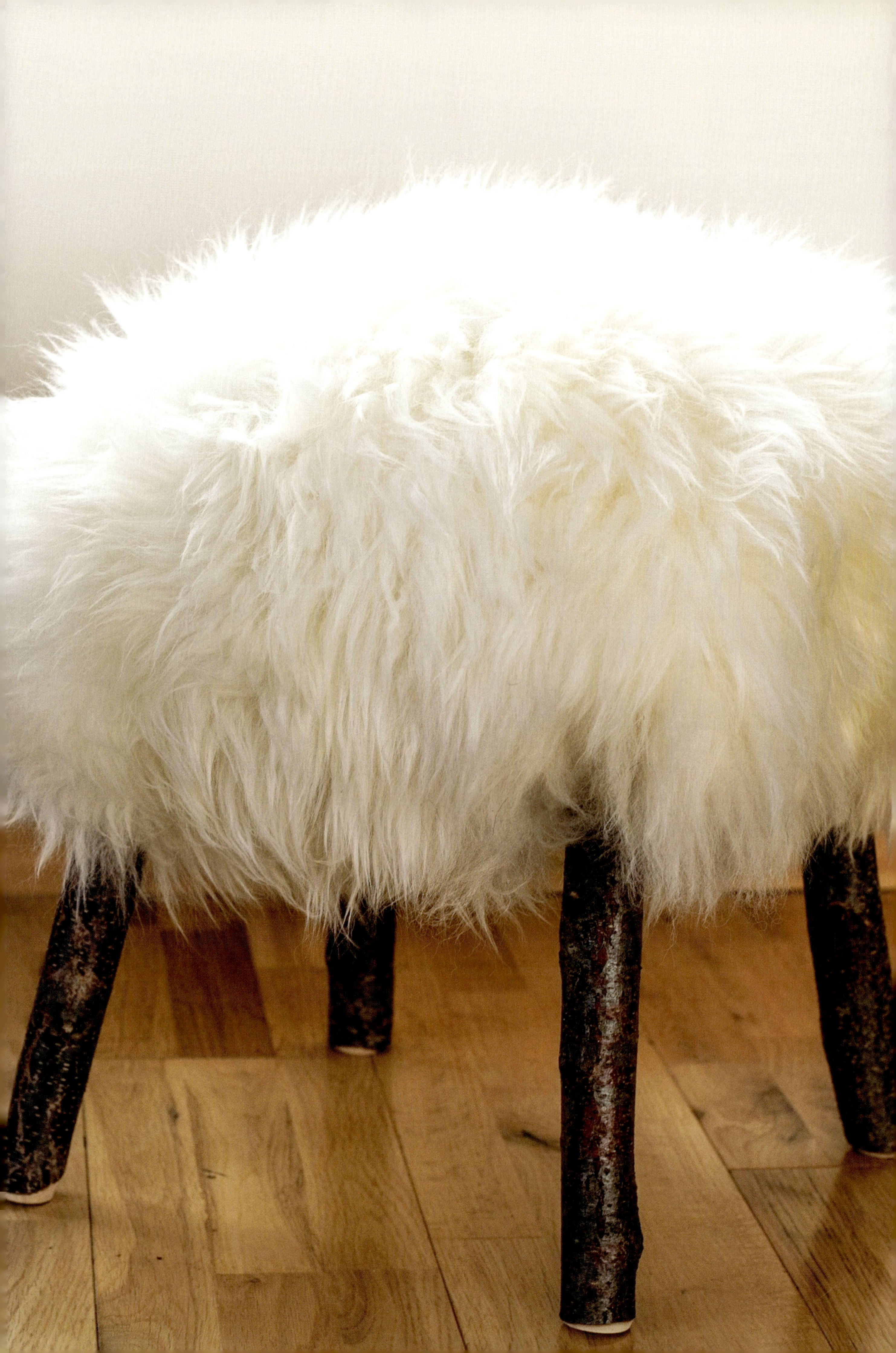

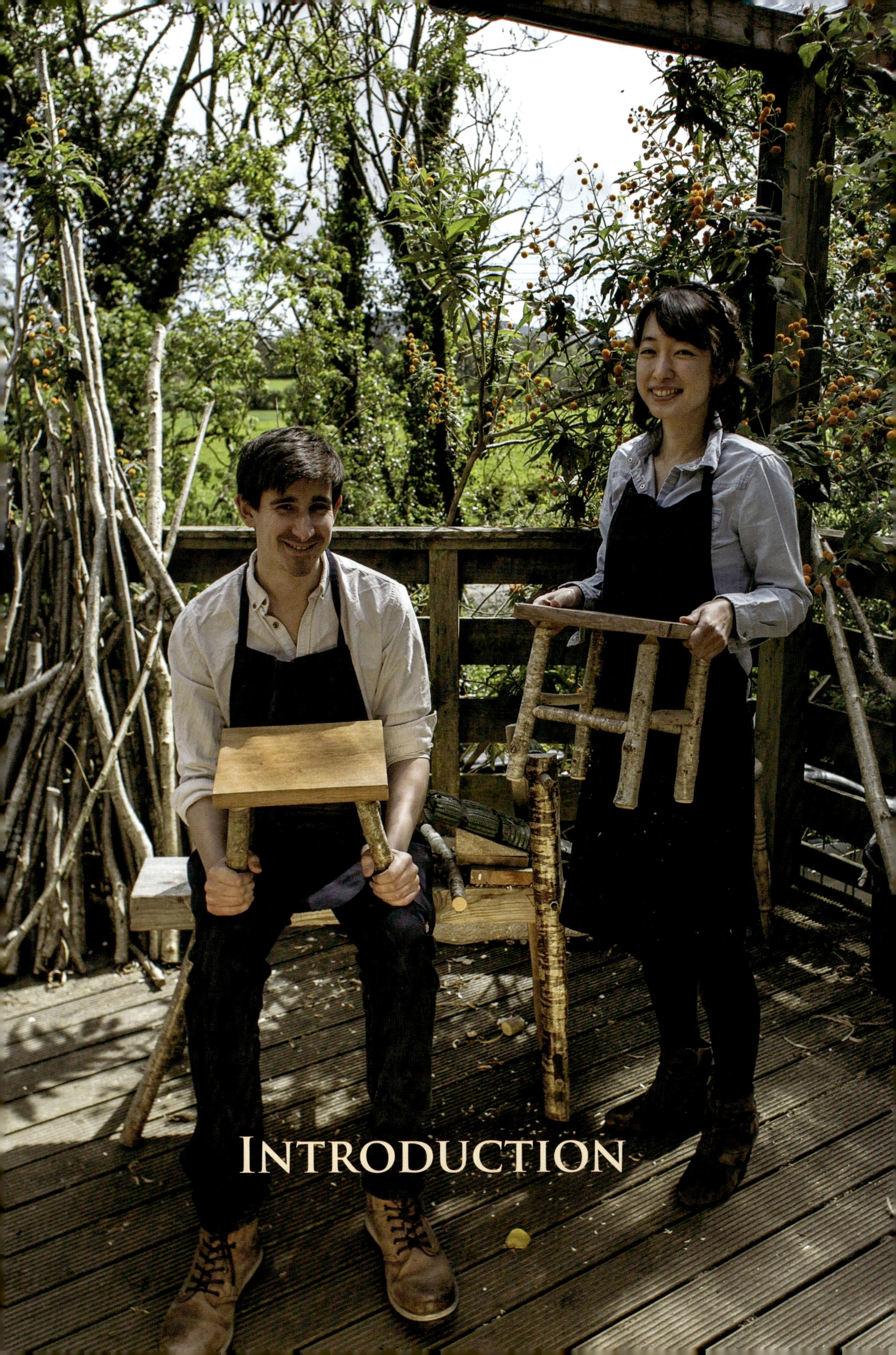

INTRODUCTION

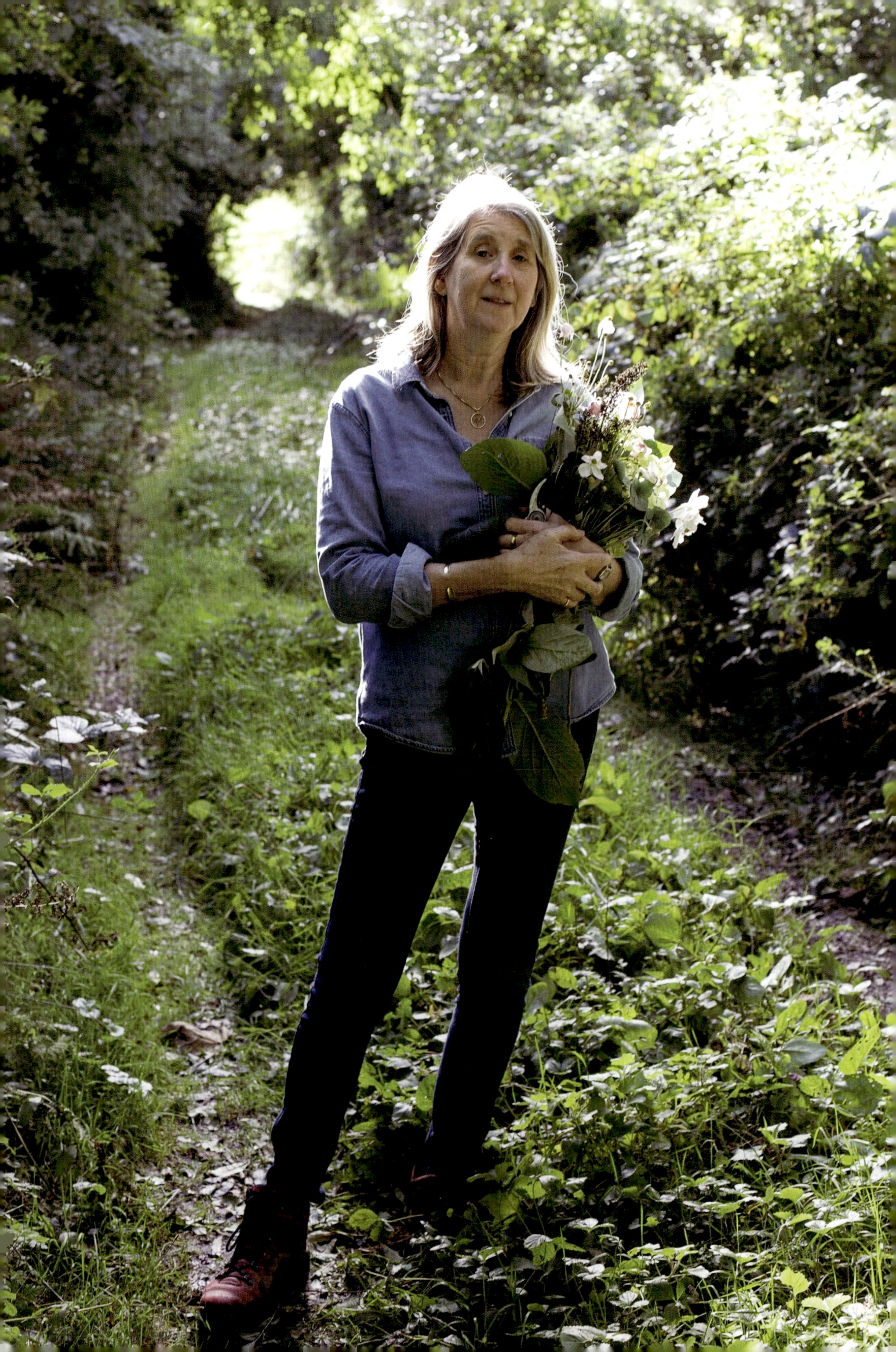

INTRODUCTION

My Journey

In 1996 the Ospina family moved from London to live in The Wooden House, near Skibbereen, West Cork.

We had been living in London since 1986 and we escaped at every opportunity. We spent weekends, holidays and days out exploring the local parks and countryside. Getting away from the city was a natural move.

Our friends called us brave but that was not how we felt. For the whole family, this was going to be a huge change and hopefully an improvement in our quality of life. We were not entirely sure at that point how we would make a living, although we had some plans.

In London, I had been employed as a part-time woodwork teacher. I worked for a few hours a week in various Adult Education centres, teaching basic woodwork skills to women's groups and to people with disabilities. When we arrived in West Cork, those kinds of opportunities were hard to find and all the woodwork teaching jobs were taken — by men.

It was not until we moved to Ireland that I considered working with unseasoned timber or making chairs. Up to that point I had only worked with planks of softwood and hardwood and had made book cases, tables, a bed, a rocking cradle and other household furniture but not chairs.

I was very fortunate that as well as a house, we now owned a large shed with electricity, suitable for use as a workshop. For Christmas 1995, my husband José, gave me a copy of Jack Hill's *Country Woodworker* which showed a wide array of porch furniture and so-called 'rustic interiors' from the United States. I was very taken with the aesthetic and particularly intrigued by the idea of using naturally-shaped branches as chair parts.

Jack Hill's book joined my other bible, *The Complete Book of Shaker Furniture*, beside the bed, both of which were pored over each night before I went to sleep. Eventually, the Shaker principles of simplicity, utility and honesty combined with the use of coppiced green wood, became the basis of my own approach.

The day I made my first green wood chair marks a turning point in my life. It could be said that for a while I became obsessed, I could not stop thinking about designing and making chairs. It was so exciting; it kept me awake at night — smiling in the dark.

From then on, every spare moment was spent in the workshop, while the children were at school, in the evenings after dinner, all week end. I was constantly making chairs. At first they were not all that good, although they had a certain primitive charm, but gradually I learned about what makes chairs robust, beautiful and comfortable.

By 1998, I was spending hours in the workshop alone and I started to miss working with other people and, more specifically, I missed teaching. I began offering courses in green wood chair making at my workshop and gradually people started to arrive on my doorstep wanting to make chairs.

The first year I had one student, the second year, four students came and it slowly built up. Teaching creates its own dynamic, students ask you questions and you have to answer them. Students get into difficulties and you have to sort them out. Students ask if it might be possible to do it a different way and you give it a go and learn something new.

I love teaching, it stops me from becoming too narrow in the way that I work and it opens my eyes to new possibilities. I love the challenges it presents. I also believe it is important to give something back and to share your experience and knowledge.

In 2002, I submitted a Green Wood Furniture Level 5 module to the Further Education and Training Council (FETAC) to teach adults in Further Education (between secondary level and third/higher level). The module was accepted and since that time I have been teaching the module in a local Adult Education College, as part of an Art, Craft and Design course.

My own green wood chairs workshop has been upgraded and expanded a few times since those early days, although I still take a maximum of three students per course. Not because of lack of space but to ensure that everyone gets plenty of one-to-one attention. I do not run so many courses at my workshop these days because I teach in college from September to May and I need the summer months to work on my own creations.

Curiously, since experiencing the set-back of breaking my knee in 2013 and not being able to teach or work properly for several months, my focus has changed. It is as if I needed an enforced 'rest' to give me a new perspective and renewed motivation. Even the bad things in life can offer opportunities and help us grow.

For almost four months I had sat with my leg raised up on a footstool, draped in sheepskin. It was a great comfort and I began designing, in my mind, a footstool that was actually upholstered in sheepskin. I had no idea how it would work and if sheepskin was usable in that way but I was determined to find out. That idea helped to speed up my recovery and get me back to the workshop.

In 2014, I designed my first woolly footstool, which led in 2015 to a commission from Google to make 18" high stools with sheepskin seats for their new office building in Dublin. Woolly footstools have since become popular and led me into new experiments using textiles and colour.

It has been a great pleasure over the last few years to introduce new styles of upholstered armchairs and rocking chairs to my collection but I keep coming back to making stools, fascinated by the proposition of variety, simplicity, strength and beauty.

page 12: Traditional square stool with upholstered seat
page 13: Hazel tripod with elm seat

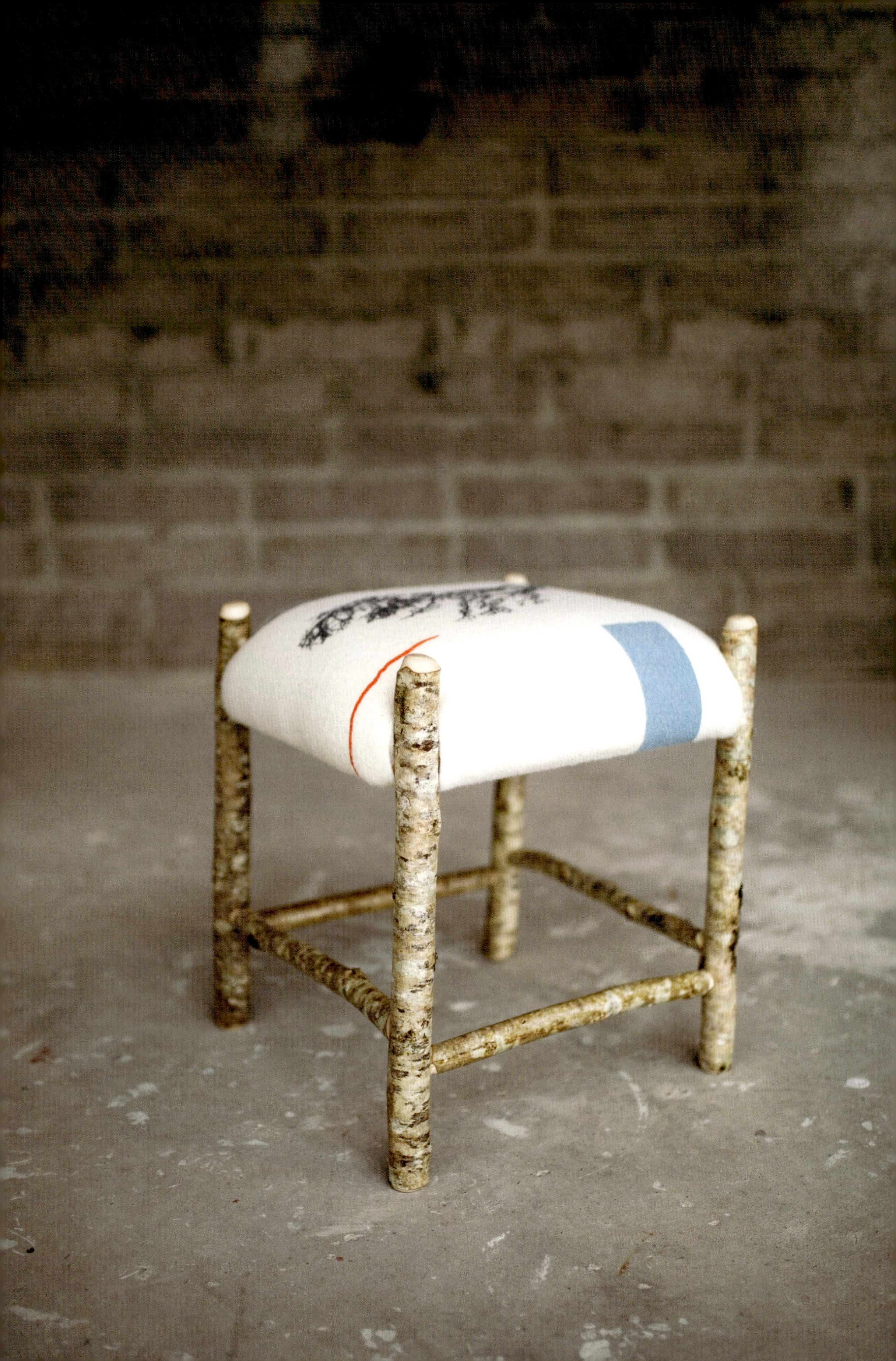

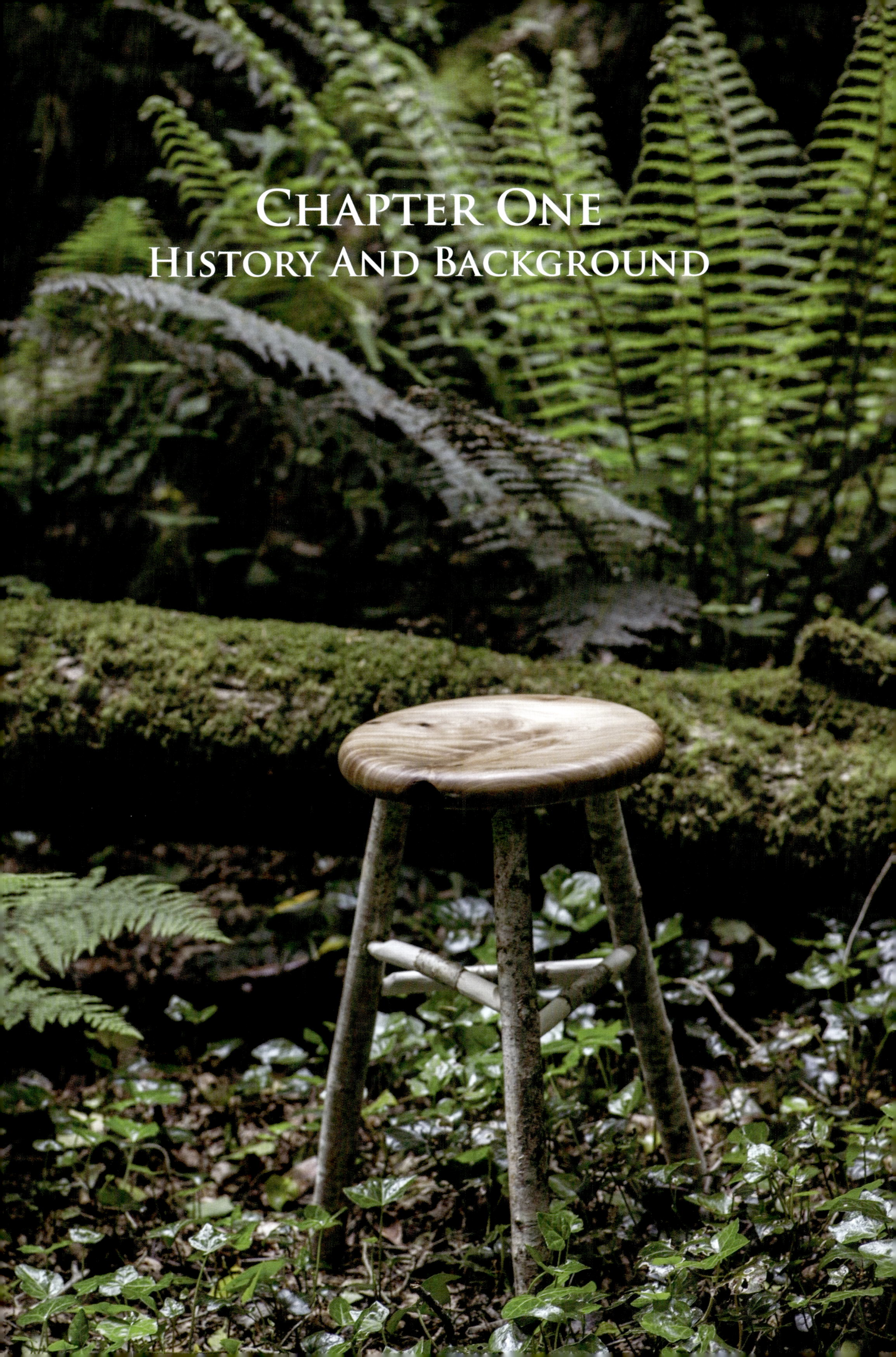
Chapter One
History And Background

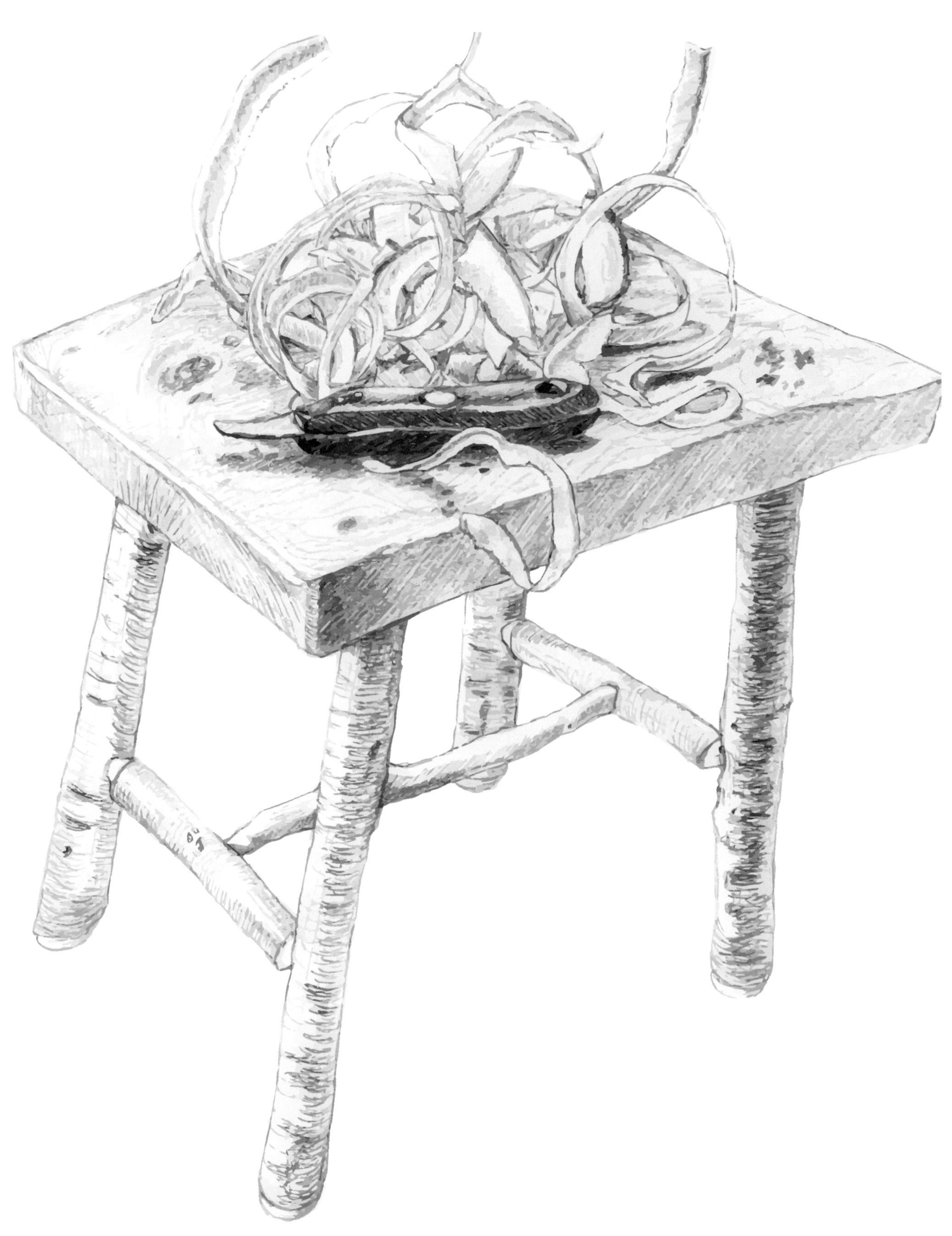

History And Background

The humble stool, in its various shapes and forms has been around for thousands of years. Stools are the simplest form of seating and in recent years I have enjoyed exploring their seemingly endless variety.

Historical background

When Howard Carter first opened the tomb of Tutankhamen in 1922, amongst the fabulous treasures found adorning the tomb's antechamber, were a number of beautifully painted, wooden stools which had survived intact for 3,500 years.

In certain African nations, where most sitting would traditionally have been on the ground, highly decorated, ceremonial stools are associated with leadership and power. For the Asante nation, with homelands in Ghana, their Golden Stool, made of wood and covered with pure gold, is the royal symbol of the Asante people, believed to house the spirit of the Asante nation.

Whether as a symbol of power or simply a tree stump or a handy rock, humans seem naturally drawn to find a place to sit which lifts them off the ground. That said, at least half the world sits on the floor cross-legged or kneeling, therefore one could presume that seating appears to have occurred chiefly in Europe.

History of stools in Ireland

Records show that stools were the most common piece of furniture to be found in Irish country homes, according to Claudia Kinmonth's book *Irish Country Furniture 1700-1950*.

Inside their homes, the inhabitants would sit around the hearth on low stools, cooking food and keeping warm. Rural dwellings often did not have chimneys; the smoke from the kitchen fire would rise to the ceiling or roof and help to keep the house warm.

During that time, timber for the production of furniture would have been grown on privately-owned land and would not, therefore, have been widely available to the country's rural poor. Scarcity of materials inevitably led to many ingenious ways of making functional seating, which required small amounts of material which could be easily repaired.

Designs were often basic and components regularly replaced, sometimes with a stick or a branch pulled from the hedgerow. Tenon joints would generally not be glued but wedged, in order to make the stool easier to dismantle, facilitating the replacement of parts, as necessary.

Three-legged stools were particularly well suited to homes with rough or uneven floors as three legs will always sit flat. Few of these very modest pieces survive today, they could well have ended up as fuel for the fire themselves!

The stool photographed below was a fairly common design which can be seen in black and white photographs of domestic interiors taken in the early 20th century. A very similar bench stool can also be seen

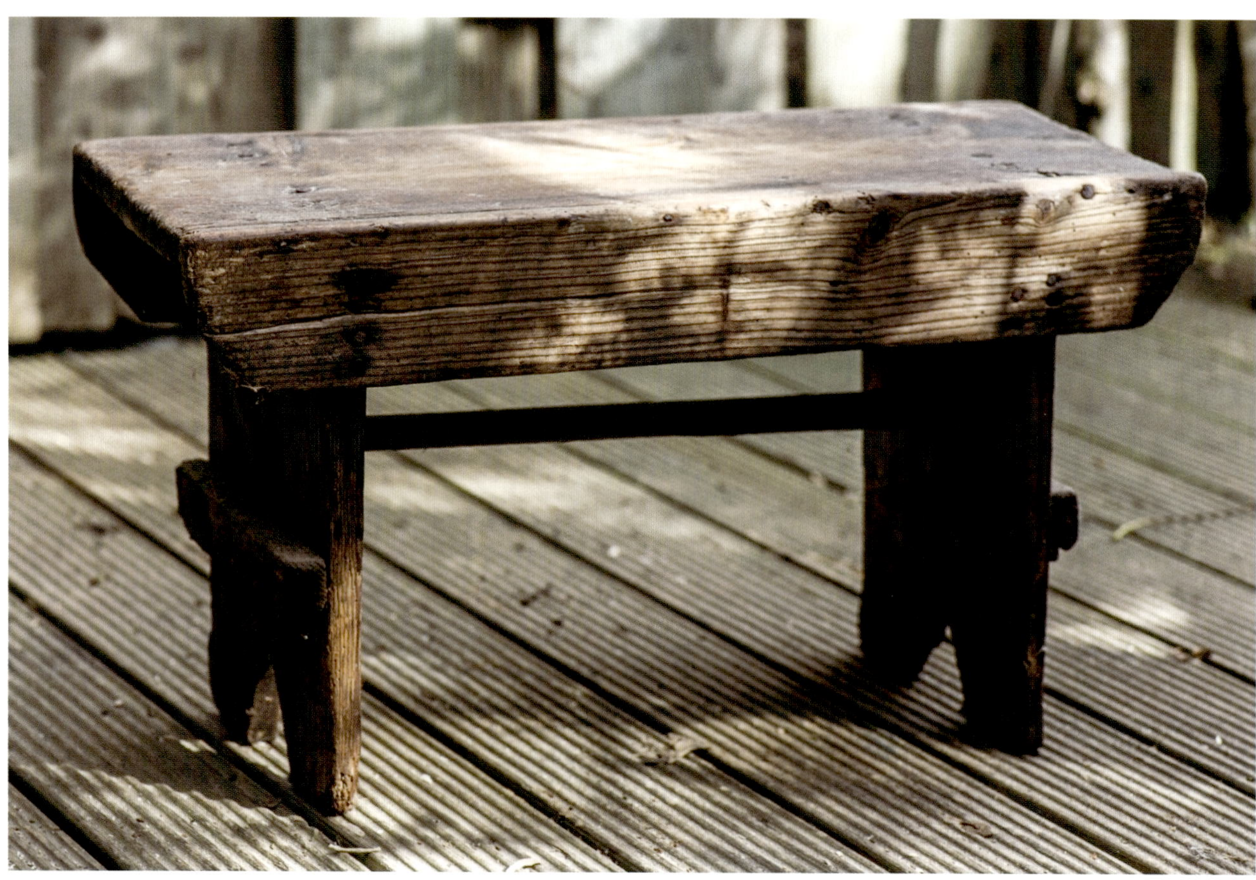

Antique Irish wooden bench stool circa early 20th Century

in J.G. Mulvany's (1766-1838) painting, *A Country Inn Kitchen*, which shows that this particular design has been in use at least since the 18th century.

The stool itself is a kind of small bench which would serve equally well as a table or a seat. A larger version could seat two or three people. The design and construction is robust and these types of stools can still be found in reasonable, functional condition today.

ARTS AND CRAFTS STOOL

This stool was carved in 1915 by M.J. McNamara (1869-1929) for his three-year-old daughter Joan. McNamara lived in Cork where he was head of the school of sculpture at the Crawford School of Art. Among his distinguished students were the two most significant sculptors to come from Cork during the first half of the twentieth century: Joseph Higgins and Seamus Murphy. McNamara had himself been a brilliant student at the Crawford and subsequently studied in London at the Royal College of Art where he received the award of Senior National Scholar. At the RCA he studied under the French sculptor Édouard Lantéri and was assistant to the Arts and Crafts pioneer (and William Morris collaborator) Walter Crane. McNamara subsequently studied in Paris with sculptor Clovis Delacour. Like Jack B. Yeats, Sarah Purser and William Orpen, he was a member of the Guild of Irish Art Workers and trained a generation of Arts and Crafts students in wood and stone carving, modelling and sculpture. He also led teams from the Crawford in the Arts and Crafts

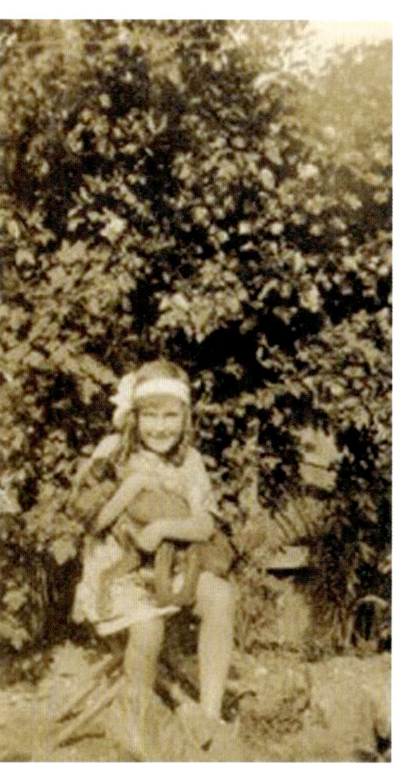

Joan McNamara c. 1915

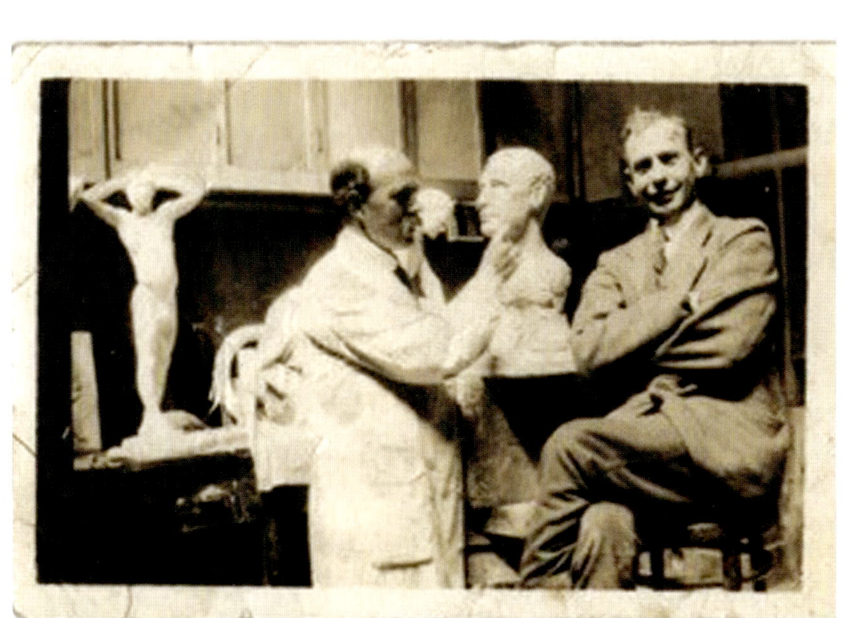

M.J. McNamara working from life in the modelling room of the Crawford School of Art, c. 1920.

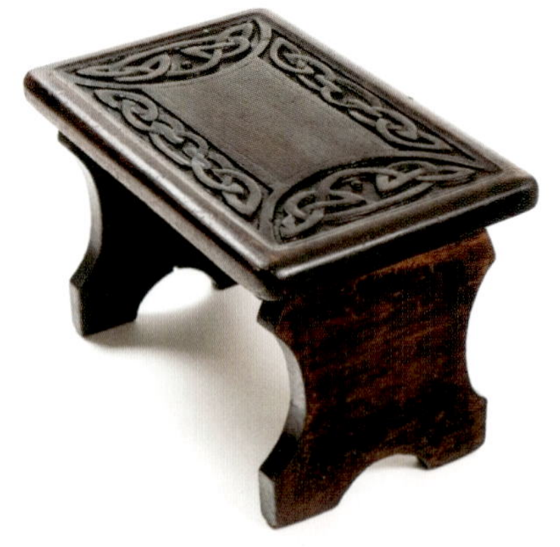

BRIAN LALOR

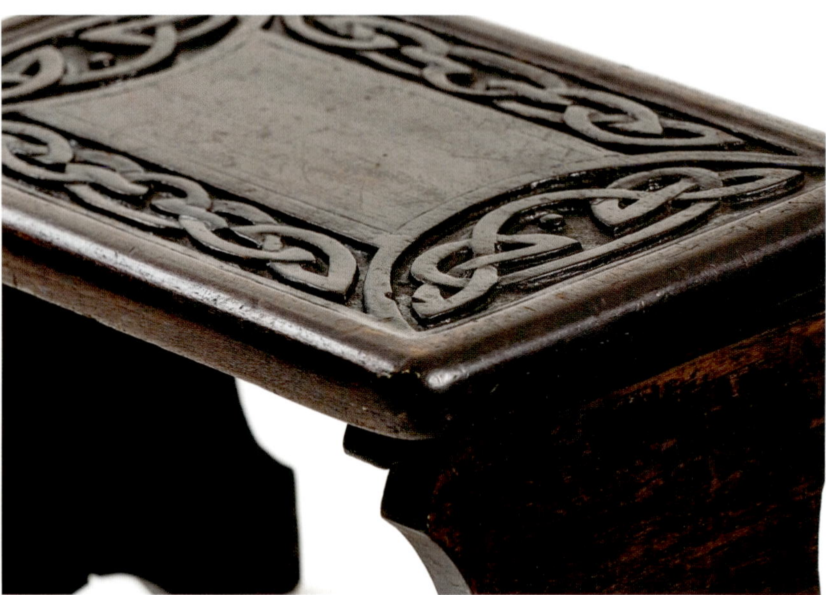

left and above: Arts and Crafts stool

PRESENT DAY

In our house we have at least one stool in each room. They are without doubt, the handiest pieces of furniture we own as they are versatile, useful and robust. Depending on their shape or size, they are used as laptop tables, lamp stands, for sitting on to light the stove (better than kneeling), a child's seat or table, as a footstool or just a convenient place for a cup of tea or the remote controls. The list is endless!

WHY USE GREEN WOOD?

Mass-produced furniture is always predictable and symmetrical and is often poorly made. Your choices can be limited, you can only buy what is on offer.

By comparison, green wood furniture is full of surprises as every piece is unique and best of all, you can make it yourself.

If you buy a stool, you might experience a moment's pleasure but if you make one, you will feel pride and satisfaction every time you use it!

I have been working with coppiced hazel wood since 1996 and although I occasionally use sweet chestnut, silver birch, alder and rowan, hazel is usually my first choice. Likewise, I choose elm where possible, for seats and stool tops.

It is hard to imagine a natural material better suited to chair making, than hazel. It grows exactly into the right shapes for stool and chair components, as if nature intended it for that purpose.

The stems shoot up tall and straight with very few side shoots until the smaller branches and twigs spread out at the top. The bark is beautiful, often with patches of green or pink lichen, depending on the growing conditions. Looked at closely, some hazel bark has really detailed patterning and coloration while other hazel is a uniform, silvery-grey colour, both very attractive in their own way.

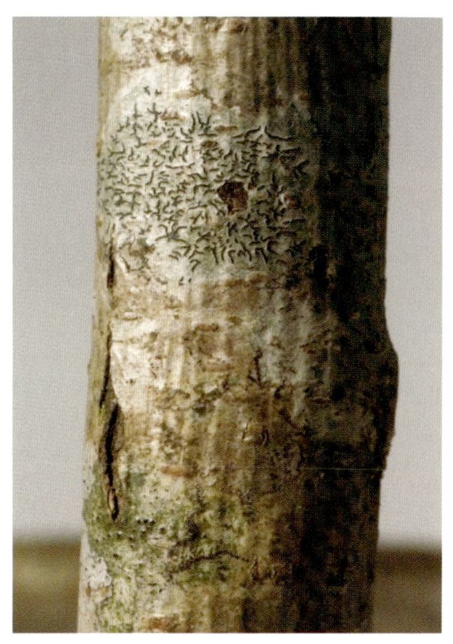
Detail of hazel bark

I enjoy the contrast of colour and texture in pieces that include both stripped and polished surfaces and other components with the bark left on. The blend of finishes combining outdoor roughness with a more sophisticated, polished, appearance brings into the home a quality not just of wood but of the forest itself.

Living wood is a pleasure to work with and words cannot express the satisfaction felt in making and using your own green wood stools and chairs.

WHY A BOOK ABOUT STOOLS?

It might never have occurred to me to write a book about making green wood stools, if my life had not changed dramatically when, on 23 December 2013, I fell and broke my knee.

Up until then, although I had designed and made many stools, I had no real interest in them. I considered them less important, simple projects. My energy and imagination were focused exclusively on making chairs. I even found my own stool designs somewhat unappealing, mainly because they lacked the elegance and energy of chairs.

By April 2014, I was starting to get back on my feet but when I eventually got into my workshop I discovered that I could not stand for long and found it impossible to kneel down. I started looking for quicker, simpler projects to make, which could be assembled on the bench top.

As I gazed around the workshop wondering what to make, my eye was caught by an old kitchen stool with turned legs, which has stood in the corner for many years. Just as an experiment I decided to recreate the same stool, using hazel wood for the legs and rungs.

As I worked on this project I started wondering exactly why the stools I usually made looked a bit awkward and unattractive. I turned it over and over in my mind, then suddenly in a flash of inspiration, I understood that the key to grace and elegance is the splay!

A square, straight-legged stool or small table is functional but inelegant and potentially unstable. A simple plank with four splaying legs becomes elegant, characterful and stable.

The next discovery was that in order to splay the legs, there is no need to drill the holes in the seat plank at carefully measured angles. Splaying the legs can be achieved by drilling into the plank at 90 degrees as usual and simply putting a longer rung in half-way down the leg or indeed allowing the glue to dry with the legs wedged apart at slight angles with a piece of scrap wood. This method is ideal for use with green wood because it has strength and flexibility.

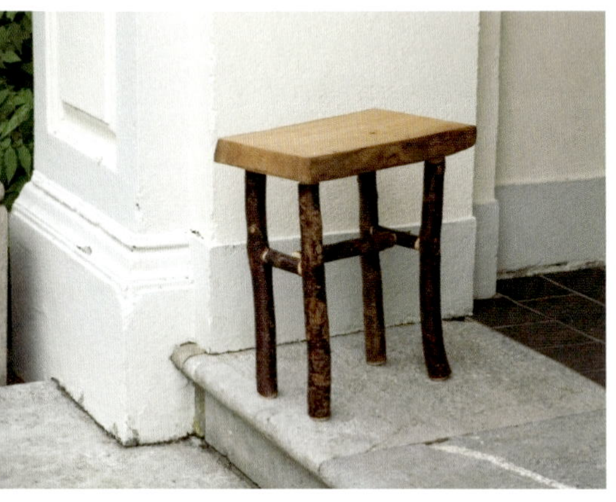

above: Straight leg 'old' style Green Wood stool birch with elm top
right: Splayed leg 'new' style Green Wood stool birch stool with elm top

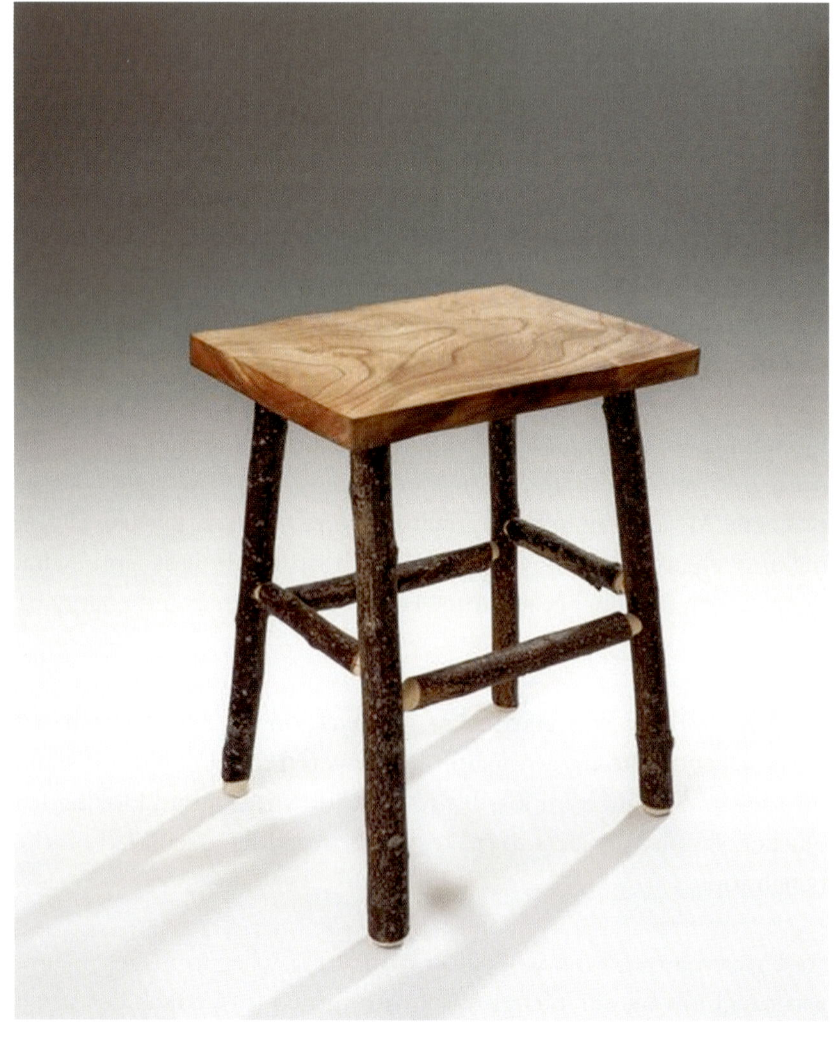

I was so excited by my discovery that I forgot all about chairs for a while and single-mindedly focused on designing and making stools in all shapes and sizes. Anything was possible — I was limited only by my materials, skill and imagination.

At this point I introduced new materials to add colour and texture which totally transformed the pieces. I began making stools upholstered in sheepskin, some with a single rung at the top, others with additional rungs half-way down. I made tall stools, low stools, three-legged stools, babies' stools, footstools, upholstered stools and ottomans.

I also began to experiment with different woods. The bark of the sweet chestnut has distinct and dramatic colouration, as does silver birch and common birch. The branches of different tree species grow in a variety of configurations, which in turn impacts on the appearance of the furniture made from it. A stool or chair made from hazel will look quite different from one made using ash or silver birch.

Each stool has a different appearance and character, not only because every stick is a slightly different shape but also because the structure really lends itself to playful experimentation. I strip the bark off some and polish or paint them. I remove spots of bark which give them a curious, animal pelt appearance. I sometimes use legs that kick out or twist at odd angles, the designs to a large extent are dictated by the materials. I have to make the stool I have the sticks for.

Even though these are simple structures with few components, they can be quite challenging to make because the wood is never symmetrical and the structure is never square. This means that my green wood joinery skills are sometimes called into question. But don't let that put you off. Start with the straightest sticks you can find and once you have made one stool successfully, I guarantee you will soon move onto your next stool project.

next page: Detail Pat Connor painted stool

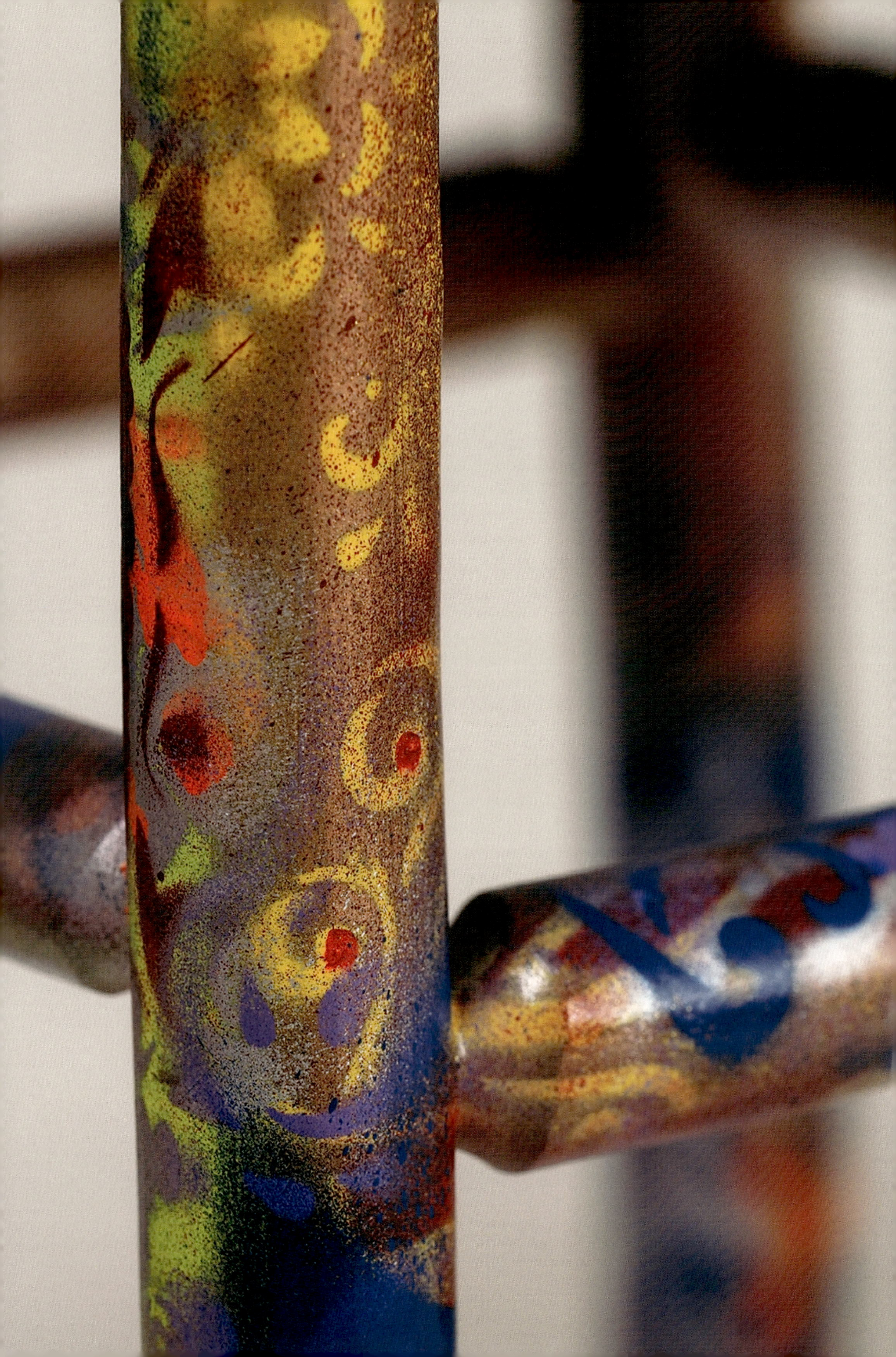

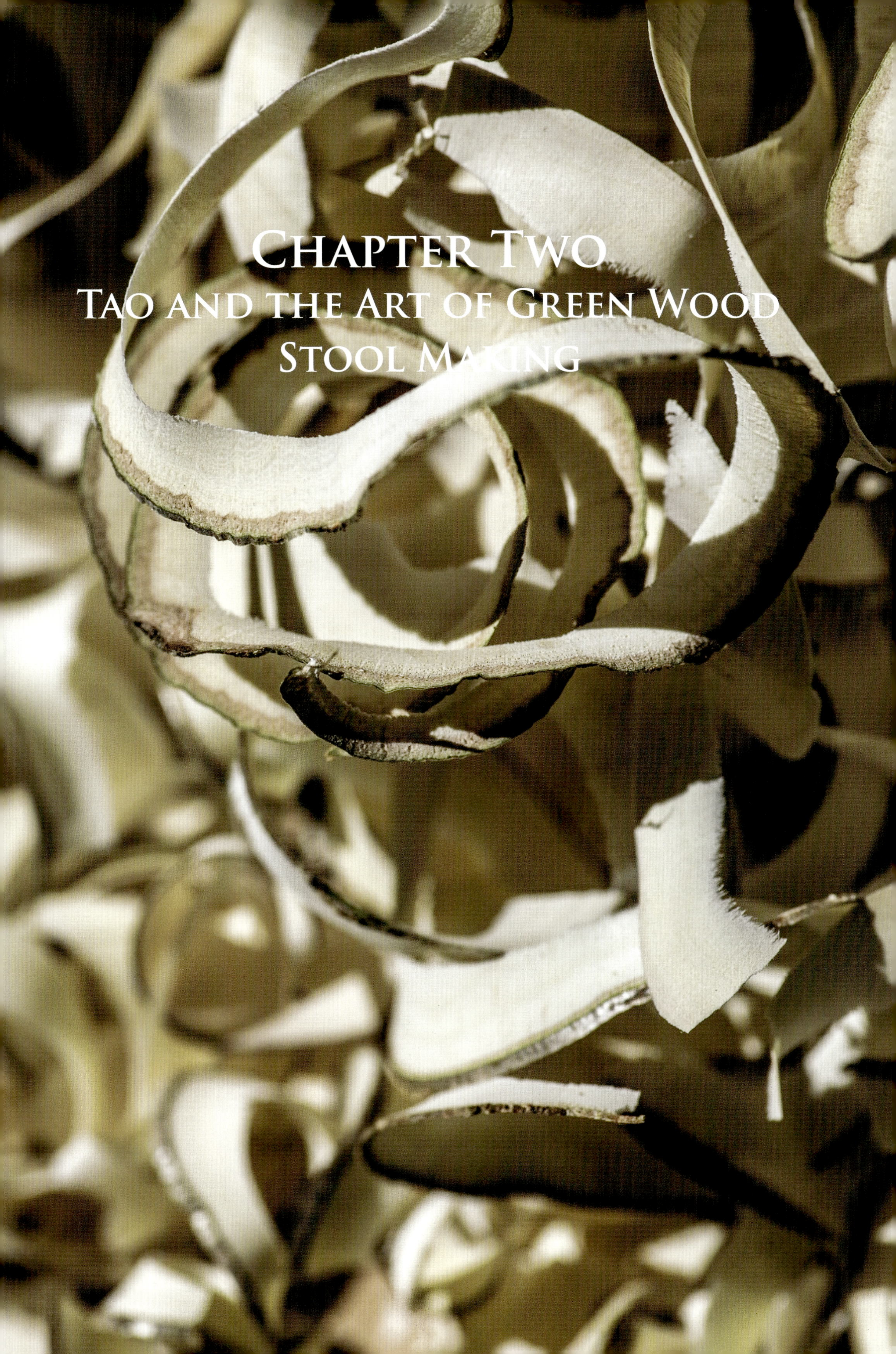

Chapter Two
Tao and the Art of Green Wood Stool Making

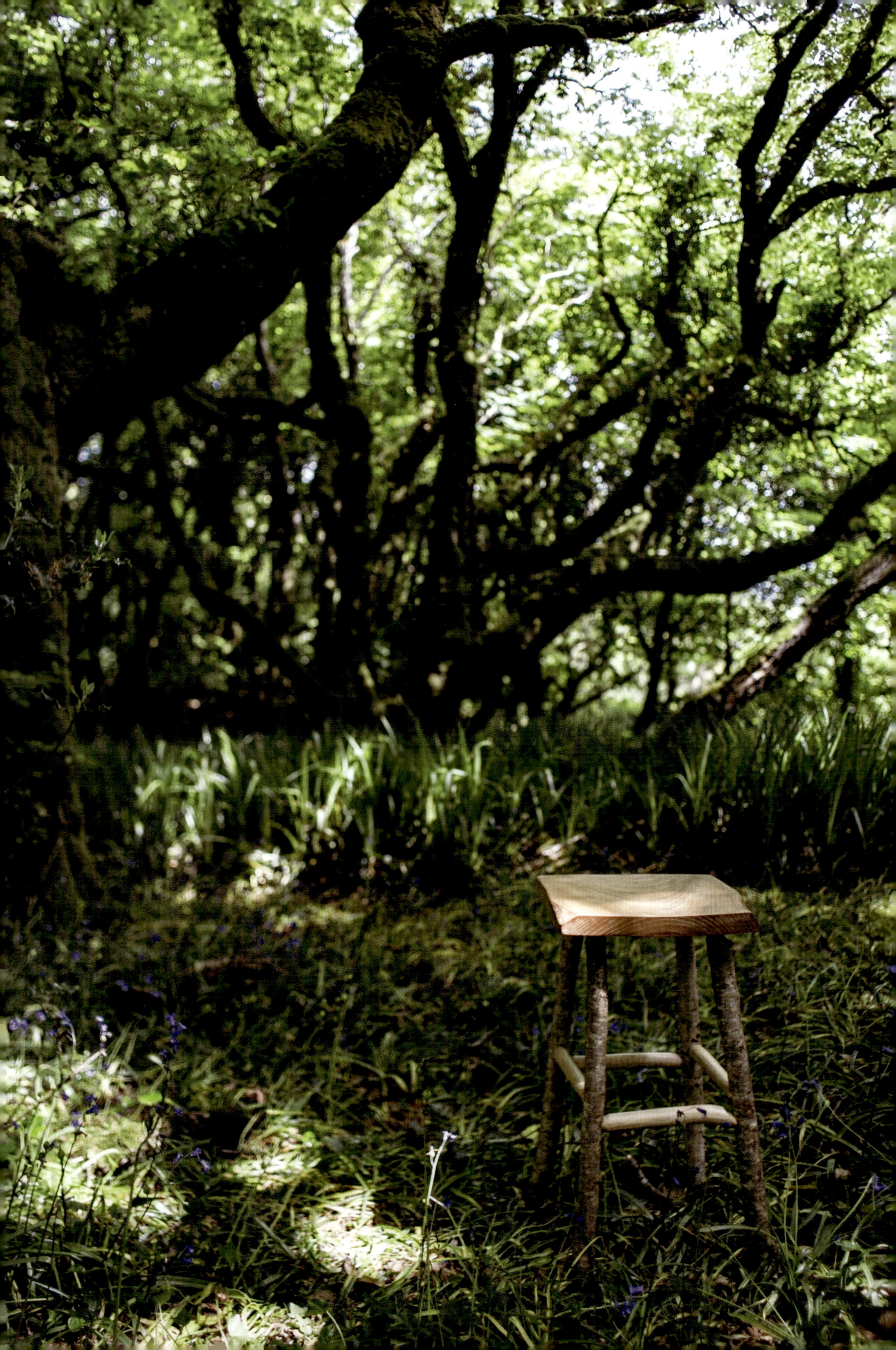

Tao and the Art of Green Wood Stool Making

A student of mine once said, 'There is something therapeutic in making chairs that I can't quite explain. All I can say is that it made me immensely proud and happy!'

Making chairs not only causes people to feel proud and happy but creativity is contagious — when one person makes something beautiful, others are inspired to have a go.

In my first book, *Green Wood Chairs — Chairs and Chairmakers of Ireland*, I touched upon the idea that working with living wood is both complementary and opposite to modern carpentry/joinery approaches. This idea is most effectively described through Tao philosophy:

In Chinese philosophy, all life systems need a balance. This is known as Tao energy or the Way. Tao runs through everything: culture, philosophy, political systems and living organisms. Reality is a process of continuous flow and change; the two poles that set the limits for these cycles of change are **Yin and Yang**. *We need a balance of both to be healthy, successful, effective, creative and loving.* **Yang** *(associated with the masculine) is rational, competitive, analytic, aggressive and intellectual. In woodwork terms this is square, hard-edged, accurate measurements, predictable outcomes and so on.* **Yin** *(associated with the feminine) is responsive, cooperative, intuitive and synthesising. In woodwork terms, this is soft-edged, free flowing, working with the grain, measuring by eye, allowing materials to dictate.*

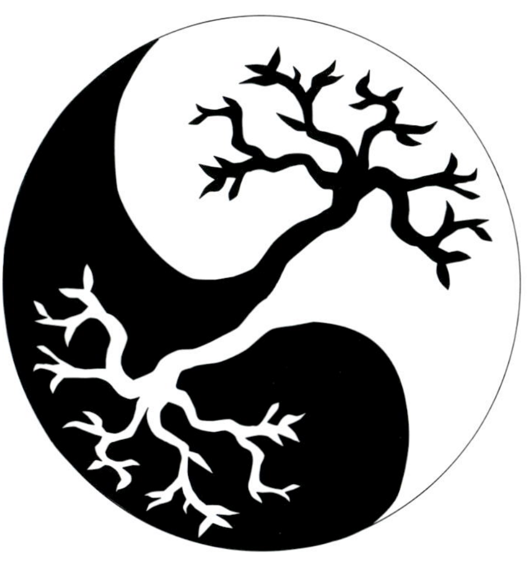

We all have elements of **Ying and Yang** *and in Western thinking they have been referred to as the rational and the intuitive and are complementary functions of the mind.* **Green wood work is the Yin to the Yang of joinery, carpentry and cabinet making**.

Tao principles and energy continue to inform my understanding of the work I do.

We draw on hidden depths within ourselves when working with natural materials. I observe the smiles and hear the comments of students experiencing, for the first time, not only the intuitive understanding we can access when working with green wood, but also the profound sense of fulfilment derived from making simple, outstandingly beautiful, chairs and stools.

Natural materials arouse our senses and inspire creativity, perhaps it is the feel, the smell, the beauty of the organic, primary substance. Being creative in general excites and stimulates but I feel there is an extra dimension to working with green wood. Conceivably it is the tensions, the resistance and the energy within the green wood that differentiates it from other materials. In a sense, the material is energetically communicating with the maker. I push one way and it pushes back. The tension within the structure makes it strong.

It is not unusual for me to 'persuade' components into position, my chairs and stools do not remotely slot together like flat-pack furniture, there is always a contest, sometimes a battle. We usually agree in the end, especially if I pay attention and listen to the wood because there are things it will not do.

Out of necessity, the green wood approach is different from traditional carpentry. It begins with the design which is materials-led. A green woodworker must make the stool he/she has the sticks for. The materials as well as the maker's skills and imagination, dictate what can be made. This can be challenging at times but 'necessity is the mother of invention' and exciting new projects can grow from an uninspiring pile of leftover sticks.

My approach to working with green wood has more similarities to cookery than carpentry — my instructions are like recipes. Good cooks never stick to recipes, they play around with the ingredients and make something that is to their own taste.

I hope to inspire you to keep changing and improving my recipes, to regard them as guidelines. Naturally I make things that I like and you must make things that you like — our concepts of beauty will never be the same.

Release yourself from the burden of following my instructions to the letter and go with the flow, always looking out for opportunities to change direction and adapt your designs. By developing your intuitive powers through practice, you will feel free to innovate.

Anyone can learn to make green wood stools. The basic techniques are fairly straightforward and do not require a huge amount of skill. Of course, you will make progress over time. As you repeat the processes again and again, you will develop a higher level of accuracy and dexterity. Your subconscious abilities to measure, design and construct will also increase with practice, as you learn to have confidence in your gut instincts.

As you improve, you will pay ever more attention to detail and enjoy each part of the process without always thinking of the result. Your previous piece will never look as good as the new one you are working on. When you reach a certain level of skill, you will start to analyse and criticise your own work and understand why some pieces look better than others.

I find it is useful to bring finished pieces into the house and live with them for a while. By observing them from different heights and angles, you will notice irregularities and imperfections and learn to grasp what looks good and what does not and why you have your favourites (although it is somewhat of a mystery).

I spent several years grappling with different woodwork techniques, slowly building the confidence, skill and intuition I have in the workshop today. I made so many chairs which had just 'one thing' wrong with them: the seat was too narrow, the stretchers too high or the arms too low and so on. It was painful at the time but every time I made a mistake I learnt something new.

Most woodwork books with projects and instructions simply teach you the required techniques, to replicate the given designs. I am teaching a new approach.

I will, of course, show and describe the techniques but I am aiming higher — I hope to release your inner chairmaker!

The following recipes evolved gradually over two years. Some were designed in response to the shape of a particular stick or plank, others are based on traditional designs and styles and still more were conceived by favourable circumstances and lucky breaks.

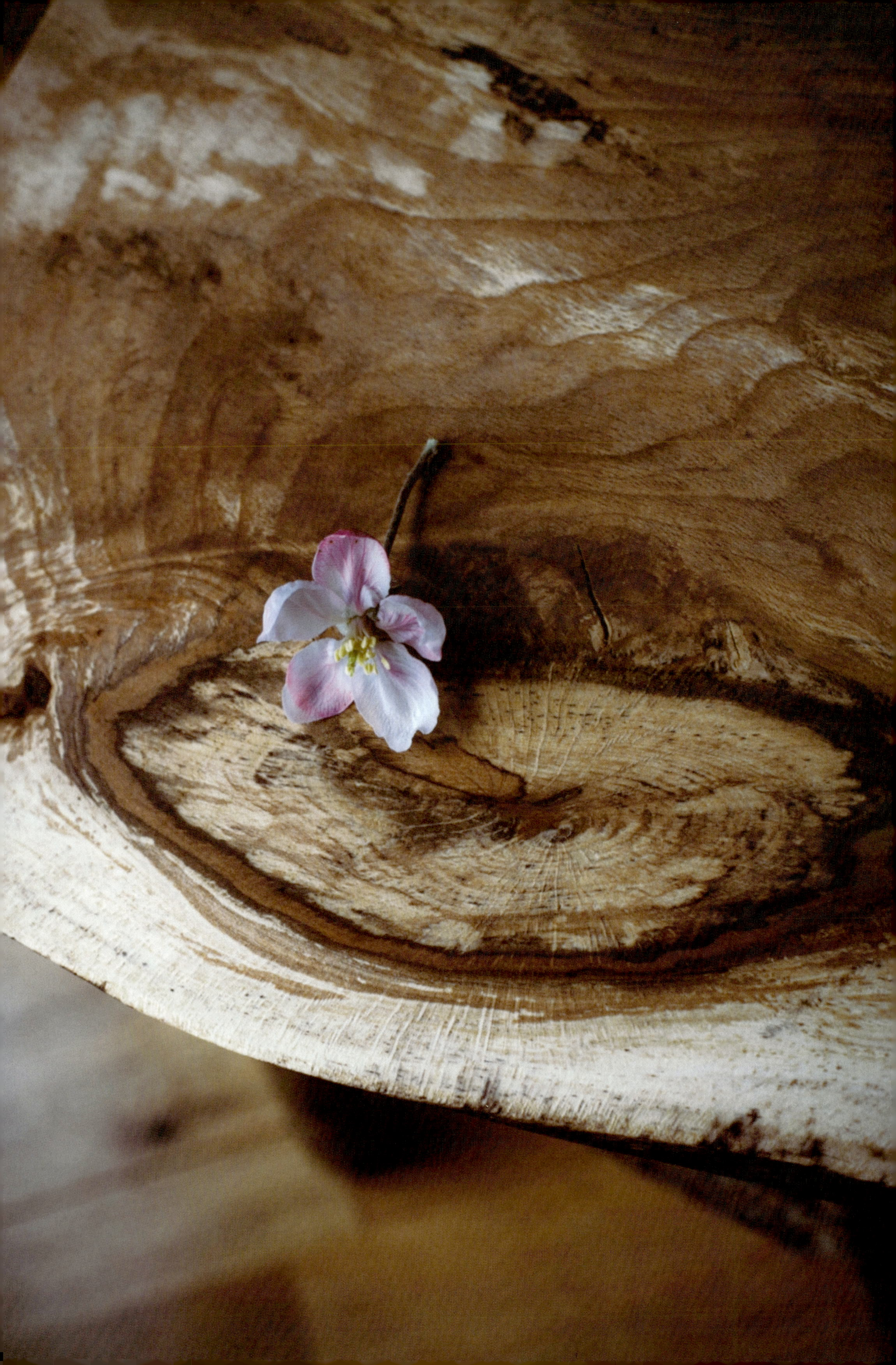

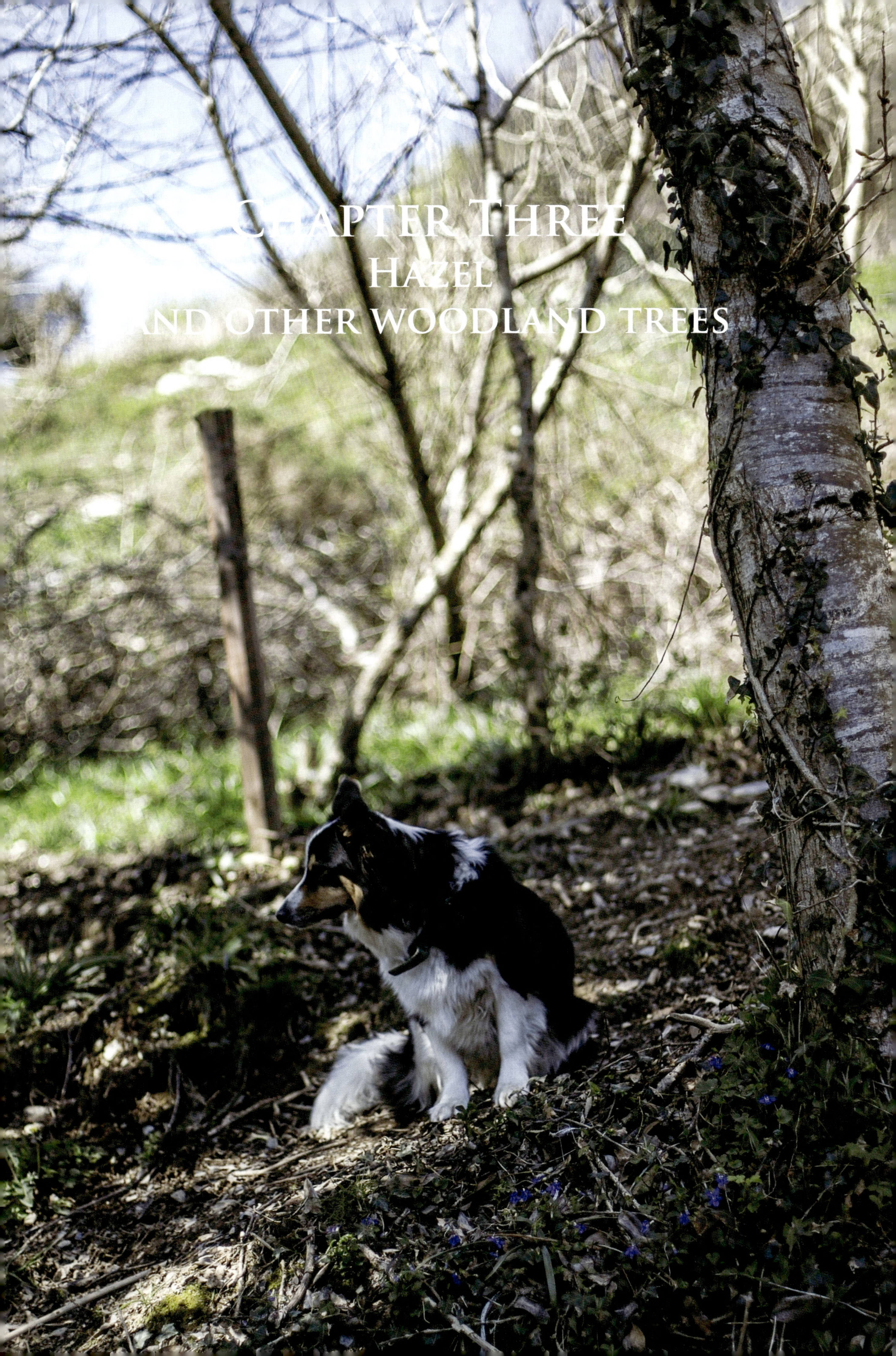

Chapter Three
Hazel
and other woodland trees

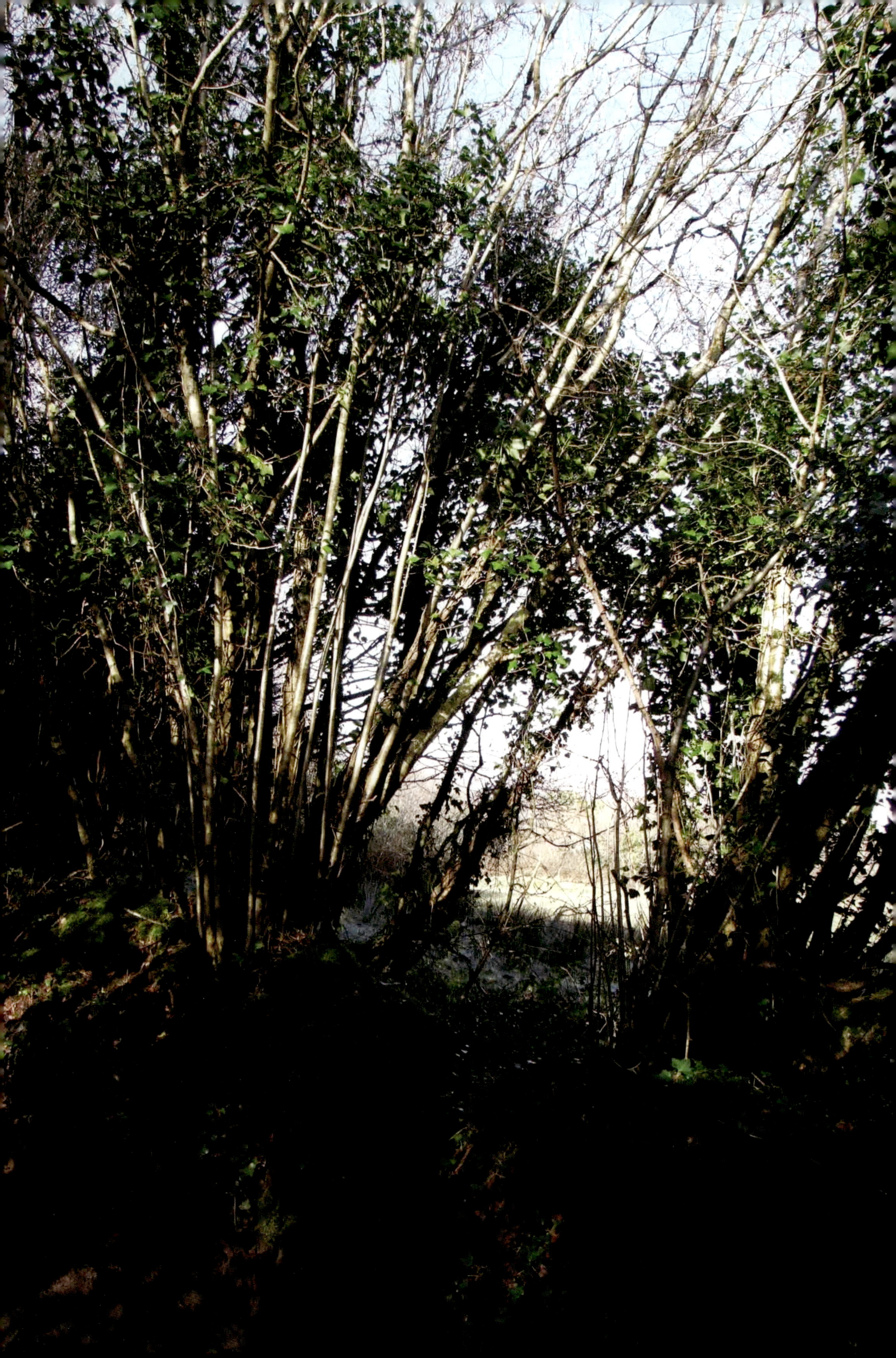

HAZEL
AND OTHER WOODLAND TREES

Wood is one of the most important natural materials known to man. It has strength, beauty, flexibility and versatility. No man-made material even comes close to being as useful or as beautiful. I feel a kinship with hazel in particular, as I have linked myself closely with the species through 20 years of chair and stool making and have grown familiar with its strength and energy. It is a strikingly attractive tree, with multi-coloured varieties of bark. The bark strips easily and the wood itself, when worked green, is yielding and aromatic.

Coppicing is a sustainable way to manage woodland. It has been practised for thousands of years, producing material for fences, tool handles, thatching spars, sheep hurdles, bean rods, hut building, creating tracks, hazelnuts to eat and possibly more uses. Hazel is also the material of choice for water divining and for a wizard's staff.

Coppicing requires a minimum area of woodland measuring roughly seven acres. Each year one acre is cut and by the time the next six acres have been cut, the first acre is ready for cutting again. The wood is grown as a crop. The whole tree is cut to a height of just 6 inches (150 mm) when the sap is low and the tree is dormant (between November and March). During the following growing season, stems will grow up to a height of approximately 5–6 feet (1.5–1.8 m). The trees recover very quickly and are invigorated by the extreme pruning. Woodland trees managed in this way have been known to live for many hundreds of years.

HAZEL is the finest coppice wood. Often self-seeded, it thrives beside streams, rivers and ponds, preferring to stand on well-drained soil, with its roots in the water. Hazel is one of the first trees in spring to come into leaf and soon after, the pollen-laden catkins appear. Pollination is complete relatively early in the year.

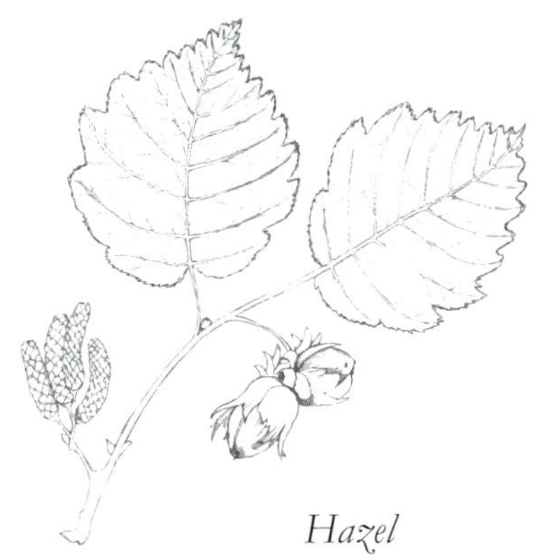

Hazel

left: Hazel coppice

In Celtic times, the hazel was the tree of knowledge and in Ireland legends abound concerning the wisdom and power associated with hazel trees. Legend has it that nine sacred hazel trees grew around Connla's Well where the Salmon of Wisdom received his gift from the Guardians of the Well. Each hazel tree dropped a sacred nut into the well, the salmon ate them and became imbued with worldly wisdom.

It is clear that hazel has played an important part in rural life for millennia. However, it is not only the products of the woodland that are the reward. By managing woodland in this way, there is no need for replanting and each coppice can retain its genetic individuality (which might help to explain why the bark differs in colouration from one woodland to another). Coppicing also helps to maintain biodiversity, creates habitats for wild life and ensures peaceful places for a gentle stroll, enhanced by primroses, bluebells and other wild flowers.

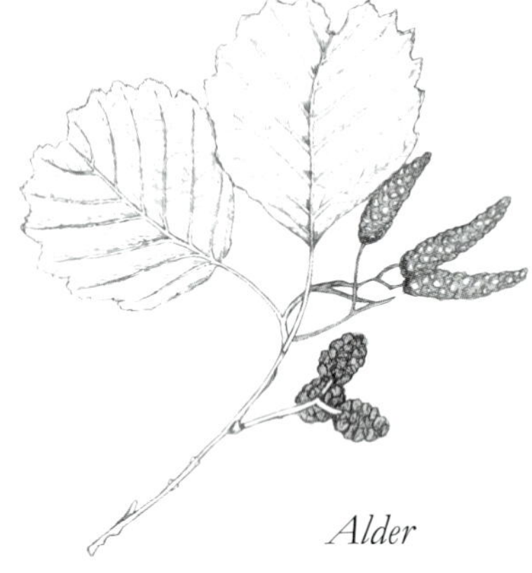

Alder

ALDER is related to the birch and hazel; it can often be found growing alongside hazel on river banks and even in boggy ground. It has very attractive bark, pale grey in colour, sometimes with lighter greenish patches. It is a water-loving tree and is often seen overhanging a stream or river, creating shade for fish and plants.

It is recognisable by its round leaves and because it often shows all four stages of production on the branch at one time: last year's cones, this spring's leaf buds and the male and female catkins. It is the only broadleaf tree to produce cones which often stay on the branch long after fruiting in the autumn.

If the bark is damaged, the sap appears with a reddish colour and in ancient times it was thought to bleed. According to Irish legend, the first man was created from alder which was considered a magical tree through which access was gained to the faerie kingdom. Alder was also highly prized for producing hot-burning charcoal, necessary for the alchemy of metal working and the manufacture of weapons.

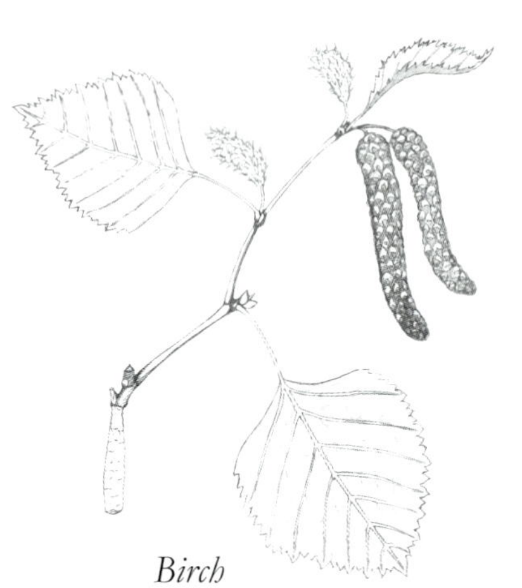

Birch

BIRCH is a very beautiful, delicate tree which grows well in poor soil and can often been seen at the forest's edge along with alder. It has fine bushy twigs which have traditionally been used for making besom brooms. However, the larger branches and stems are eminently suitable for stool and chair making.

There are thought to be about 60 different species of birch worldwide. Silver birch is a very hardy tree and can survive in the coldest reaches of Northern Europe and Scandinavia. The common birch can found having seeded itself among hazel and other woodland trees. It can be coppiced and produces stems with a dramatic reddish/brown bark and strong, flexible, white wood.

Birch, along with hazel, is one of the first trees to leaf in spring and produces pendulous catkins which pollinate the flowers. The female catkin contains hundreds of seeds which are scattered by the wind, it is well known for prolific self-seeding. In ancient times, it was known as the tree of inception and purification and was used in Beltaine celebrations to light the ritual bonfires.

ROWAN is a small tree often called mountain ash because it likes to grow at high altitudes and its leaves are very similar to common ash leaves. Rowan blossoms in May, with scented white flowers that give way to small green berries which hang in clusters from the branches. Our attention is inevitably drawn to the rowan in early autumn when the clusters of berries turn a dramatic bright red, contrasting with the dark green leaves creating a bold splash of colour in the landscape. You will rarely find an entire woodland of rowan but may see it lining city streets or growing amongst other trees, creating diversity often in poor soil and growing conditions.

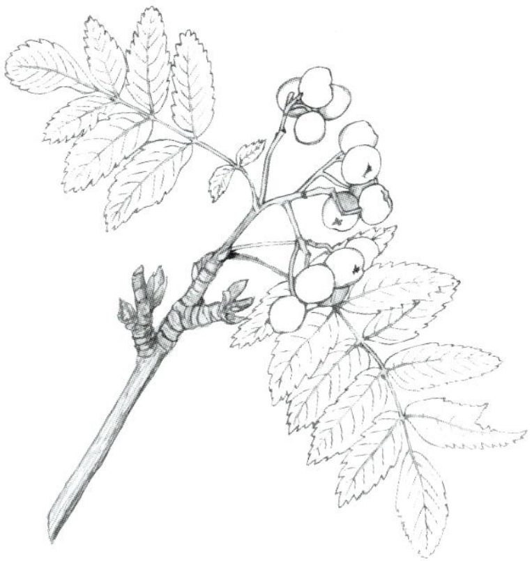

Rowan

The bark of the rowan is usually grey with very clear horizontal markings. Unlike hazel bark, when rowan dries, the bark becomes slightly gnarled, although it is not unattractive. If the bark is stripped off, the revealed wood beneath has a visible grain to it, slightly darker than hazel or birch, light brown rather than white.

Rowan is considered to have a magical protective influence and was often planted around stone circles and homesteads as a guardian tree. In ancient times, it was used by farmers in spring to deck their cattle sheds, thereby keeping stock and milk safe from evil spirits. In Ireland, Brigid was strongly associated with the rowan tree especially in her role as protector of country folk and their livestock. Brigid was the goddess of spring, invoked for her influence over spinning and weaving where rowan wood was traditionally used in the making of spindles and spinning wheels. She was later incorporated into Christian mythology and to this day is worshipped as Saint Brigid. In many Irish schools and families the first day of spring (1st February) is still celebrated with a rush woven into a St Brigid's cross.

Ancient wisdom guided so many practices; people had an awareness of the energy of the trees that surrounded them which were not simply differentiated by their leaves and fruit. We are no longer guided by that wisdom. Trees are seen as a resource and not as 'beings' which share our planet and can facilitate or influence our lives. If we open ourselves to their energy, we can rediscover our connection through trees to the vast life force, past and present that surrounds us.

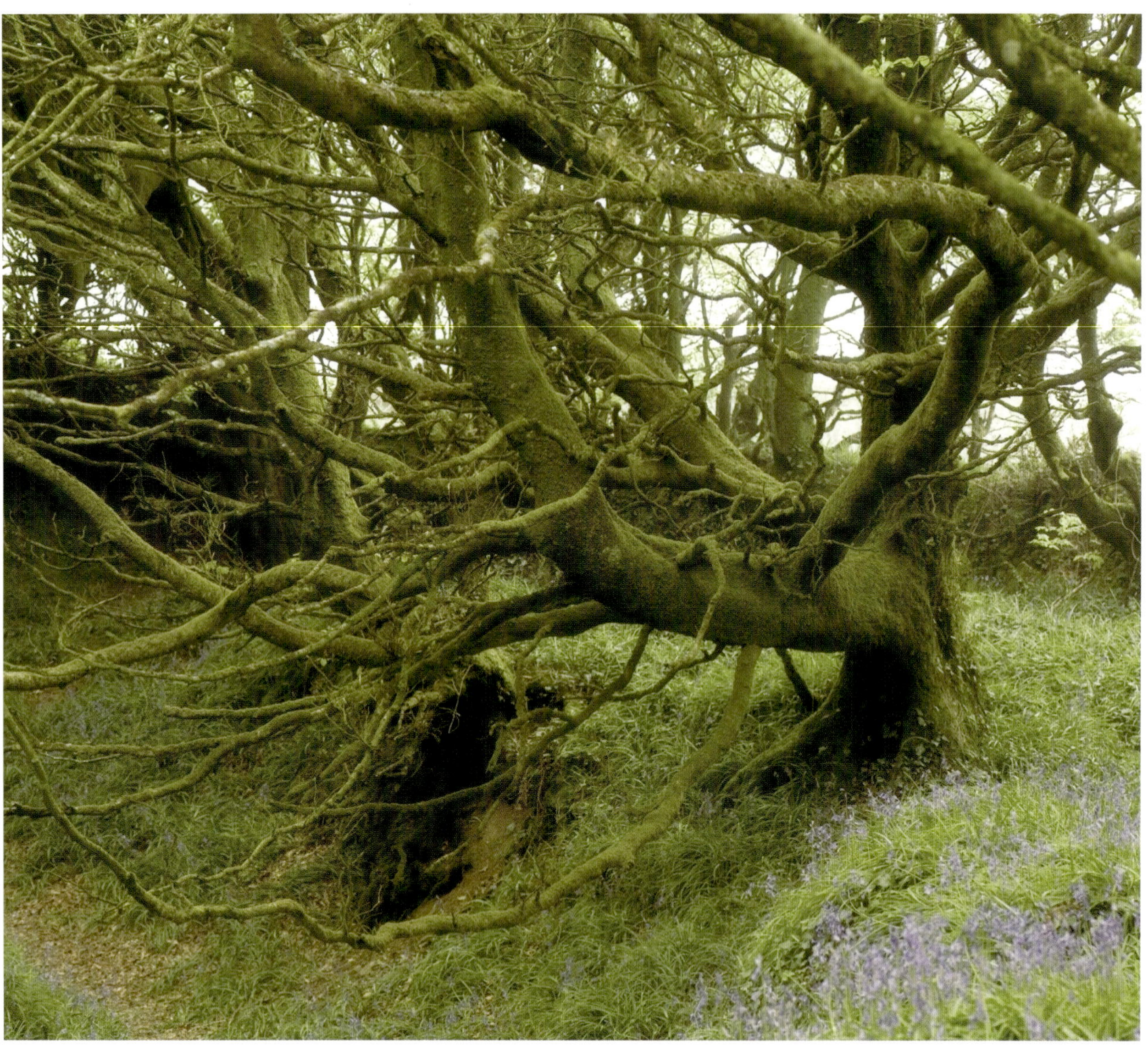

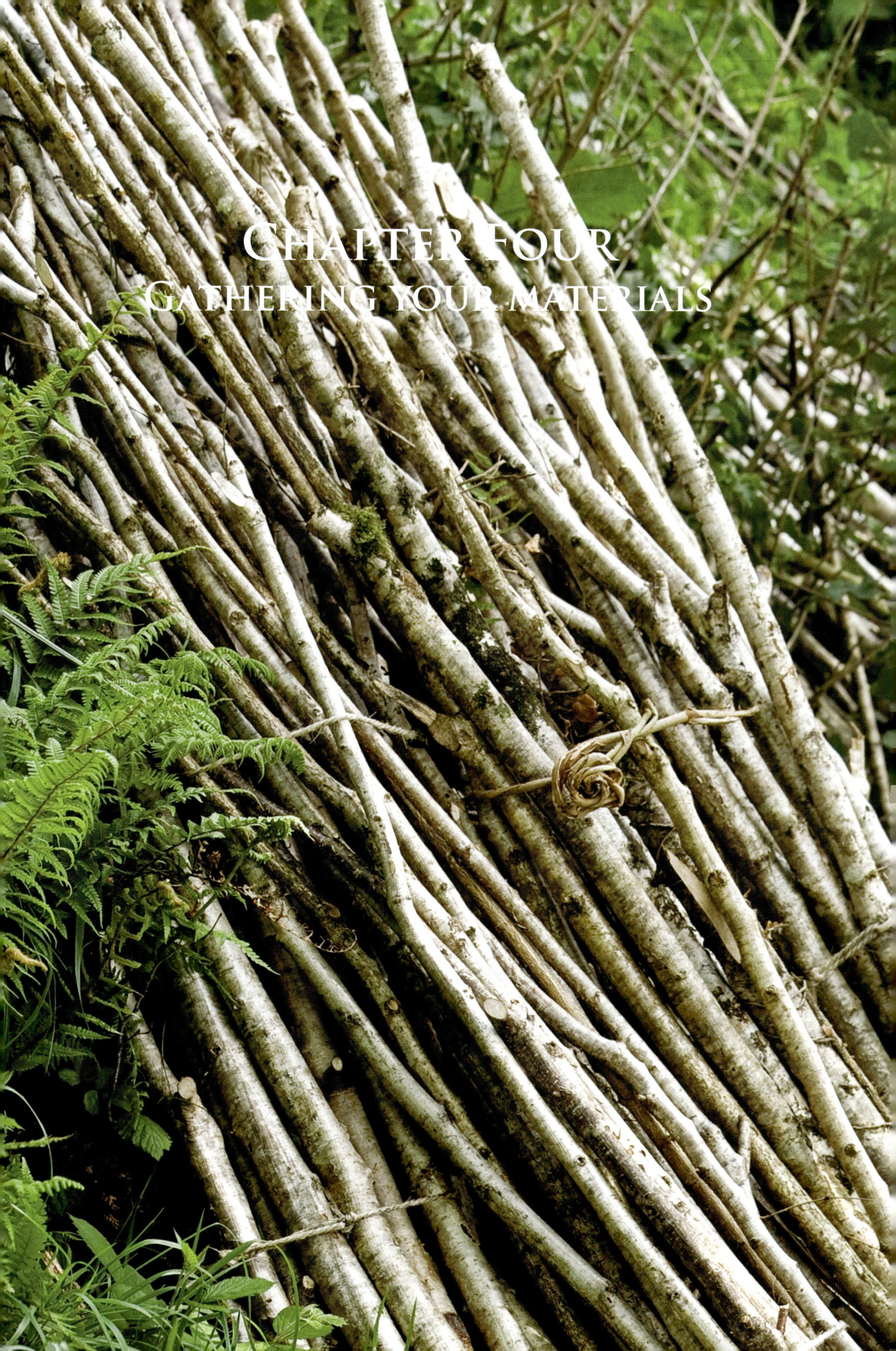

CHAPTER FOUR
GATHERING YOUR MATERIALS

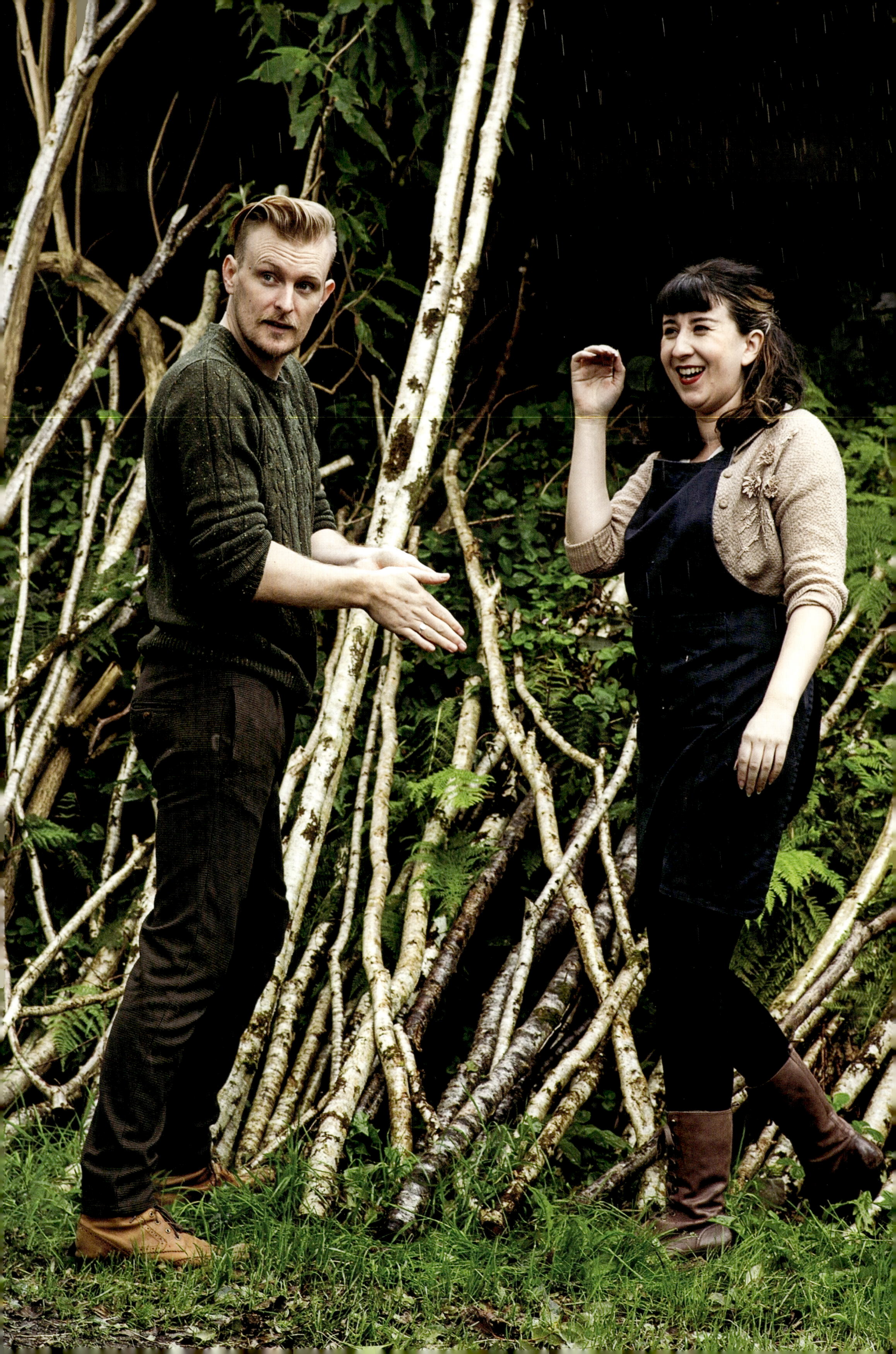

Gathering Your Materials

The chairs and stools that I make are very much rooted in the landscape. In the south-west corner of Ireland, very little re-forestation has taken place in recent years, but all along the roadsides and in the hedgerows, self-seeded hazel grows in wild profusion.

In Ireland, native forest now comprises just 1% of total land cover, while non-native conifer forest makes up 60% and approximately 6% of the total land cover. In West Cork, you will find large areas of Sitka spruce, a fast growing conifer cultivated for a variety of end uses including timber for building, fencing material (stakes), pallet manufacture, and medium-density fibreboard (MDF) production.

Most of us are aware these days that trees are much more than just a source of timber. Trees absorb the carbon dioxide that we produce and make our atmosphere breathable. Forests produce rainfall that plant and animal life is dependent upon. Without trees, we would have no oxygen, rainfall or food. Trees also enhance the landscape and play an important role in stabilising the soil and absorbing excess ground water.

Forests and woodlands provide important wildlife habitats and are home to a wide range of plants, insects, birds and mammals. A walk in the woods not only gives us an opportunity to exercise and breathe fresh air. It reminds us we are creatures of this earth, it stimulates our senses and makes us receptive to the sights, smells, and sounds of the natural world.

Researchers in Japan and the UK have found that spending time in the forest can reduce stress levels, lower blood pressure and even help to prevent cancer. In one study it was found that people who live in cities with trees nearby suffer less from depression than those living in urban landscapes without trees.

Research carried out at the Nippon Medical School in Tokyo showed that spending time in the forest enhances the body's ability to produce

*far left: Rosa and Stephen selecting
their sticks*

NK (Natural Killer) cells which help our immune systems to fight cancer. The Japanese call a walk in the woods *shinrin-yoku* or 'forest bathing'.

COPPICING OR PRUNING HAZEL FOR STOOLS

Once you have identified some suitable hazel, whether in a hedgerow, in woodland or beside the road, exercise good judgement before jumping in with your saw. You do not want to annoy the landowner, local council or other woodland visitors, especially as you hope to come back for more.

If verges are being cleared, ask the workers if you can take away some of the branches, or request permission from the landowner. In

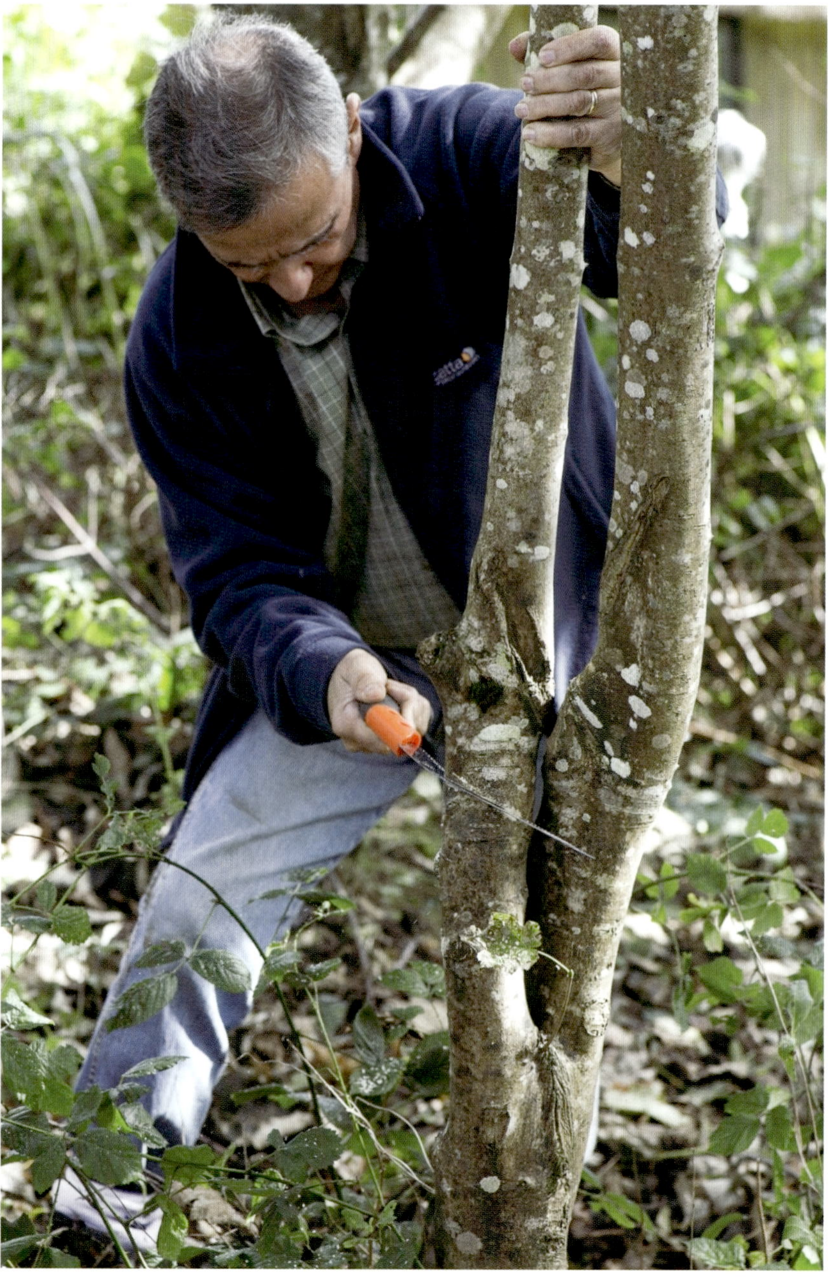

Cutting a sycamore pole using a Japanese pruning saw

Ireland, trees are regularly cut back to keep them clear of electricity cables and to stop them from overhanging roads. You will be surprised how much hazel there is once you start looking, you will notice it everywhere.

Not everyone has access to coppiced hazel. If you want to just prune a few branches, you will not harm the tree. You will be stimulating new growth and giving smaller trees and plants beneath a chance to get some light.

TOOLS

If you want to prune a few branches, I recommend using a pruning saw. These neat foldaway saws are ideal for getting between the hazel stems, allowing you to cut just the stems you want.

Select stems that are appropriate sizes for the job in hand. Most stools are made from small gauge hazel, approximately 1½-2" at the base, with even smaller gauge material for rungs.

If you are coppicing and therefore cutting the entire tree during the winter months, then a bow saw would be suitable. Cut the stems low, approximately 6" from the ground and at a slight angle, preventing water from gathering on the stumps.

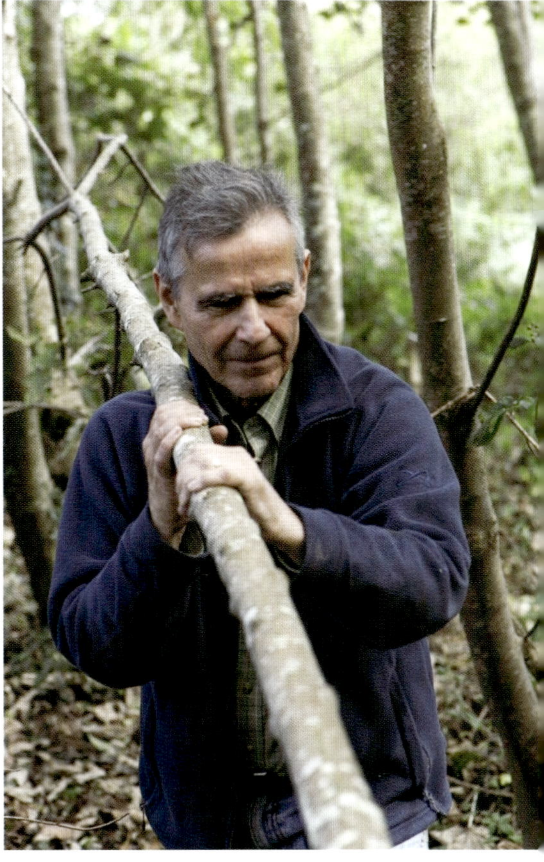

José carrying back the sycamore pole

Once the stems are cut, they will need to be trimmed again before transporting them. I use a pair of long-handled loppers (preferably with a ratchet) for this job, removing the side branches and twigs before bundling the sticks together to carry back to the trailer. Remember to keep some of the smaller twiggy branches, they can be useful and decorative.

People who choose to work with more traditional coppicing tools, like to use a bill hook to remove side branches but I find there is a tendency to cut the side branch too low and leave a white scar on what might otherwise be a perfect rung or post. I prefer the loppers.

Once you have processed your sticks, leave the offcuts neatly hidden in the woods where they will not be a hazard to others or look untidy, for they will decompose naturally. Decomposing wood provides important habitats for many insects, mammals, earthworms and fungi.

Freshly-cut sticks are surprisingly heavy, so be prepared and take rope or straps with you for bundling the sticks. This makes it easier to carry or drag them out of the woods. Whilst moving the sticks, try to protect the bark, it is easily damaged at this stage.

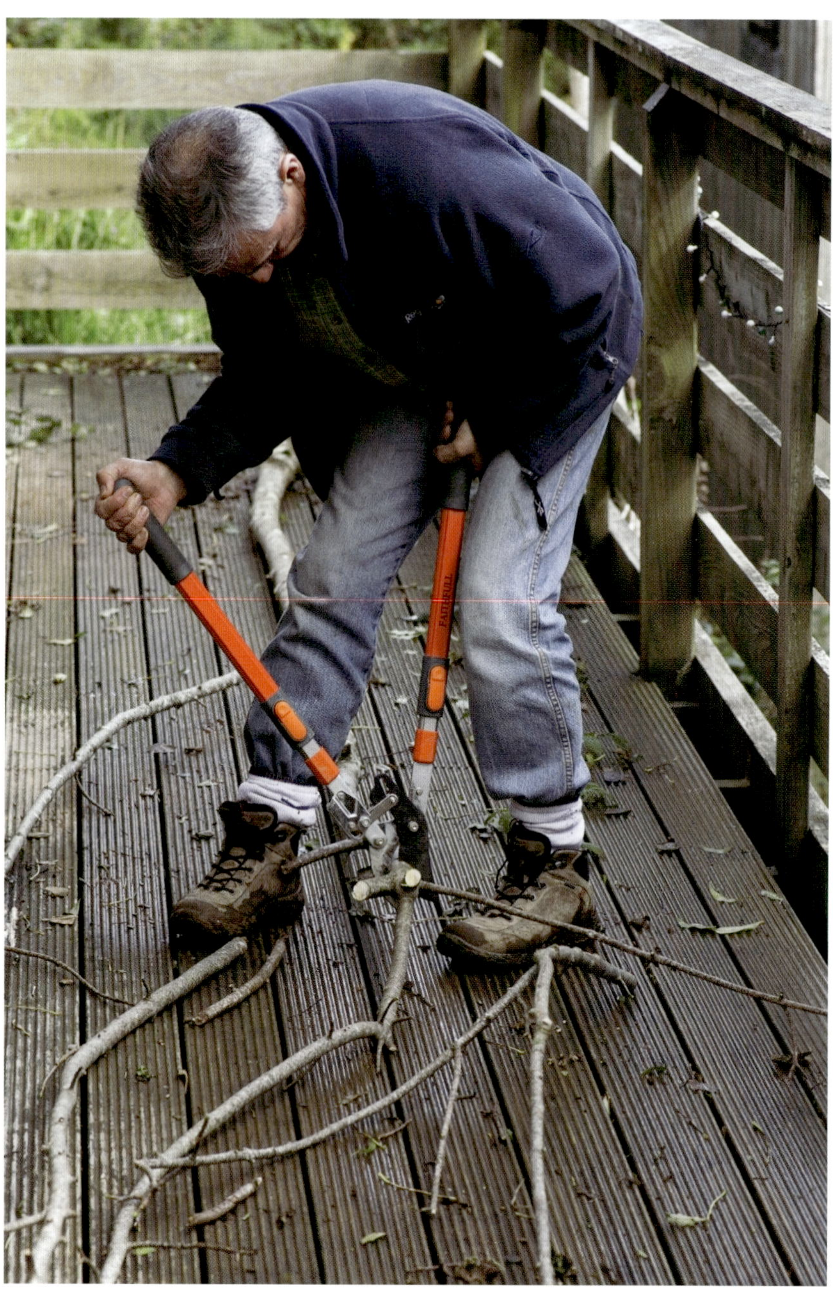

Removing side branches using long handled loppers

STORING YOUR MATERIAL

Ideally, your freshly-cut sticks should be stored in an upright position and preferably protected from the rain. An open-sided barn is perfect for this. The sticks will stay dry and air can circulate around them. However, most of us will not have access to that kind of storage and we find ways to manage anyway!

My sticks are usually coppiced at the beginning of December when I get a delivery of approximately four hundred various sized hazel sticks in bundles of 10–15. They stand up against an earth bank and can be used until the following September. By September, they have usually dried out too much for easy stripping or if the summer has been wet, they will start to rot. By October, my hazel sticks are good for nothing but kindling and firewood!

Even though my hazel sticks are delivered in December, I do not usually start work until April. This is simply because my workshop is in the semi-outdoors and I wait for warmer, drier weather. West Cork is a very wet and windy corner of Ireland!

Freshly-cut hazel sticks are difficult to work with but not impossible. However, if you strip the bark off, they feel quite slimy and the wood turns brownish, much like a peeled apple. Drilling into unseasoned sticks can also be difficult and even dangerous as the drill bit can slip, it gets coated in green fibres which prevent it from cutting cleanly.

The sticks should be dry-ish, meaning green enough for the bark to be stripped off easily but dry enough that they are not too wet or slippery to the touch. You will soon get a feel for when the wood is easy to work.

Hazel tied with willow bindings
or 'withies

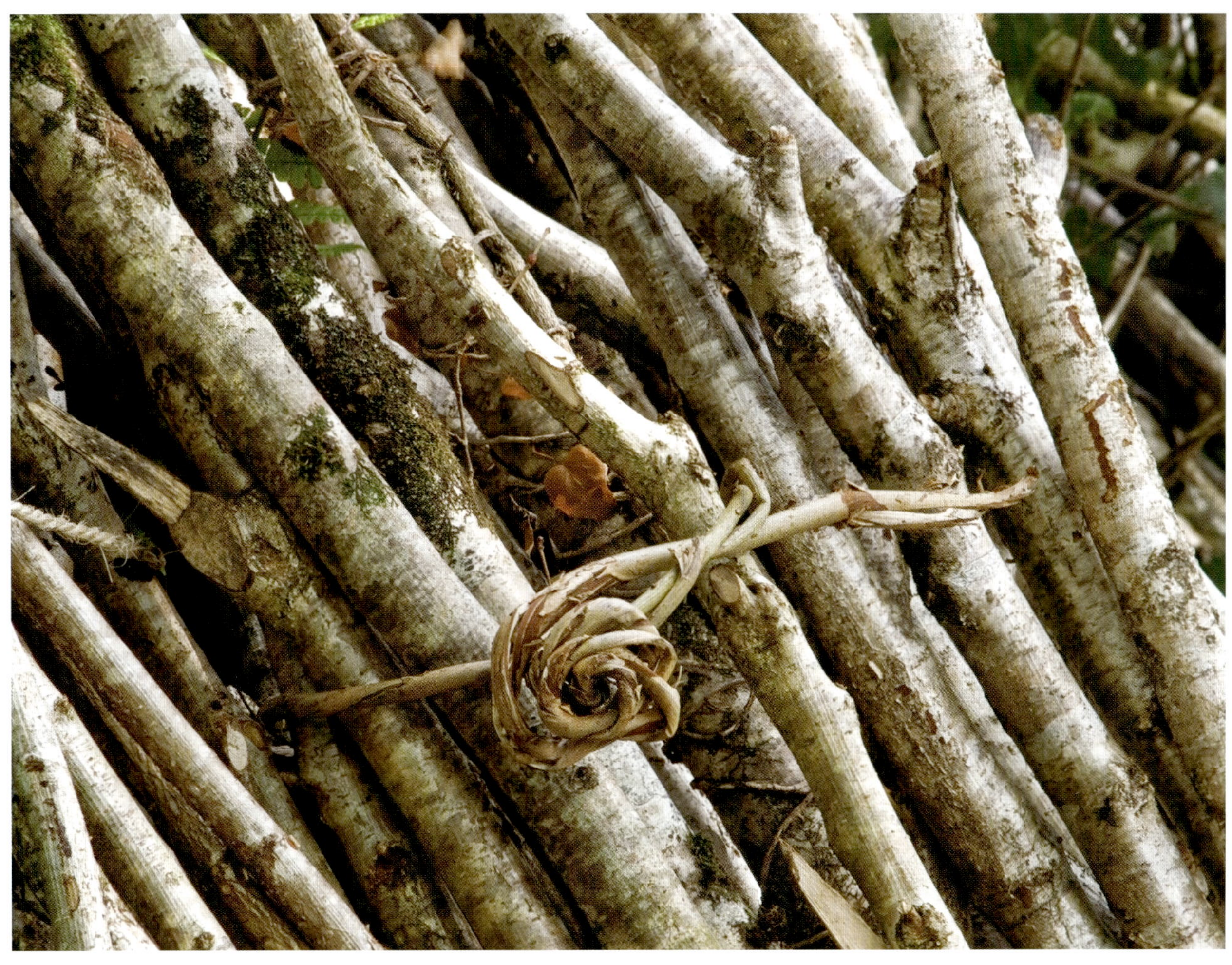

One advantage of using green components is that the mortice and tenon both shrink, making a stronger, tighter joint. My rule is not to drill until you have i) made your tenons and whittled them; ii) measured and marked your surfaces for drilling. In that way, the tenons have started to dry but the mortices are still green. Do not leave drilled holes overnight and come back the next day to assemble, the mortices might have already dried out.

A stack of hazel sticks is an inspiring sight to any green wood chairmaker and I know that sense of impatience to get started! If you want the wood to dry out a bit more quickly, make up your cutting list (leaving them all slightly oversized to allow for potential shrinkage and cracking) and take the components into your workshop or even your house. The warmer and drier the atmosphere, the quicker they will season. Do not strip the bark off at this stage because if the house is warm, your components could dry out too quickly and they could crack.

You have several months, between March/April and September/October, when the wood is at its optimum for green woodworking. If green wood chairmaking takes over your life, as it has mine, you will find yourself developing a natural rhythm for gathering, storing, designing and making.

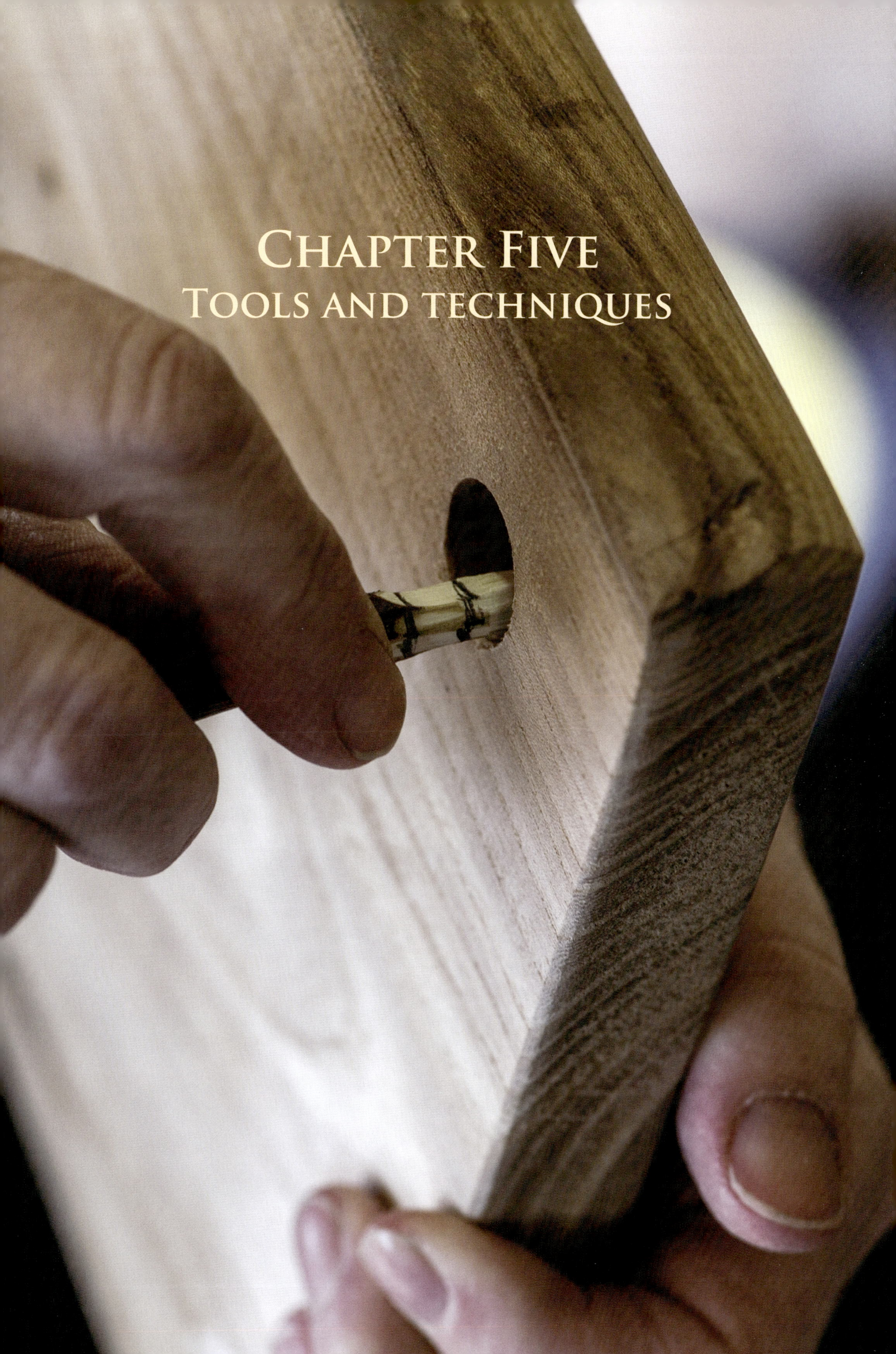

Chapter Five
Tools and techniques

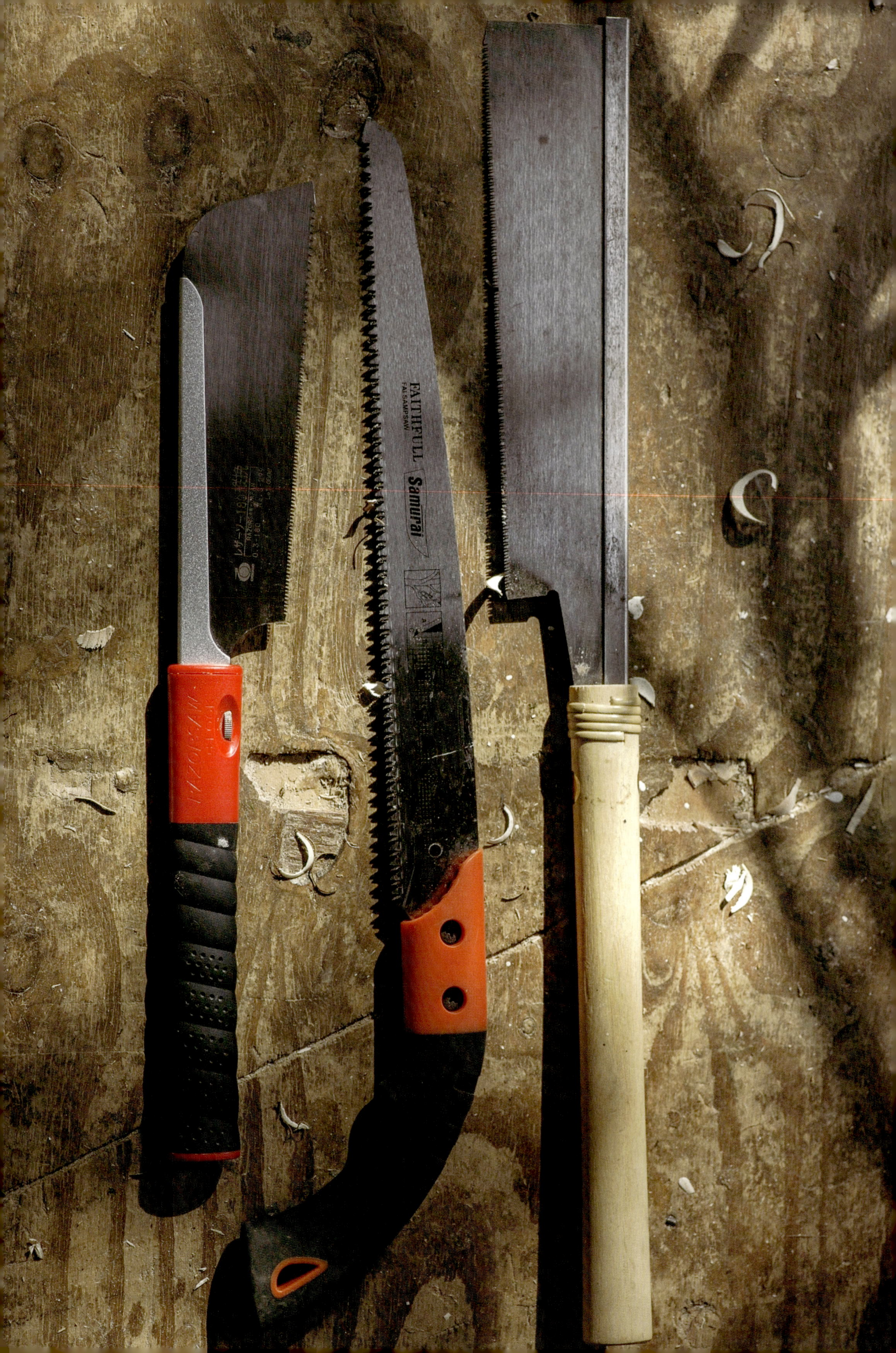
FAITHFULL
FAI SAW/SAW
Samurai

TOOLS AND TECHNIQUES

A wood worker connects with his/her materials through the use of tools. Tools link maker with material and method.

Over time, the tools we use begin to feel familiar in our hands and our expertise develops through repeating the same action, using the same tool.

I have three purpose-made knives which get used in my workshop for a variety of tasks: whittling, trimming, scraping and cutting. We have a relationship of sorts. I have a callus on my thumb where the knife rubs and the knives are dark and polished where my thumb rubs. I have grown fond of them!

I own a small plane, which I rarely use, that I inherited amongst other tools, from my grandfather. Although he worked as a bus conductor, I am told he enjoyed making furniture in his spare time. Sadly, he died in his early forties and I never met him but each time I hold that plane in my hand and slide it along a plank, I feel a small shiver, as if I am connecting with him across time.

Could the tools we use 'rub off' on us somehow or vice versa? According to Flann O' Brien in his book *The Third Policeman*, 'Atomic Theory' dictates that policemen who spend their lives riding bicycles over rocky roads get their personalities mixed up with the personalities of their bicycle as a result of the interchanging of atoms! An hilarious book that describes and explains with great humour, my feeling about tools!

MY WORKSHOP TOOLS

In my experience, it is best to have a small set of good quality tools in your workshop. It takes time to learn to use them but once you have, your actions become intuitive and your tools seem to anticipate your actions.

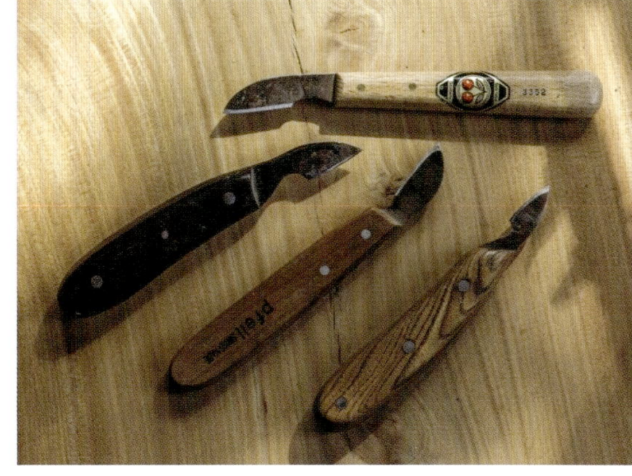

various chip carving knives used for whittling, stripping and trimming

far left: three of my favourite Japanese 'pull' saws

The fundamental joint used for green wood stool making is the tenon and mortice joint. Put simply, it is a round peg (tenon) on the end of one stick, fitting snugly and deeply into a hole (mortice) drilled in another stick. For a strong joint, the tenon must be slightly longer than it is wide.

Never drill the mortice until the tenon is made and whittled, as the drying out process should happen after the two components are joined.

The mortice shrinks onto the tenon and once glued, it makes a joint that is almost impossible to break. There are various ways of making a tenon. For many years I used a wood turning lathe. I turned the tenons roughly to size, then sat down with my chip carving (whittling)

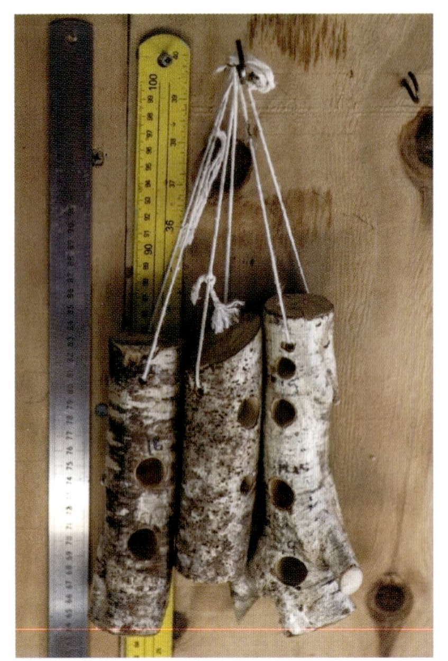

Chairmaker's gauges

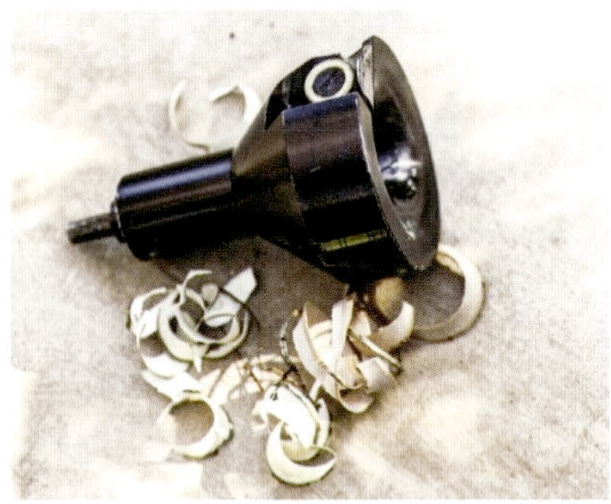

Veritas tenon Cutter

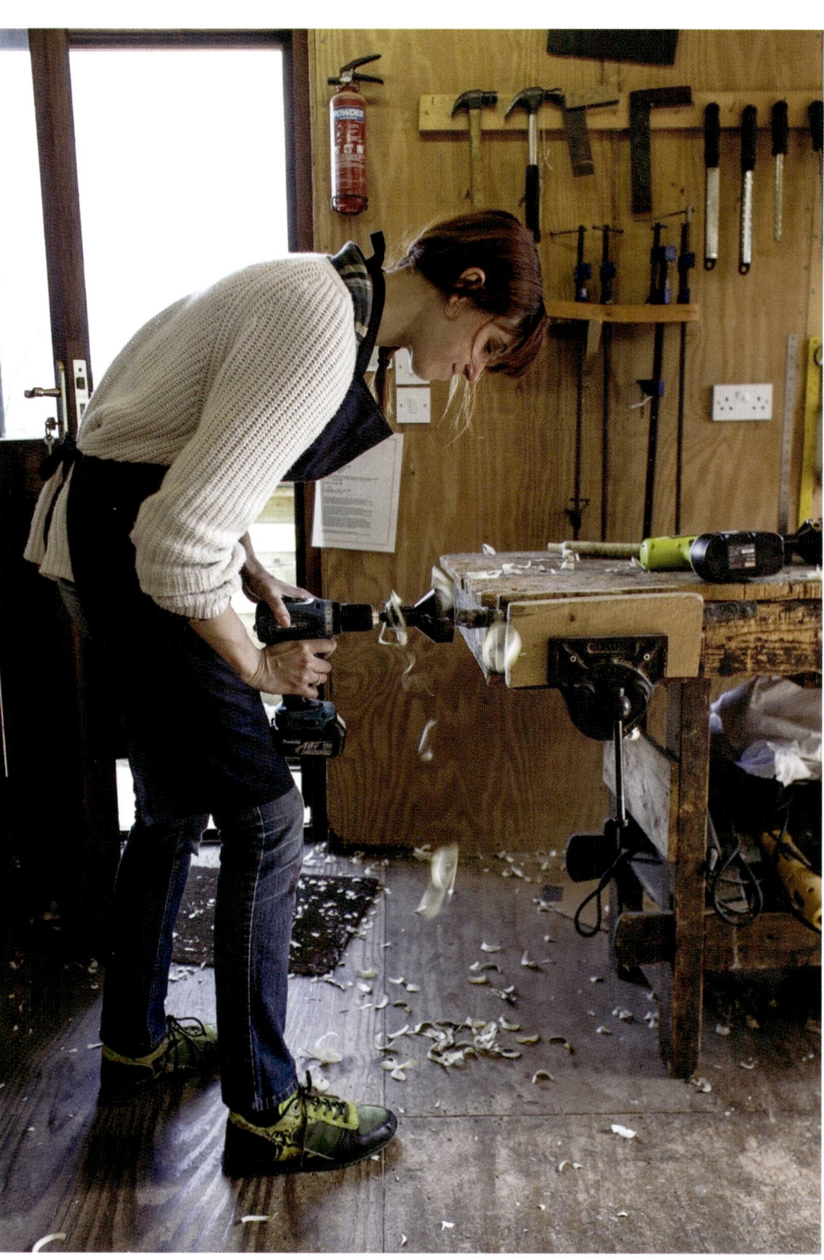

making a tenon using a cordless drill with tenon cutter attached

knife and a chairmaker's gauge and whittled them down to size. I knew they were exactly right when they creaked as I turned them in the hole. I loved that job and never found it tedious. I did not realise how time consuming it was.

Some chairmakers still work with the method used by chair 'bodgers' back in the 18th and 19th centuries, who spent months in the woods every year, coppicing the wood and roughly turning the unseasoned chair components on a pole lathe. The pole lathe was powered by a treadle, attached to a springy sapling. The parts were then stacked up and left to season before being taken to the actual chairmakers who finished the turning and sanding and constructed the chairs.

These days I make all my tenons using Veritas tenon cutters.

These are fabulous bits of equipment, extremely well made and perfect for the job. They work a bit like a giant straight-sided pencil sharpener, attached to a cordless drill.

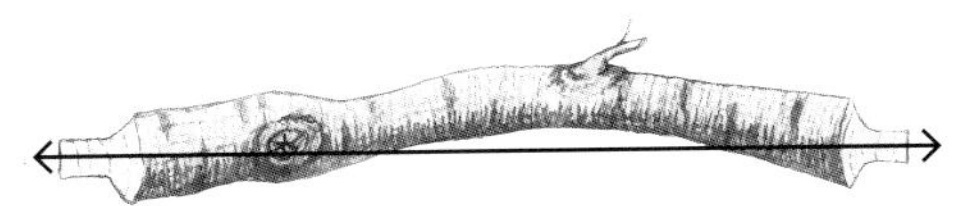

Centering tenons

When making a tenon, always grip the stick in a vice, positioning it as straight as possible. Use the spirit level on the tenon cutter to ensure you are making your tenons line up with each other. *I cannot emphasize this enough, if the tenons are not in line with each other, the stool you are making will not sit flat on the ground!* Use your drill on highest torque and speed. For a robust joint, make your tenons slightly longer than they are wide.

Tenons can also be made (especially in large diameter material) by sawing around the base of the tenon, with your stick held sideways in a vice, turning it each time you cut, then, turning it upright in the vice, and chiselling down from above. It will need tidying up with a knife afterwards and will not have gradually sloping 'shoulders' but for larger pieces such as beds it can be a suitable way to make tenons.

I managed with one ¾" tenoning attachment for several years but eventually bought the smaller ⅝" for spindles and lighter materials. I also invested in a 1" tenon cutter for reducing heavy material down to ¾". It puts less strain on the drill if you do it in two stages. I use an 18 volt drill on its highest torque and speed settings.

Mortices need to be drilled. I use 3D or multi-angle drill bits, in combination with either a cordless drill or a pillar drill. These excellent drill bits are available from good quality tool shops and builders merchants. I believe they are mainly used by carpenters for fitting locks into doors but I like to think they were invented specially for green wood chairmakers!

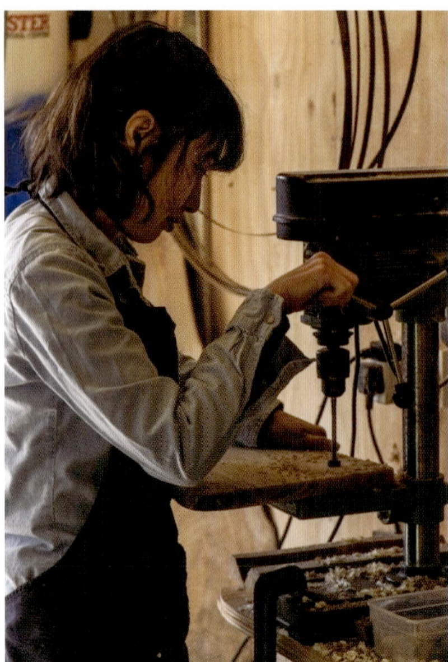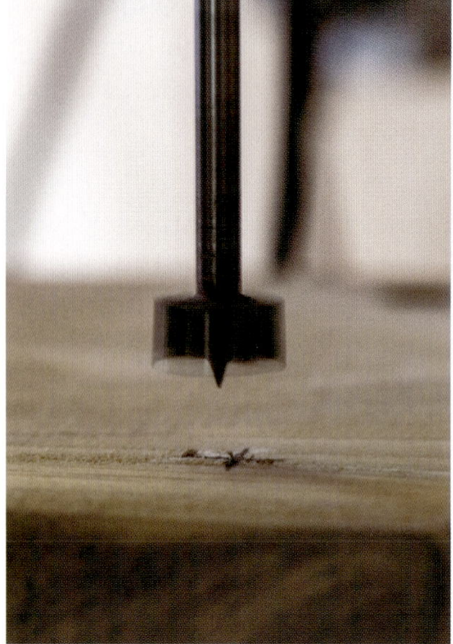

Drilling mortice using MAD drill bit and pillar drill-0456

I have tried using flat (spade) bits but find the point too long. I have also tried using Forstner bits but the fibres produced by unseasoned wood, quickly tangle themselves around the cutting edges, fill up the gaps and prevent it from cutting. The multi-angle drill bits have the sides cut away and allow the material to escape through the gaps, making them ideal for this job.

I now exclusively use Disston Blu Mol multi-angle drill bits in 18 mm (with the ¾" tenon attachment and 15 mm with the ⅝" tenon attachment). These are the best 3D drill bits by far and cut cleanly and easily into unseasoned wood. I have tried a wide range of different makes with varying results. Unseasoned, sappy wood is quite a resistant material but I find the Disston bits fit for purpose and they keep their edge very well.

Tenoning attachments come in imperial sizes and the multi angle drill bits come in metric sizes. I find that an 18 mm drill bit gives me the right size hole for a tenon made with a ¾" tenon cutter, although it will need whittling slightly. A 15 mm drill bit fits the ⅝" tenon cutter and the 25 mm drill bit fits the 1" tenon cutter.

Here is a list of equipment you need before starting, although you could manage without the last five items at a pinch:

- A cordless drill (does not need hammer action but needs 2 speeds) and high torque 18V

- Whittling (or chip carving) knife

- Sharp cross-cutting saw

- Japanese pull saw for fine cuts

- White chalk

- PVA woodwork glue

- Bench with vice or workmate type

- Disston Blu Mol multi angle-drill bits

- Veritas tenon cutter (you need ¾" definitely) or other suitable equipment for making tenons

- Rubber mallet

- Wooden mallet

- Sharpening stone diamond or stone

- Pillar drill

- V cradle for holding sticks still for drilling and marking

- Sash clamps

- Electric orbital sander

- Shaving horse

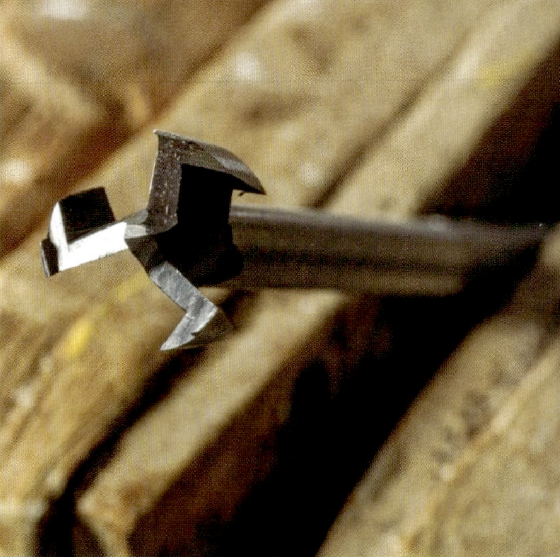

Disston MAD drill bit

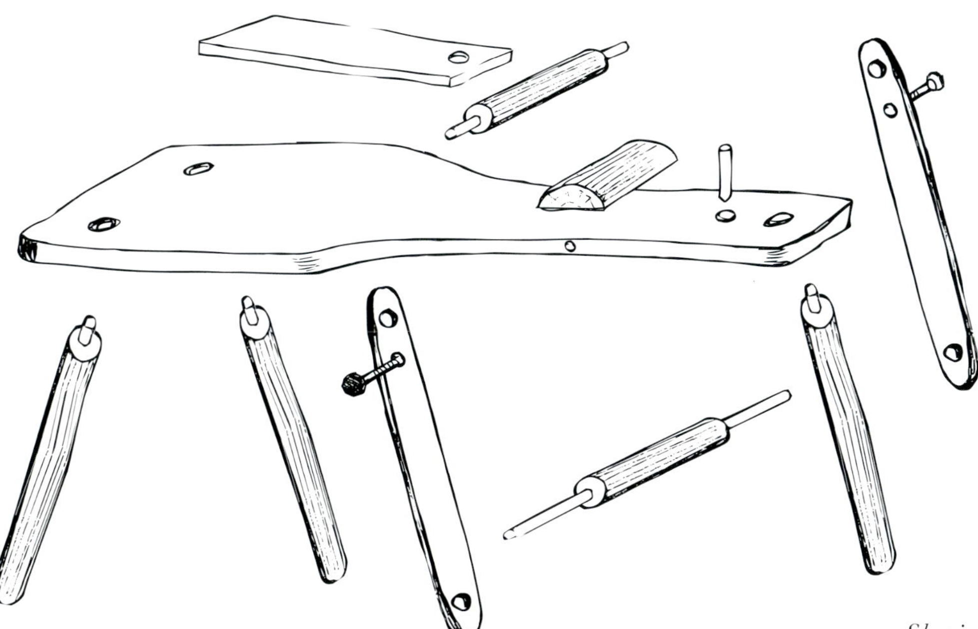

Shaving horse — exploded view

Take really good care of your tools. Remember to put them away clean and dry, do not allow them to lay in the damp or on the ground for any length of time, or they will rust. Treat them with respect. Spend time sharpening and cleaning them, and they will last longer, replace your knife in its sheath every time you pack up for the day. This way your tools will work better and you will develop an affinity with them.

WHITTLING KNIFE AND SHARPENING STONE

My favourite knife for general use is a chip carving knife. It has a very short blade and soon begins to feel like an extension of your hand. You will use it for many jobs: stripping, whittling, trimming and so on. If you have a knife, you need a sharpening stone. This can be an old-fashioned oilstone or, my current favourite, a small, medium-grade, diamond stone used with water. A very sharp edge can be produced, quickly and with little effort using a diamond stone. If you are not experienced in sharpening, do not let that bother you, the only way to learn is to keep trying. Hold the knife at a slight angle to the sharpening stone, and rub gently with a circular motion and try it. If it is sharp enough, use it, if not, try again. You will feel a slightly ragged 'burr' on the edge of your knife, once it is sharp. Do not be afraid to practice and experiment with sharpening — it is the only way to learn.

TECHNIQUES

MEASURING TENONS USING A CHAIRMAKER'S GAUGE

When whittling tenons to size, make yourself a gauge from an off-cut of seasoned wood, with 15 mm and 18 mm holes drilled into it. As you whittle, keep trying the tenons in the holes until you have a 'creaky' fit. The sound tells you when the tenons are fitting snugly. Hang your gauge on a hook in the workshop as you will need to make regular use of it!

WHITTLING

You will often find that your tenons need to be whittled slightly, to make them a good fit. Also, the components for the ¾" tenon cutter and the 18 mm drill bit are almost exactly the same size. Whittling takes the roundness off and leaves gaps in the joint for glue and to let the air escape.

In my experience, whittling is a tricky technique to master. You are trying to pare away very little material and keep the tenon an even shape, you therefore need to keep careful control of your knife. My method is to hold the stick under my arm, steadying it against my body. I pare lightly and turn the stick after each cut, thereby keeping

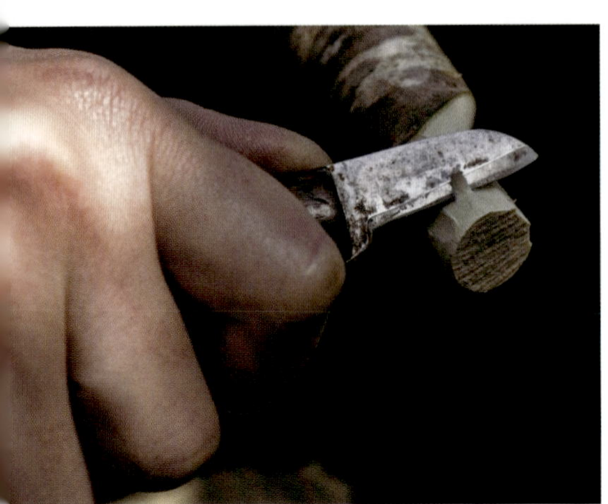

Whittling a tenon using a chip carving knife

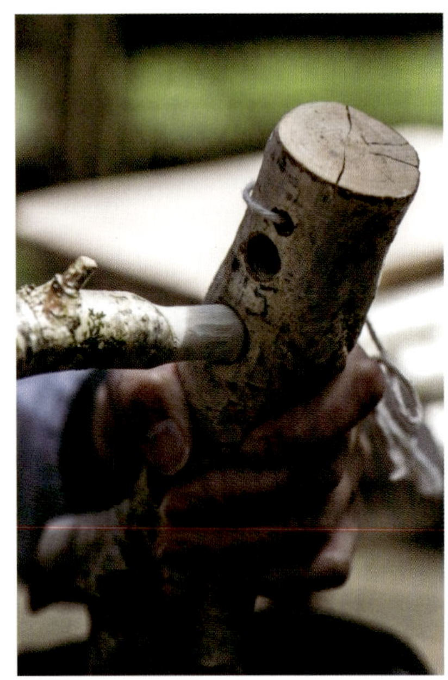

Measuring the size of tenon using a chairmaker's gauge

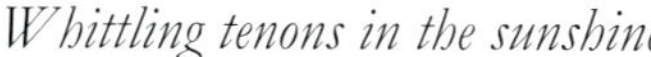

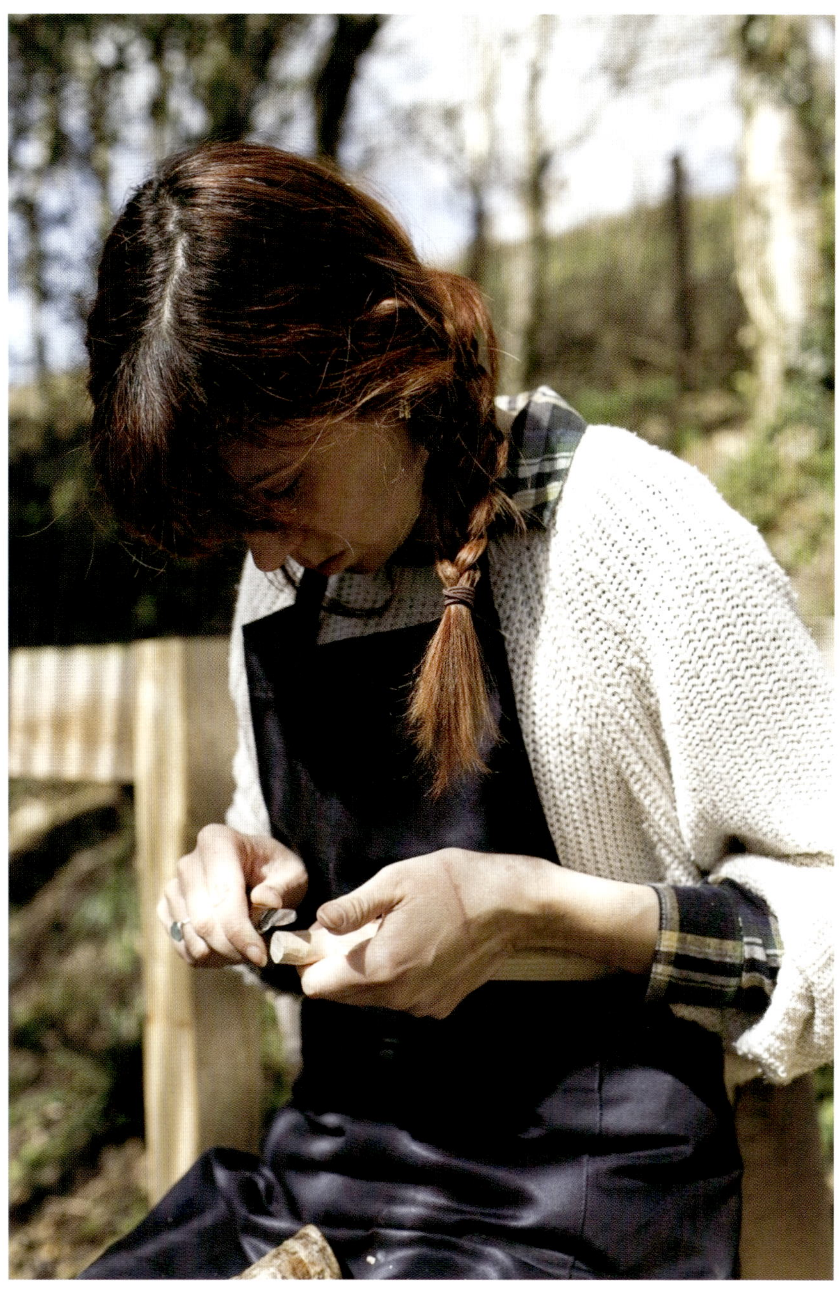

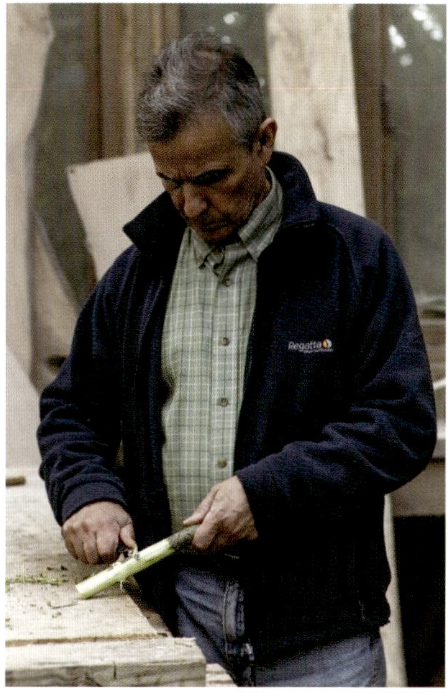

the tenon round. Keep a chairmaker's gauge to hand so that you can keep trying the tenons in the holes.

BARK STRIPPING

Once you start to strip the bark off, you will notice your stick has three layers, on the outside, the bark, next a pithy layer, which is bright green when the wood is unseasoned and of course — the wood.

Stripping can be done on freshly-cut sticks, using a chip carving knife. Stand your stick up on the bench or workmate and run the knife down the length of it, taking ribbons of bark as you go. As the pithy layer will remain in some places use the knife, as if you were scraping a carrot, to remove it.

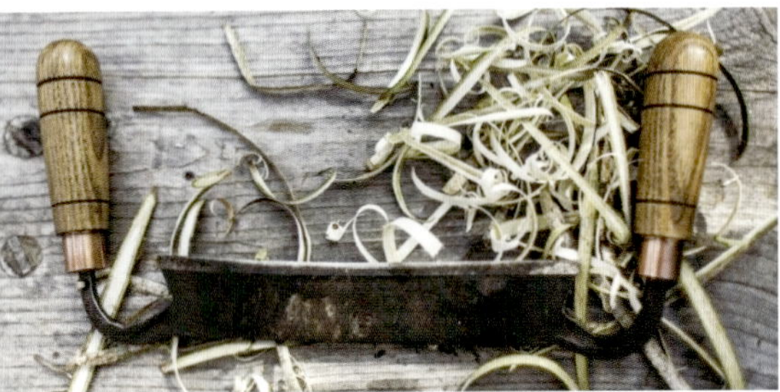

Straight blade drawknife

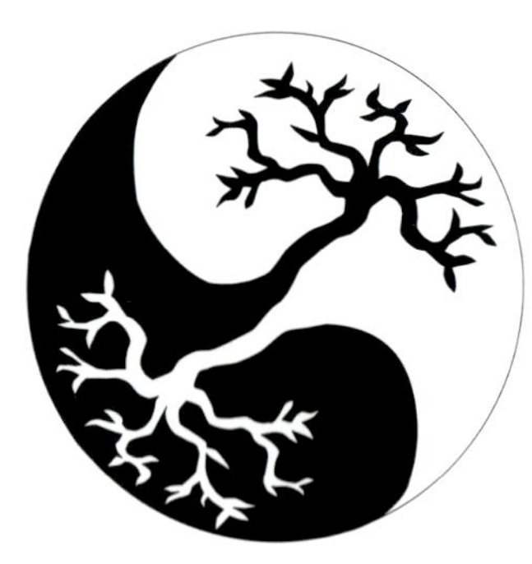

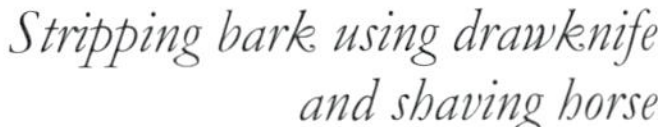

*Stripping bark using drawknife
and shaving horse*

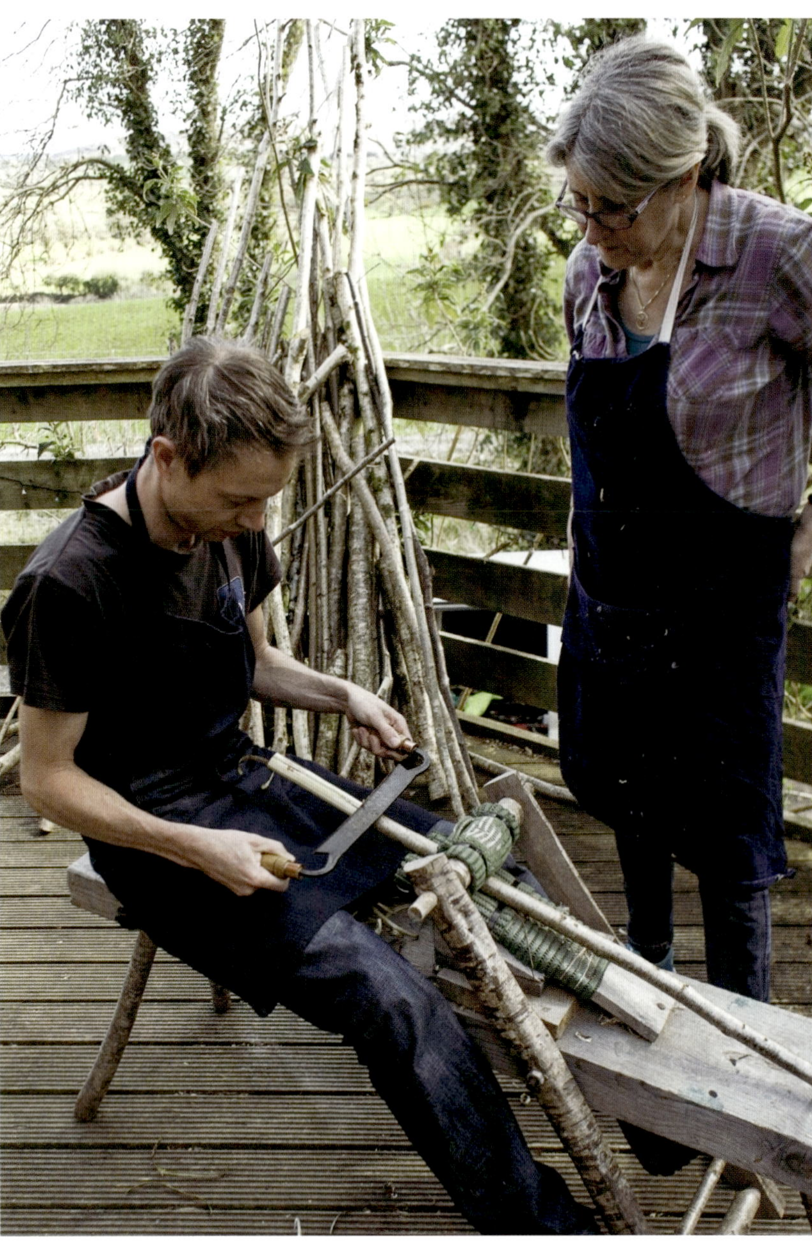

Alternatively, you can use a draw knife and a shaving horse. The shaving horse grips the stick, leaving your hands free to use a two-handled drawknife. The shaving horse is simple enough to make yourself and a draw knife can be acquired in a variety of ways. You may be lucky and find an old one for sale, you may know a blacksmith who makes tools, or you can buy one from a reputable tool supplier (names and addresses can be found in the Appendix). I was fortunate and met a blacksmith just when I needed one, who made drawknives in a variety of styles, out of old Land Rover springs. According to him, these springs are made of excellent steel!

MEASURING MORTICE DEPTH
When drilling mortices into small gauge components, you might worry about drilling through the stick and out the other side. A

measuring device made from a stripped twig with pencil marks at the appropriate heights will help you to check the depth.

FINDING THE CENTRE POINT

Finding the centre point is something you will need to do again and again. It is very important. When drilling into a round stick there is a centre point, it is the highest point and if you drill off-centre you will have a hole that has one side higher than the other. It is worth intentionally doing it once (on scrap wood) to illustrate the point to yourself.

On a front or back post I draw a centre line all the way down the stick, with white chalk, and mark off the height of the mortices, forming crosses that mark the points to be drilled.

FINISHING THE BOTTOMS OF THE LEGS

The bottoms of the legs look neater and the overall appearance of the stool or chair you are making is more 'finished' if you run a 1" tenon cutter around the bottom of each foot. A couple of turns of the drill tidies up the edge.

MAKING REPAIRS

Even when you have developed a high level of skill and experience, you will find yourself problem-solving from time to time. Green wood work is very forgiving and there is usually something you can do to get yourself out of a tricky situation. Here are two techniques I use when in a tight spot:

- If you have over-whittled the tenons and find they fit too easily into the mortices, place a strip of bark (the material produced

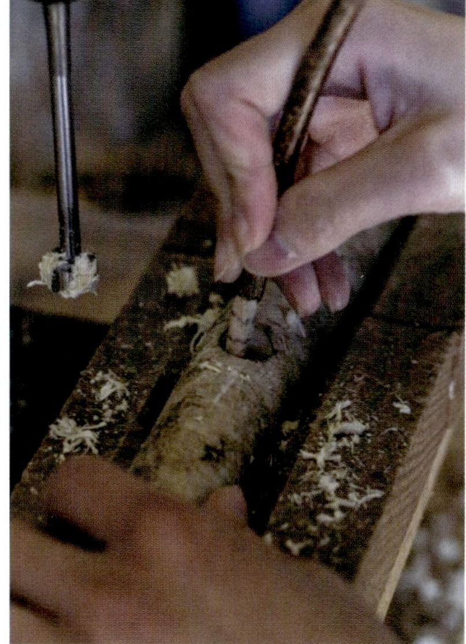

Measure the depth of the mortice using a dibbing stick against the top and bottom edge — not against the sides which are lower

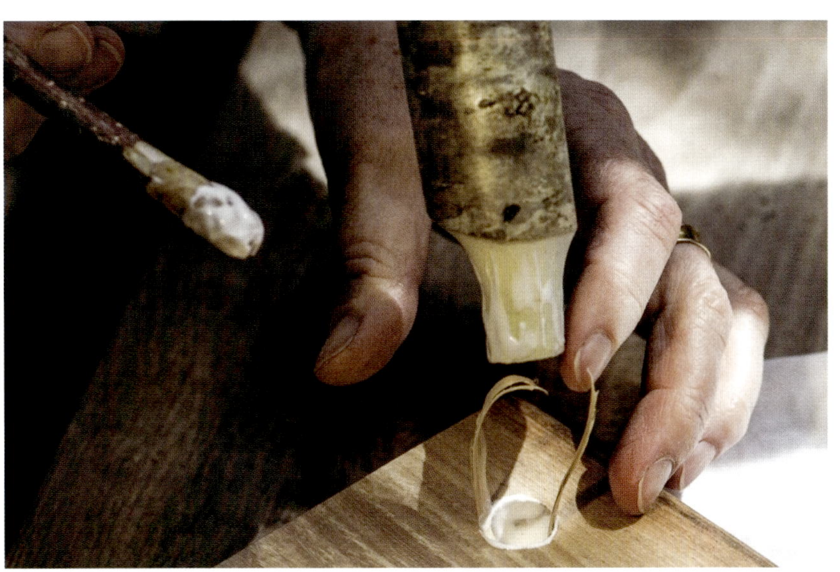

Packing a tenon and mortice joint using a strip of bark

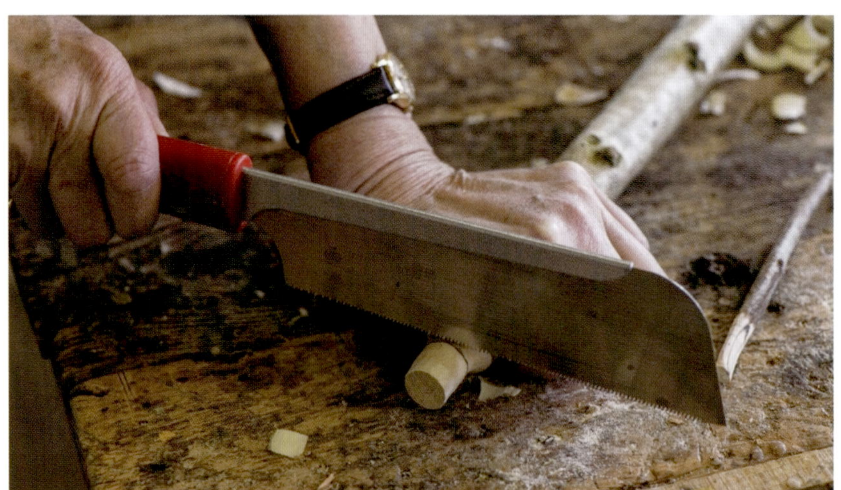

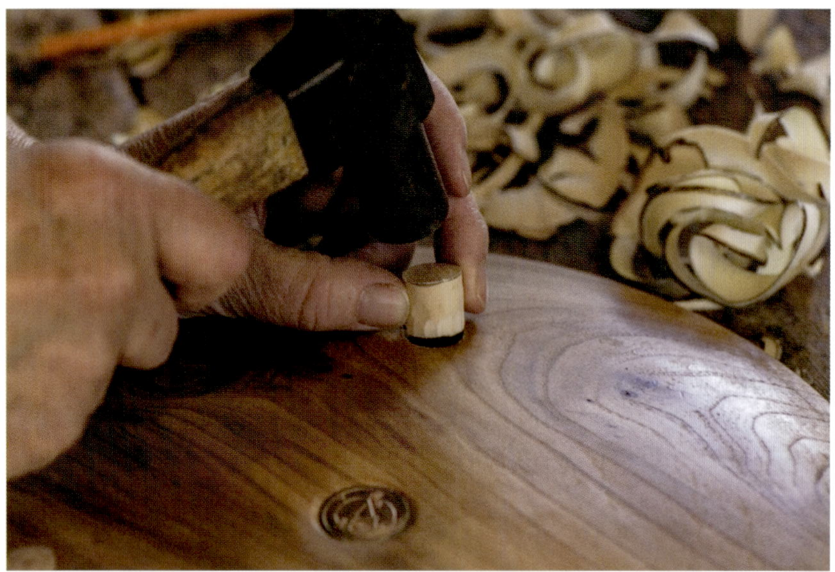

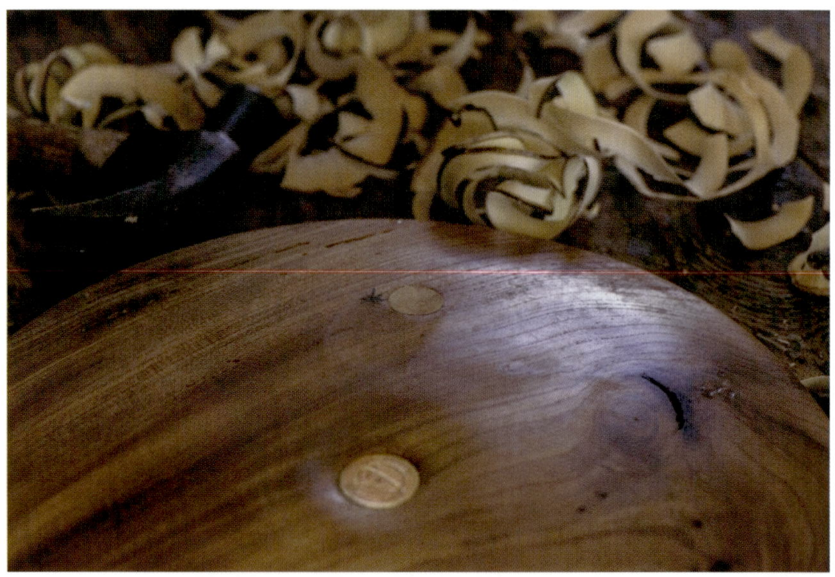

If you have drilled in the wrong place: i) cut a tenon from a 'scrap' stick having whittled it slightly; ii) apply glue and tap into position using a small hammer; iii) sand it flat and re-drill mortice in correct position

when stripping wood using a drawknife) when you come to assemble, across the mortice. As you tap the tenon in, the bark goes into the mortice too, making a tighter fit.

- If you have drilled in the wrong place or drilled a hole at a slightly wrong angle, you can give yourself another chance to get it right by making a tenon on a piece of scrap wood. Cut it to the right length and glue it into the wrongly-drilled hole. Once the glue has set you can drill into the same or similar place again.

Please take the safety of yourself and others into account when gathering hazel sticks out in the woodland.

First of all, dress sensibly. Wear strong shoes (preferably with steel toe caps), protective gloves and clothes that will keep the brambles and stinging nettles away. I find that leather gloves are invaluable when handling branch wood and pulling stems out of the undergrowth. If you are right-handed, I advise wearing a glove on your left hand when sawing or using a bill hook. The hand holding the tool needs a good grip and your bare hand is best for this. The left hand is holding the branch and if the saw or bill hook does slip, this will be the hand which will get injured.

Fortunately, you are cutting fairly small, round wood with a diameter of no more than 2"-4" at the base so the risks can be minimised.

Ensure there are no young children or animals nearby and that the area you will be working in is sufficiently cleared to avoid tripping over stumps and brambles and so on.

Once you have identified the stems you will be cutting, think about practicalities. You will probably be cutting upright stems, therefore consider the direction in which they will fall. Make sure you are well positioned and not leaning your weight against the stem or you could go flying too! If you are using a pruning saw, the saw blade can get pinched by the weight of the tree as the cut progresses. This is most easily released by pushing the stem away from you, thus taking the downward pressure off the blade.

Most of the time, in the woods, the twiggy branches at the top get tangled around each other and it is possible to cut several stems with nothing falling as they are held, dangling in position by the upper branches. In this case, once the stem is cut, hold it on your shoulder and pull it out of the wood behind you, ensuring it can fall safely on the ground. You might have to shake and wiggle it to get it free but in this case there are no surprises, you are more in control of when and where your stem will fall.

Another danger to be wary of is that these trees and saplings are springy, you push in one direction to cut the base of a stem and it can spring back unexpectedly. I have had a few bruises and scratches over the years from this!

Keep your tools in one, easy-to-find spot, you do not want to trip over any sharp tools unexpectedly and you need to be able to find everything once you have finished. As a rule, I buy brightly-coloured tools so that they are easy to see amongst trees and leaves. Always make sure your tools are clean and sharp, a blunt knife, bill hook or saw is more likely to slip and cause an accident.

Always carry a First Aid kit and, if possible, do not go coppicing alone.

SAFETY IN THE WORKSHOP
Once you have brought your sticks back to the workshop, a few additional safety instructions apply to your usual regime:

- Reduce your sticks to manageable lengths before bringing them into the workshop.

- Ensure you are working in a clutter-free environment.

- Always hold sticks in a vice, workmate, shaving horse or sawing horse before working with them. Round sticks do not easily hold still.

- Never attempt to put a tenon on a stick that is not secured.

- Never wear open-toed shoes.

- Tie back long hair, do not wear scarves, ties or dangling sleeves.

- Protect your eyes from flying bark ribbons when tenoning, with goggles.

- Protect your nose and mouth from dust when sanding, with a mask.

right: Traditional rush-seated stool

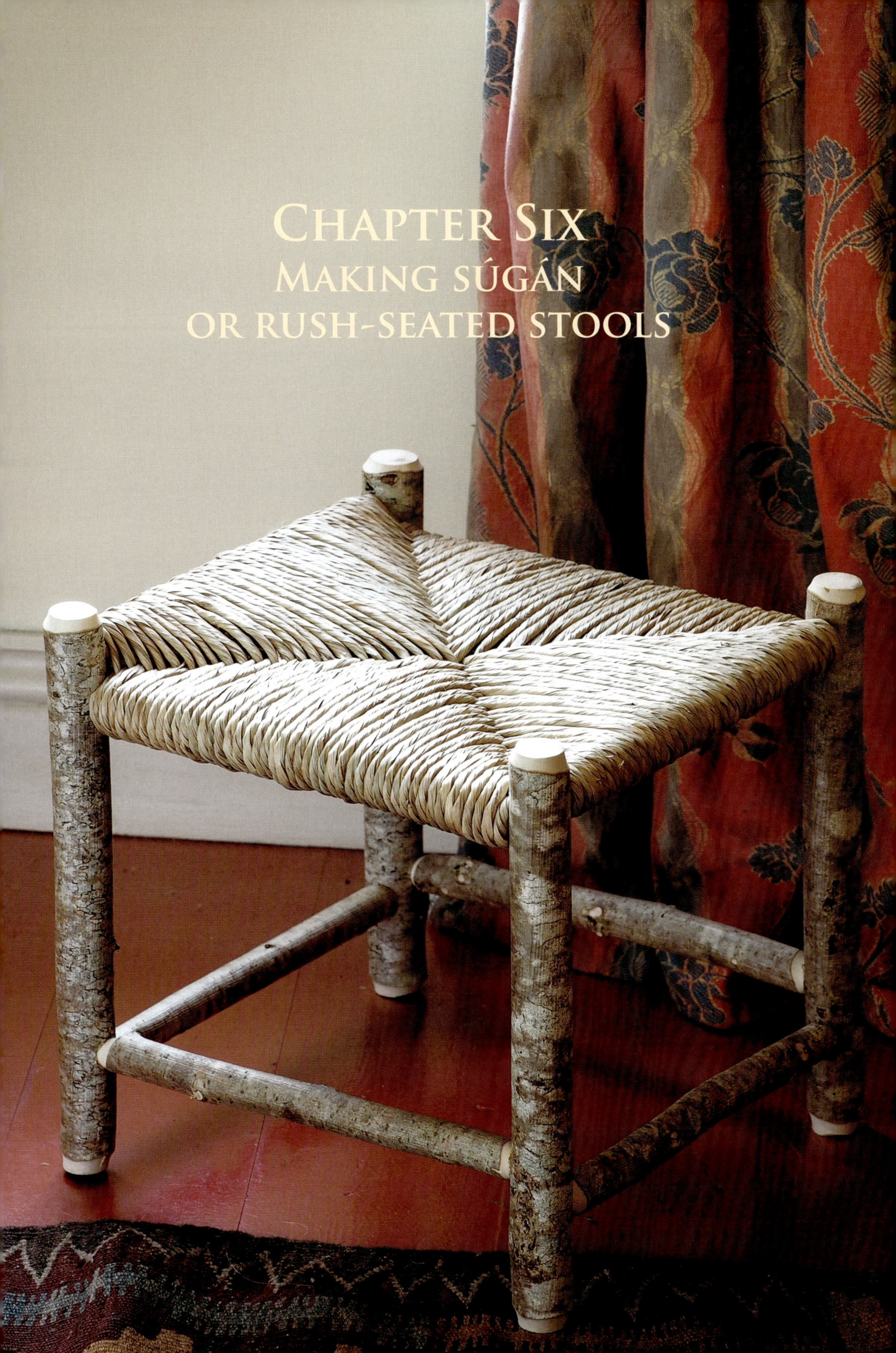

Chapter Six
Making súgán
or rush-seated stools

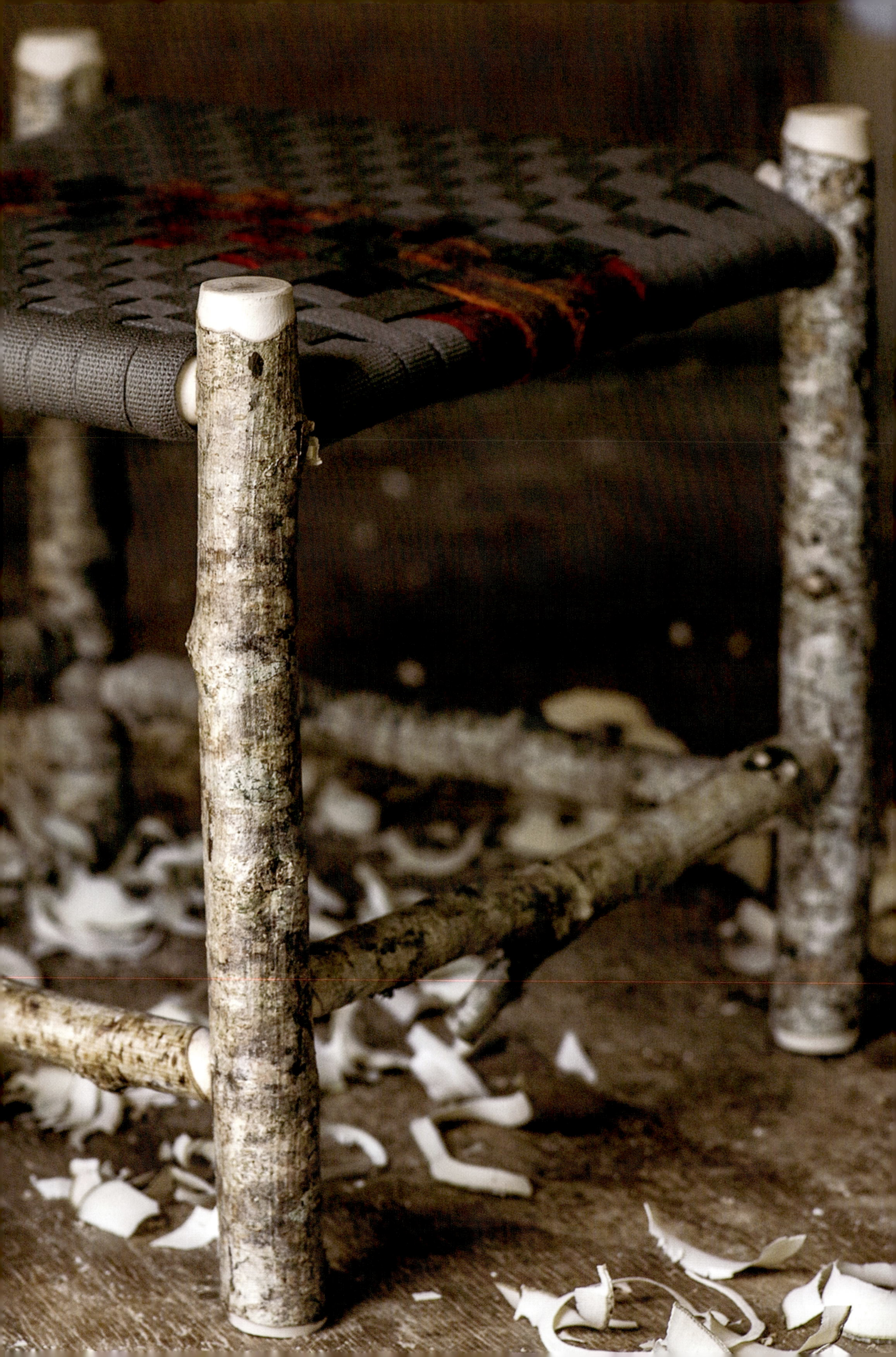

MAKING SÚGÁN
OR RUSH-SEATED STOOLS

In Ireland there is no identifiable tradition, that I have found, of rush being used for the seating of stools, even though suitable rushes can be found growing on riverbanks and lakesides. It is possible that rushes were used for stool seating, they were certainly used for the seating of chairs.

More generally, súgán was used for chair seating, especially in rural areas. Súgán is rope made by hand from straw, hay or rye grass. It was a commonly used material which functioned not only as chair seating but also for tying down thatch, fastening gates and other jobs around the farm.

Up until the 1960s when polypropylene baler twine became widely available, farming families made their own súgán. It was a seasonal task that involved two people, one feeding the straw in evenly while the other person used a thraw or whimble to twist the straw into a rope whilst walking slowly backwards. Many older people in West Cork have strong memories of helping out with the súgán rope-making each year, after the harvest.

The design for this stool is based on a traditional post and rung construction. It is usually made with a 1" square section from machined ash or poplar. With a rung around the top and bottom, it is ideally suited to rush seating although súgán is also suitable as the materials really complement each other. While súgán brings a pleasing texture to the stool and a striking golden colour, rush is smoother and easier to obtain (see Appendix for suppliers) with the added bonus that is has a wonderful, wholesome smell!

The seat can also be woven using sea grass, or recycled paper rope (see Appendix). With this stool design there are many seating options — I have used ⅝" Shaker seating tape and ½" woven wool fabric for the stools featured in the photographs here.

far left: Traditional square stool with Shaker tape and woven wool tape seat

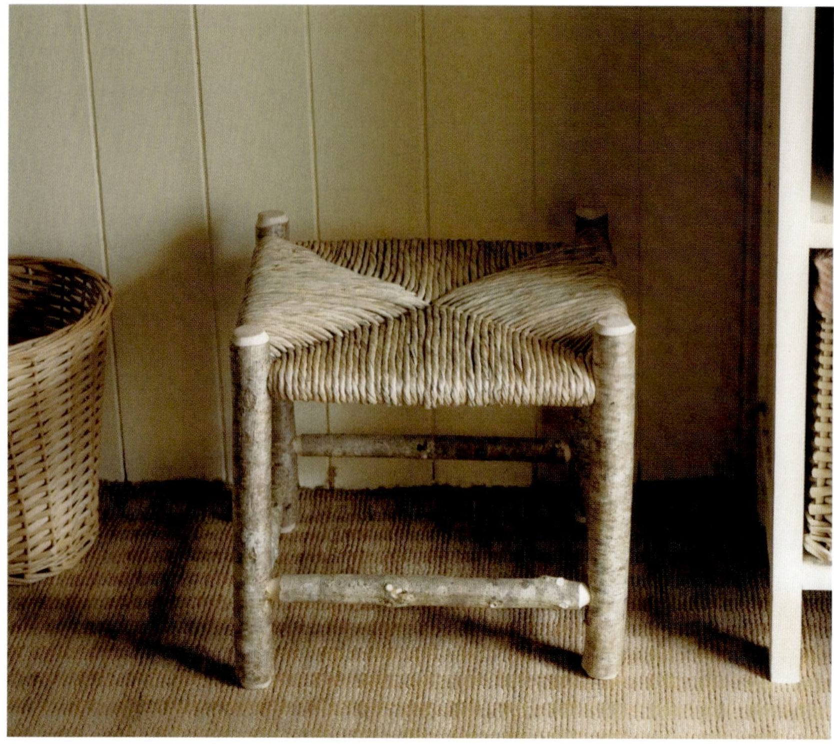

If this is your first foray into green wood stool making, I suggest you select the straightest material you can find. It is quite easy to find straight material over such short lengths. Hazel is suitable and so is ash, birch, sweet chestnut or alder.

Cutting list

- Always cut your posts slightly too long to allow you to trim them down when the stool is finished. This prevents the risk of the wood splitting out from tight joints during assembly and allows for cracking at ends if the wood is very green. When trimming down, take care not to cut them too low as the saw might accidentally catch and cut your fabric.

- Cut x 4 posts of approximately 35 mm (1½") diameter hazel x 350 mm (14") long.

- Cut x 8 of approximately 15 mm (¾") diameter rail material hazel x 300 mm (12") long.

Instructions

1. Make 2 frames and decide how the legs will best fit together. Pair them up and if there are any bends in the sticks, position them so that they kick out rather than back under the stool.

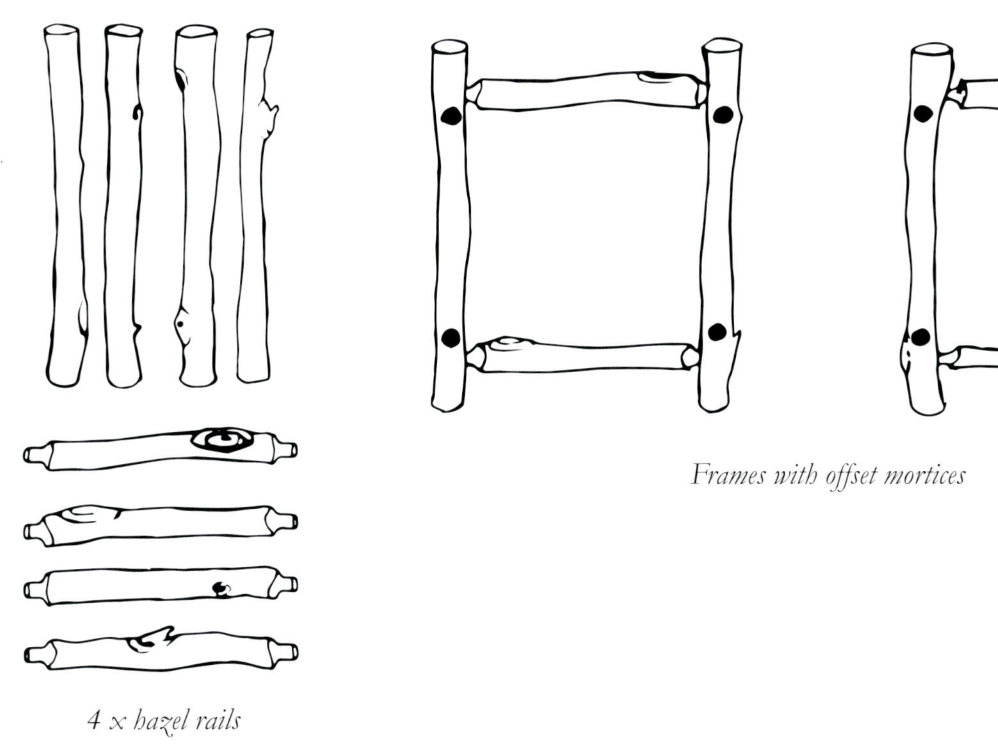

4 x hazel rails

2. Put ⅝" tenon on both ends of all 8 rails.

3. Having chosen the face you wish to drill into, draw a white chalk line down the centre of each post. To mark your drill holes, measure approximately 70 mm (2½") from bottom and top of posts and mark across the centre line forming a cross.

4. Using the pillar drill and a 15 mm 3D drill bit, make holes approximately 18/20 mm deep (use a dibbing stick).

5. Assemble using waterproof PVA glue and tighten with a sash clamp placing wooden glue blocks between clamp and post to avoid damage to bark.

6. The sash clamp is used to locate the tenon tightly into the mortice. You may remove it immediately and wipe off excess glue.

7. Once assembled, ensure that each frame lies flat on the bench. If not, take it in both hands and give it a twist or hold it in your bench vice and give it a twist (this requires less effort)!

8. The next step is to join the 2 frames together using the same technique. This time, when marking the drill holes for the top rail, offset them slightly so that they are almost in line with the first ones but you are not drilling into the tenon and mortice joint

you have just made. The reason for this is that you do not want a big height difference between front and back and the 2 sides, for woven seating purposes, but you do need to offset slightly in order to maintain the existing joint. pic.

9. I usually offset by about 10–12 mm.

10. Now use your sash clamp with glue blocks to pull the joints together so that they fit snugly.

11. Once again, if the stool is not sitting flat on your bench (or on a flat surface) give the whole structure a twist or clamp it to the bench while the glue sets. By clamping it to the bench, all of the joints will twist and adjust themselves gradually.

Information and instructions/ diagrams on rush seating can be found in books and on the internet. It is a basic design that is not too difficult to manage even for beginners and rush rope is a pleasing material to work with.

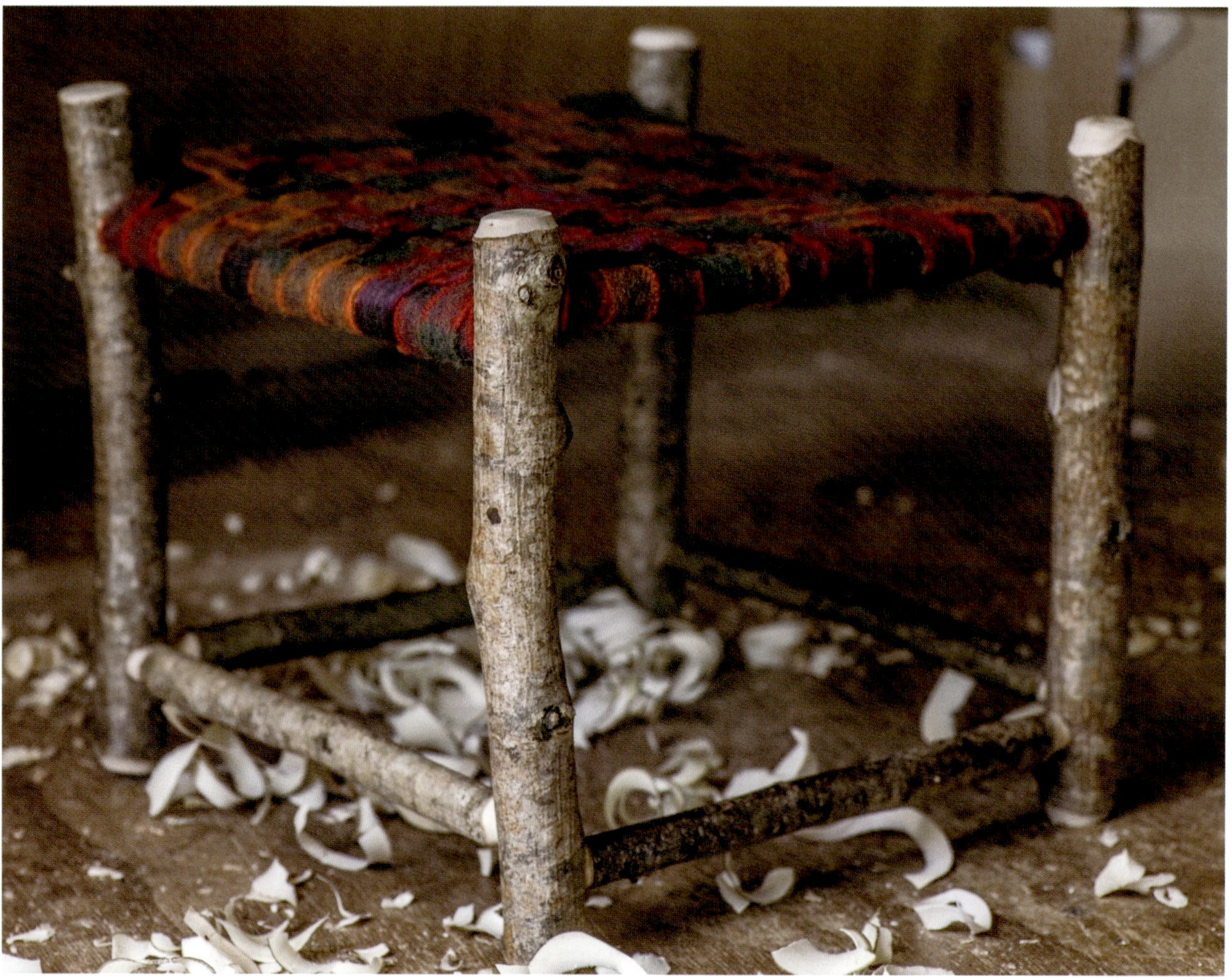

Traditional square stool with woven wool-tape seat

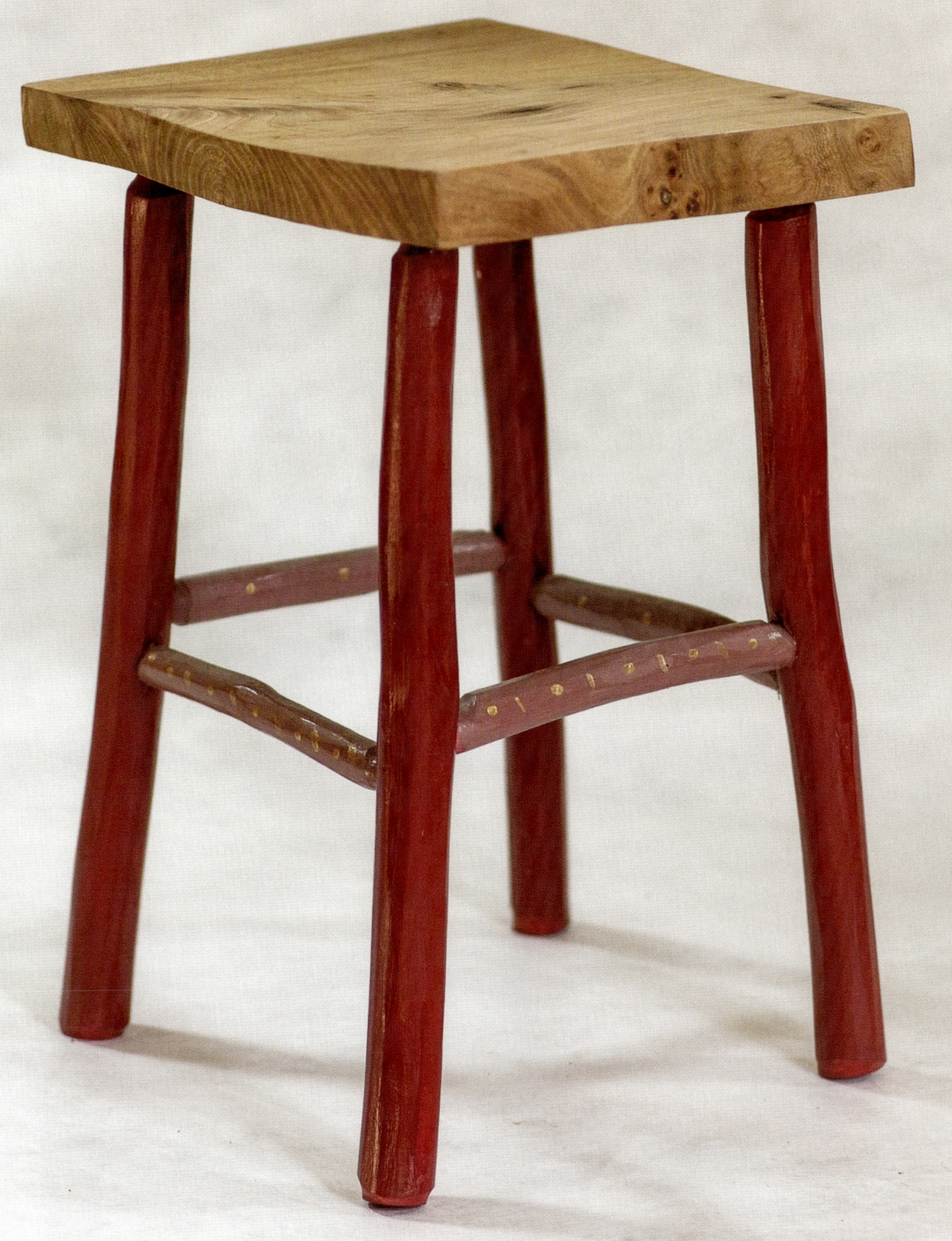

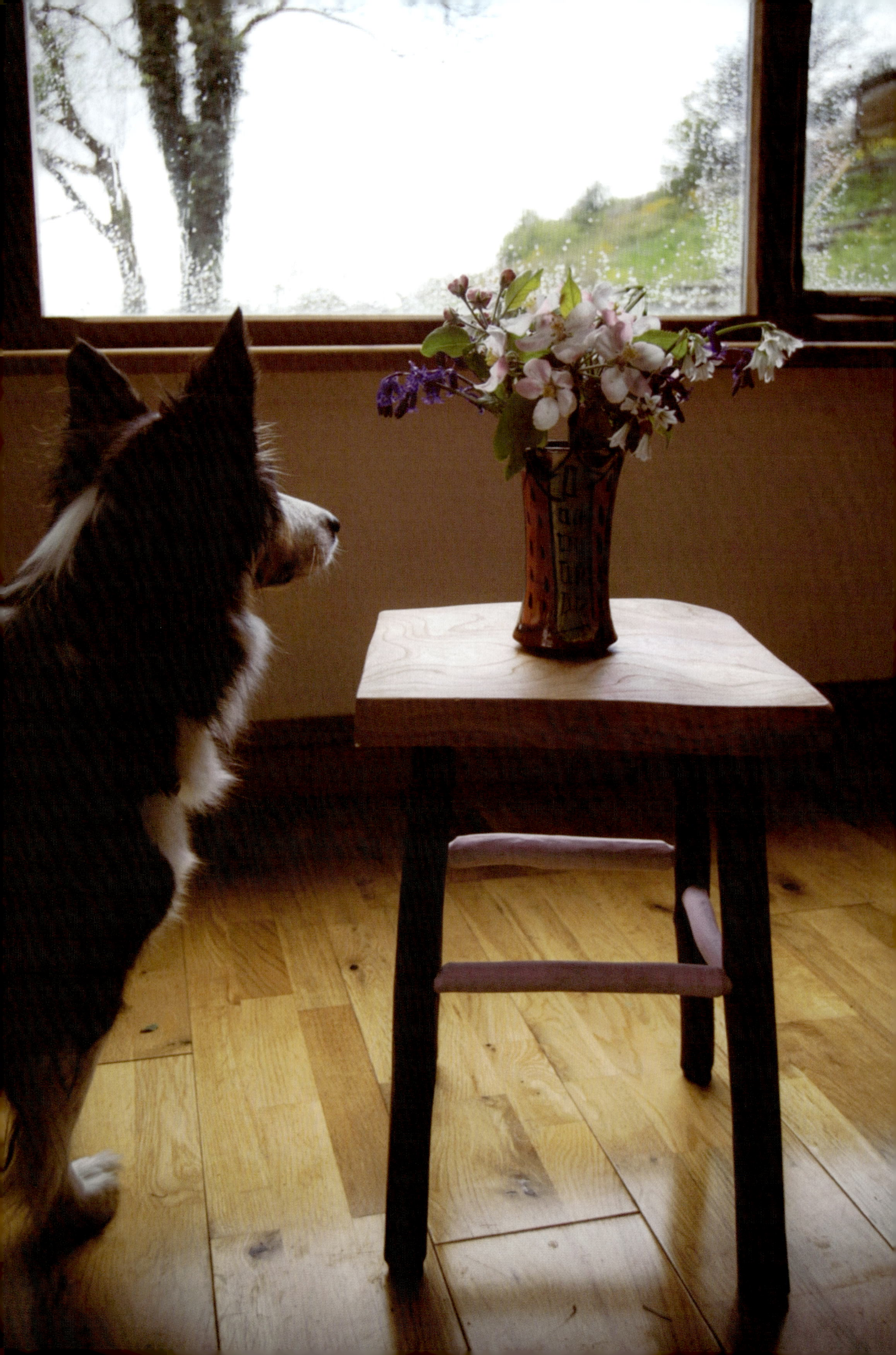

Kitchen Stools

This is the first splayed-legged stool I made, it is a green wood version of the traditional kitchen stool which usually has turned legs and a solid round top. The stool is useful for sitting at a kitchen counter, although it can be made at different heights (and widths) for various purposes. The smaller version makes a useful occasional table.

I make this stool all in one go, which is why I call it the two-hour stool and not because it is a quick job! I usually encourage people to take their time when chair making and enjoy the process but in this case it is important to start and finish within a relatively short timeframe. All in one day is good enough!

Throughout the process you will need to be able to twist and turn the joints until everything sits right. The joints need to be loose enough (the glue not set) to allow them to move relative to each other, until you are satisfied with the shape.

Those of you who have read my *Green Wood Chairs* book will know that the stools I used to make were really more like tables in that the legs were straight and reinforced with side rails.

Looking at the new version stool, the most noticeable difference is that the legs are splayed which can be achieved very simply without recourse to drilling at angles or measuring in degrees.

Due to the natural (asymmetrical) shapes of the sticks used, the green wood frame will never be square, although it is being forced into it. In consequence, it is permanently under tension which gives strength to the structure. Hazel can withstand tremendous pressure, it always bends and almost never breaks.

For this project, I used approximately 1½" (40 mm) diameter for the posts and something lighter for the rails. If this is to be your first green wood stool, use the very straightest material you can find as it will make the job much easier and will ensure success! Curvy material is very attractive but hard to work with.

far left: medium height kitchen stool painted — with Evie

- 4 x straight hazel posts approximately 1½" (40 mm) diameter at base and 20" (500 mm) long

- 4 x hazel rails lighter material 9" (230 mm) long

- Hardwood plank, min 1¼" thick, approximately 12" x 12" (300 mm x 300 mm) square or 10" x 12" (250 mm x 300 mm)

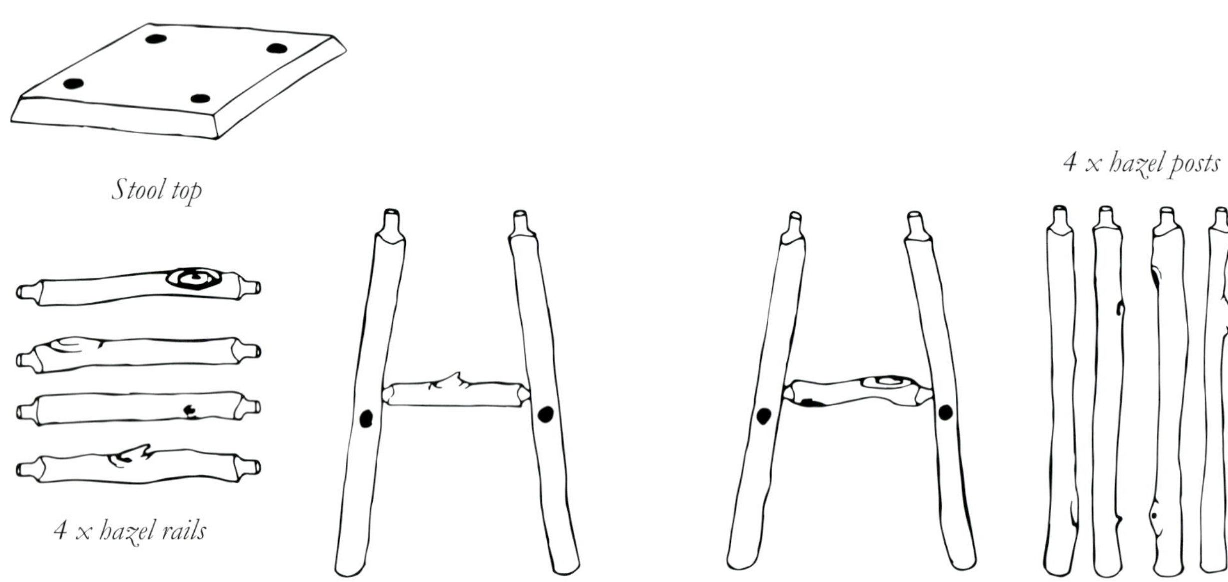

Stool top

4 x hazel rails

4 x hazel posts

Instructions

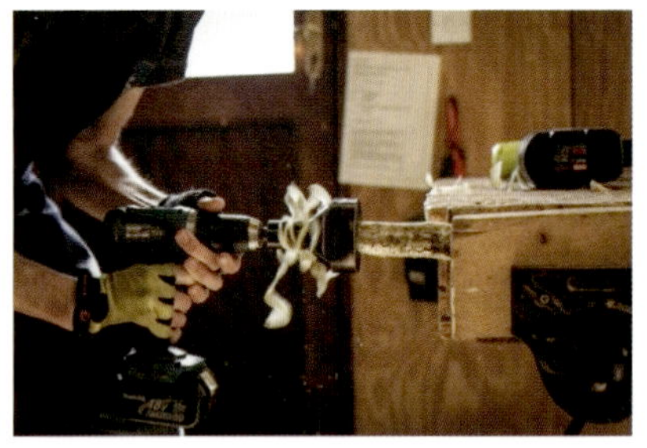

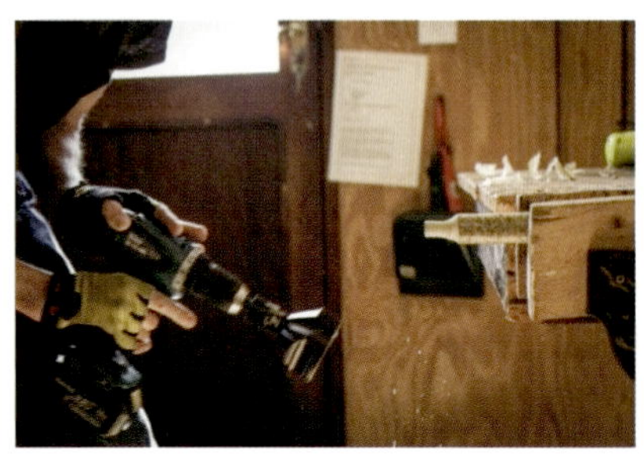

Making a tenon using a Veritas tenon cutter on a cordless drill

1. Using a Veritas ¾" tenon cutter, make tenons approximately 1" (25 mm) long, on tops of each leg.

2. Whittle the tenons slightly so that they will fit snugly into 18 mm holes using a chairmaker's gauge.

3. Using Veritas ⅝" tenon cutter, put approximately ¾" (20 mm) long tenon on each end of rails.

4 Drill 4 x 18 mm holes 7½" (190 mm) apart into the underside of the hardwood top at least 1" (25 mm) deep. pic.

5. Pair up the posts, matching colour, size and shape as desired.

6. Use chalk to mark the face you are going to drill into, hook tape measure over the bottom edge and measure 10" (250 mm) up from end on all 4 posts.

7. Drill approximately ¾" (20 mm) deep using a 15 mm drill bit.

8. Make 2 x H frames with the components using glue, pulling them together using a sash clamp.

9. Once assembled, take off the clamp and pull the tops in, transforming the H shape into something approaching an A shape.

10. Make sure you have the posts facing in the right direction so that any kick-out or curve is facing outwards and not under the stool. Tap the tenons lightly into the 4 holes in the stool top and pull the posts outwards slightly creating a splay.

11. Stand the stool on the bench top and settle the posts into position.

12. Measure from the bottom of the post up to 10½" (265 mm) and mark with chalk for drilling. Do this on all 4 posts.

13. Wiggle the posts out of the holes in the seat and drill into the posts using a 15 mm drill bit. Insert and glue rails.

14. Firmly twist and tweak the frame as necessary, ensuring all feet touch the ground (more or less).

15. Glue the posts into the seat top. Knock them in using a mallet and then use a sash clamp to pull each one in as deep as it will go. Too much glue is better than not enough. I make sure the

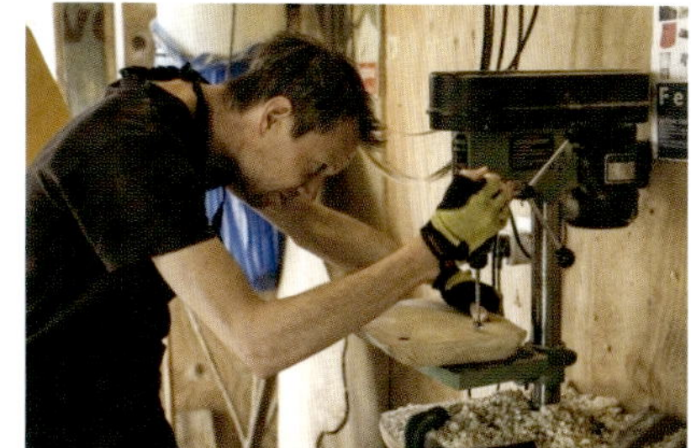

Drilling mortices into a hardwood stool top using a pillar drill

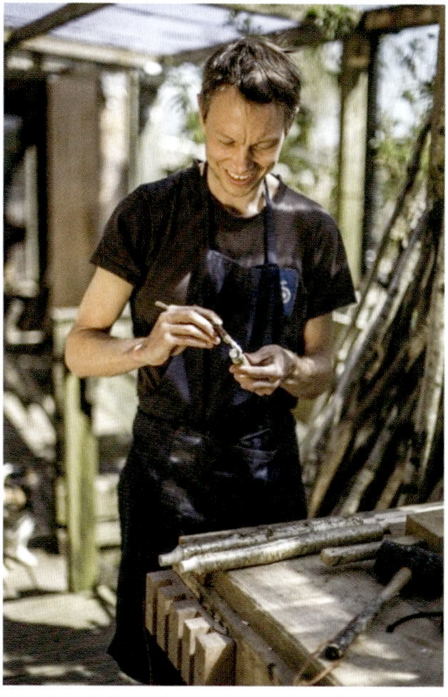

Applying glue to tenons using a twig

below (left to right): Assembling the frames using glue and a rubber mallet

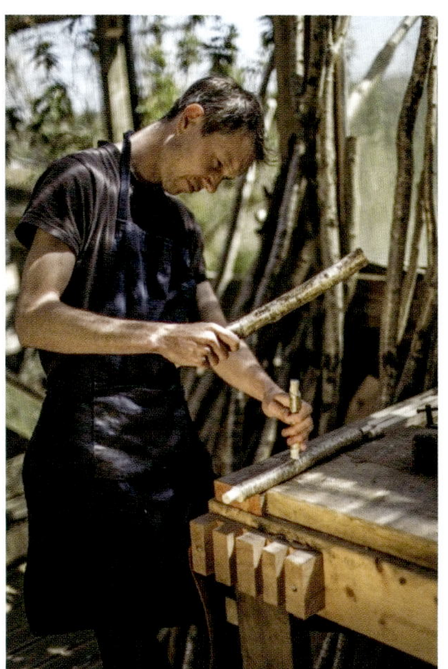

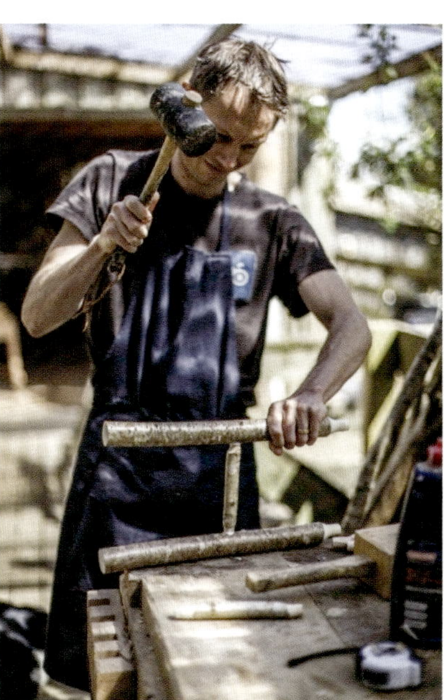

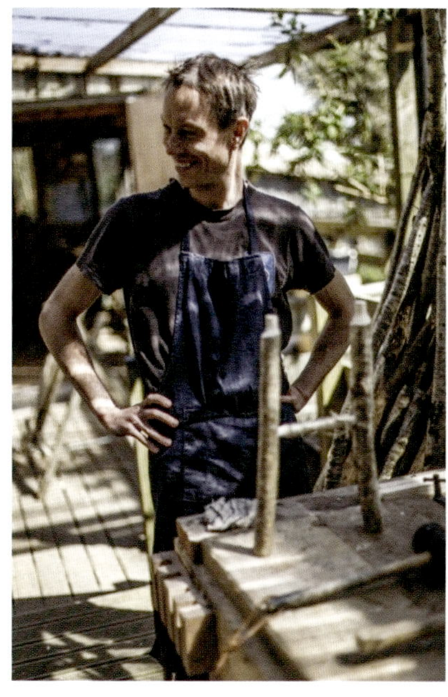

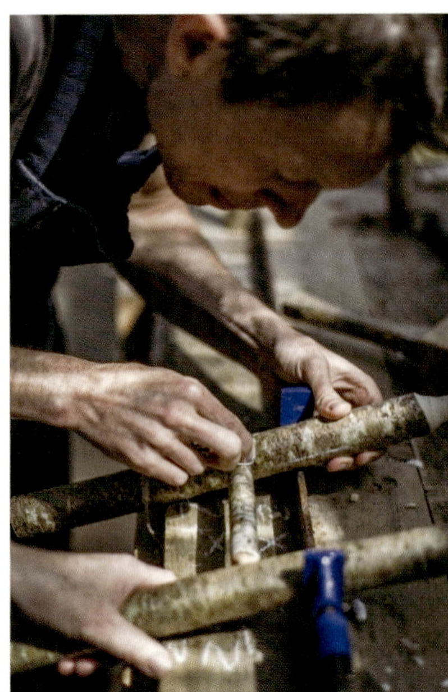

Pull the frames together using a sash clamp

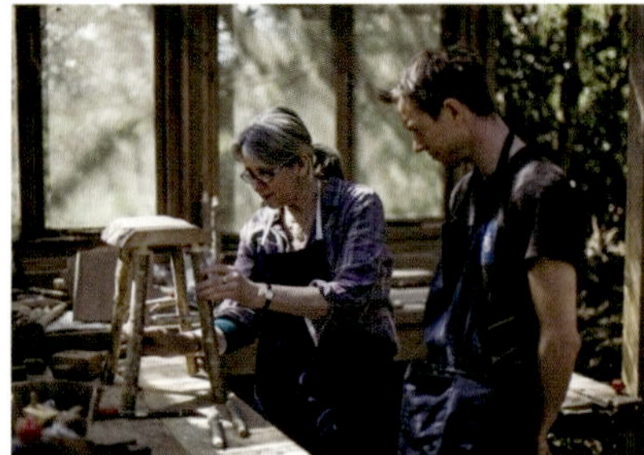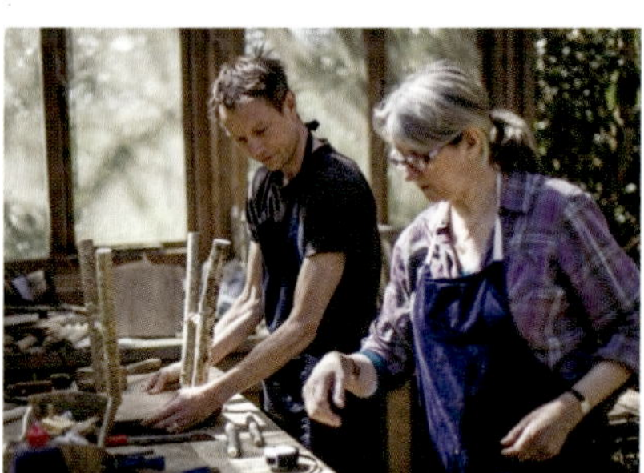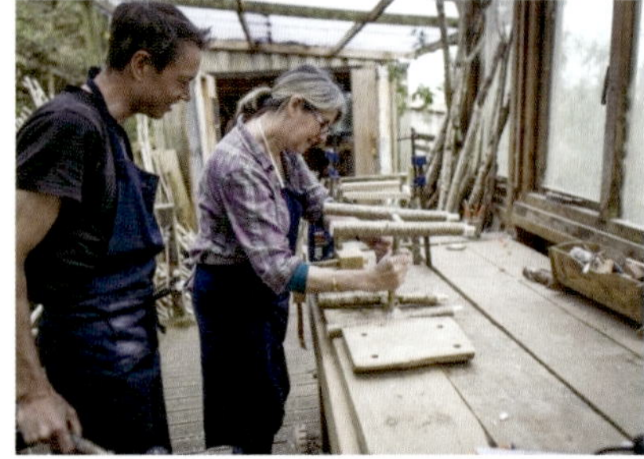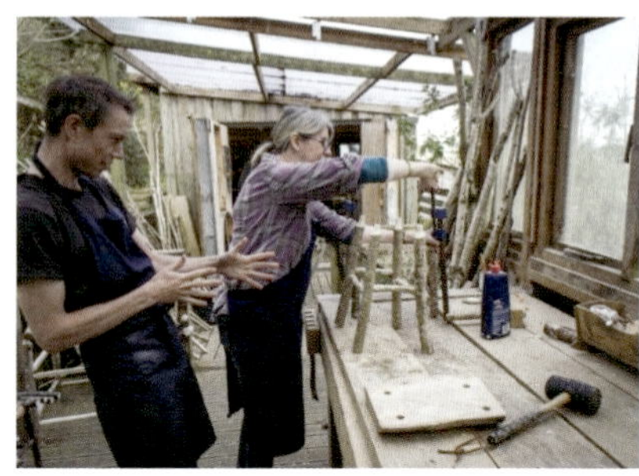

top left: With both frames assembled and the top (temporarily) in place settle the posts into position; top right: Turn the stool upside down and measure positions for drilling of mortices; above left: Once the mortices are drilled, insert and glue the last two rails into position; above right: Firmly twist and tweak the structure as necessary so that it is sitting flat

sides of the mortice and the tenon are coated. Otherwise the glue can pool in the bottom of the hole and do very little work.

16. Wipe off excess glue.

If the feet do not all touch the ground, be prepared to trim them slightly as necessary. Always trim the leg beside the one that is too short, not the one diagonally opposite.

I use a 1" Veritas tenon cutter to finish the bottom of each post as just a couple of turns gives a neat finished edge.

GOOD TO KNOW

I use the sash clamp to help locate tenons into mortices without too much use of a mallet. Sash clamps exert huge pressure without damaging the wood or bark. I insert glue blocks to protect the green bark.

This stool can be made in all shapes and sizes. Do not get hung up on the dimensions I have used here, experiment with the design — try it with birch or ash or even blackthorn!

right: Single rung upholstered footstool

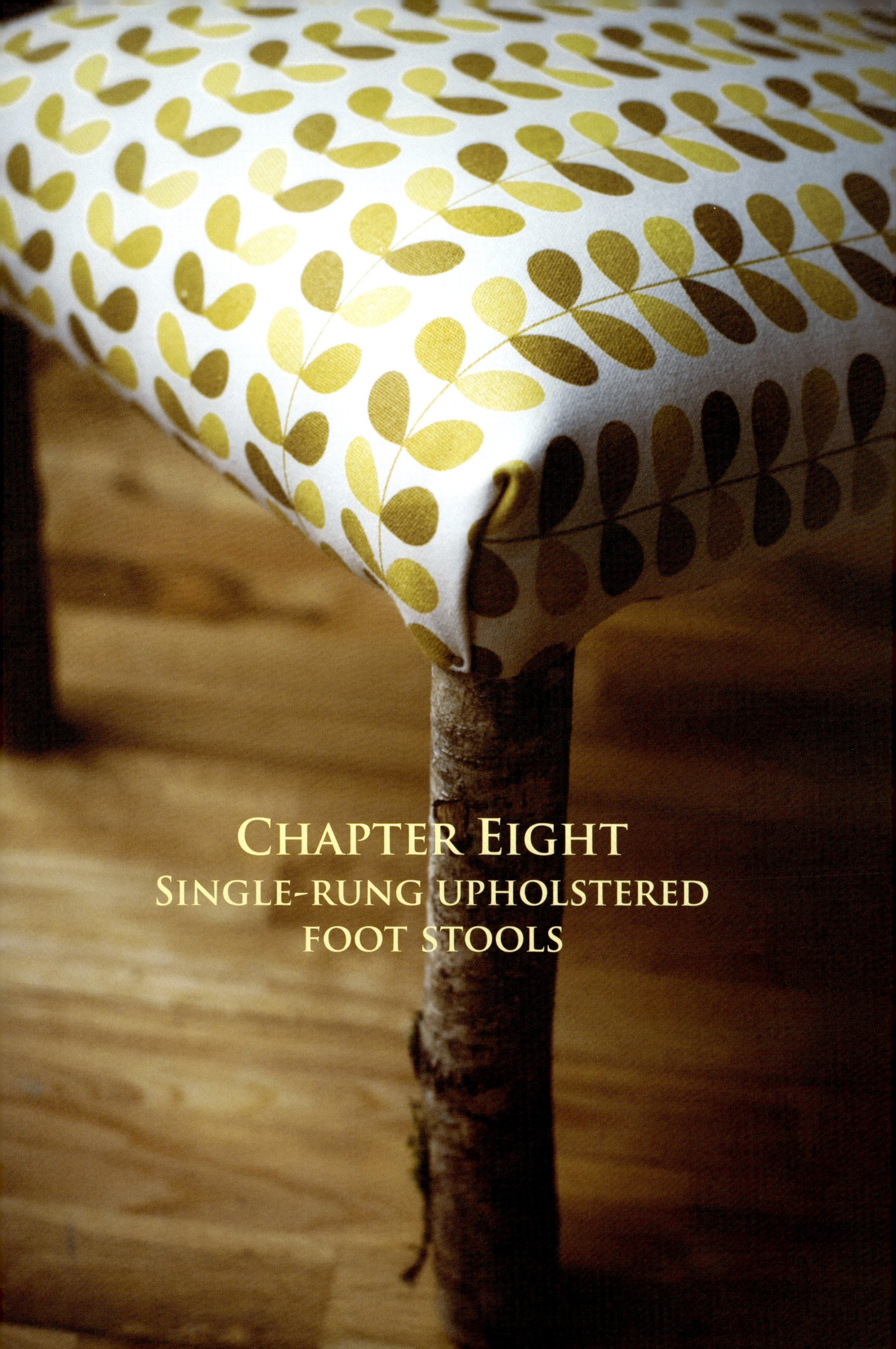

CHAPTER EIGHT
SINGLE-RUNG UPHOLSTERED
FOOT STOOLS

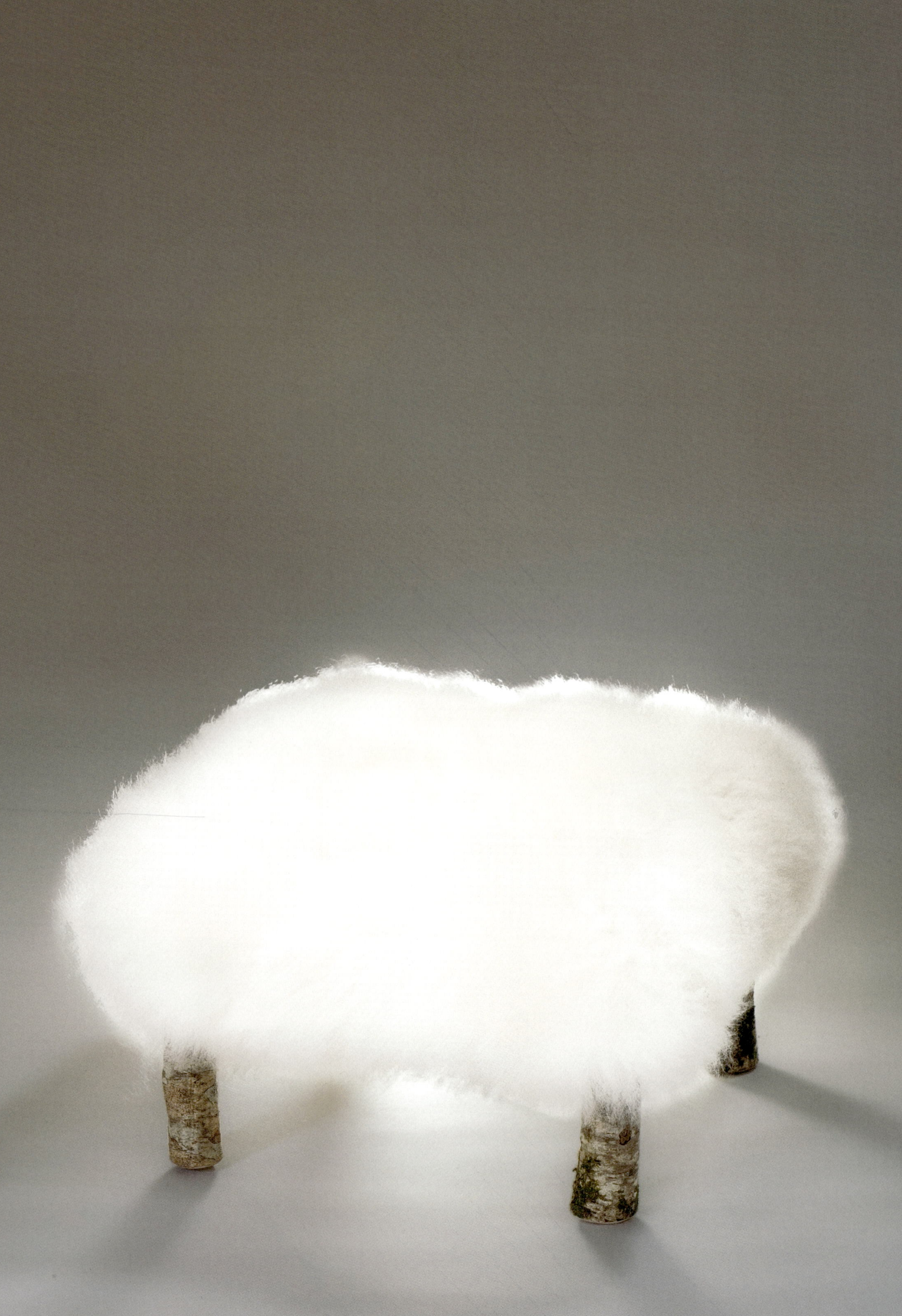

Single-rung upholstered foot stools

You can experiment with the dimensions of this stool depending on the size of your room and how the stool will be used. It is most often used as a footstool or leg rest because it fits very well in front of an armchair or sofa, allowing you to recline.

These stools are popular because they are cosy, comfortable and attractive. In our living room we have two of these stools, one upholstered in fabric, the other in sheepskin. Despite being very lightweight, they are stable because of the splayed legs.

This footstool can be made using green wood for all of its components. However, I use hazel for the four posts and 1" square section ash for the upholstery rail. I find that upholstery nails and staples grip better in ash. Also, it is easier to upholster onto a flat surface than onto a round stick, and looks neater. Having said that, it is not essential as green wood rails will also do the job.

This particular example is 12" (30 cm) high and 15" (38 cm) square.

In terms of materials for upholstery, I try to source natural fibres where possible. You can simply buy a cushion or pillow but they are likely to contain polyester wadding which is not a natural fibre. Always be aware of textiles that are potential fire hazards. There are many materials available which are flame retardant such as wool and cotton felt.

For the strapping, I use 40 mm wide hessian straps, woven and secured using a heavy duty staple gun — 3 staples in each end. Bend over the end of the strap and staple it, leave a small gap of about ¼" (6 mm) then do the next one. The hessian strapping is approximately 2" (50 mm) wide, you should fit 6 or 7 straps across in each direction, keep them close together and pull them tight when securing.

For the padding, I use 4 oz. of wool/cotton/felt wadding (see Appendix for suppliers). I use two layers to make the seat comfy then

left: Small sheepskin upholstered footstool

put upholstery fabric on top. The fabric is secured with ¾" upholstery nails but you can use staples if you find them easier to use.

Again, I try to source pure wool, cotton or recycled fabric for the upholstery. If you are using eco-friendly green wood for your frame, it makes sense to stick with natural fibres for your upholstery.

You can cover the tops of the posts with your upholstery fabric (add extra padding on top of each post before covering) or upholster around them if you prefer to leave them showing.

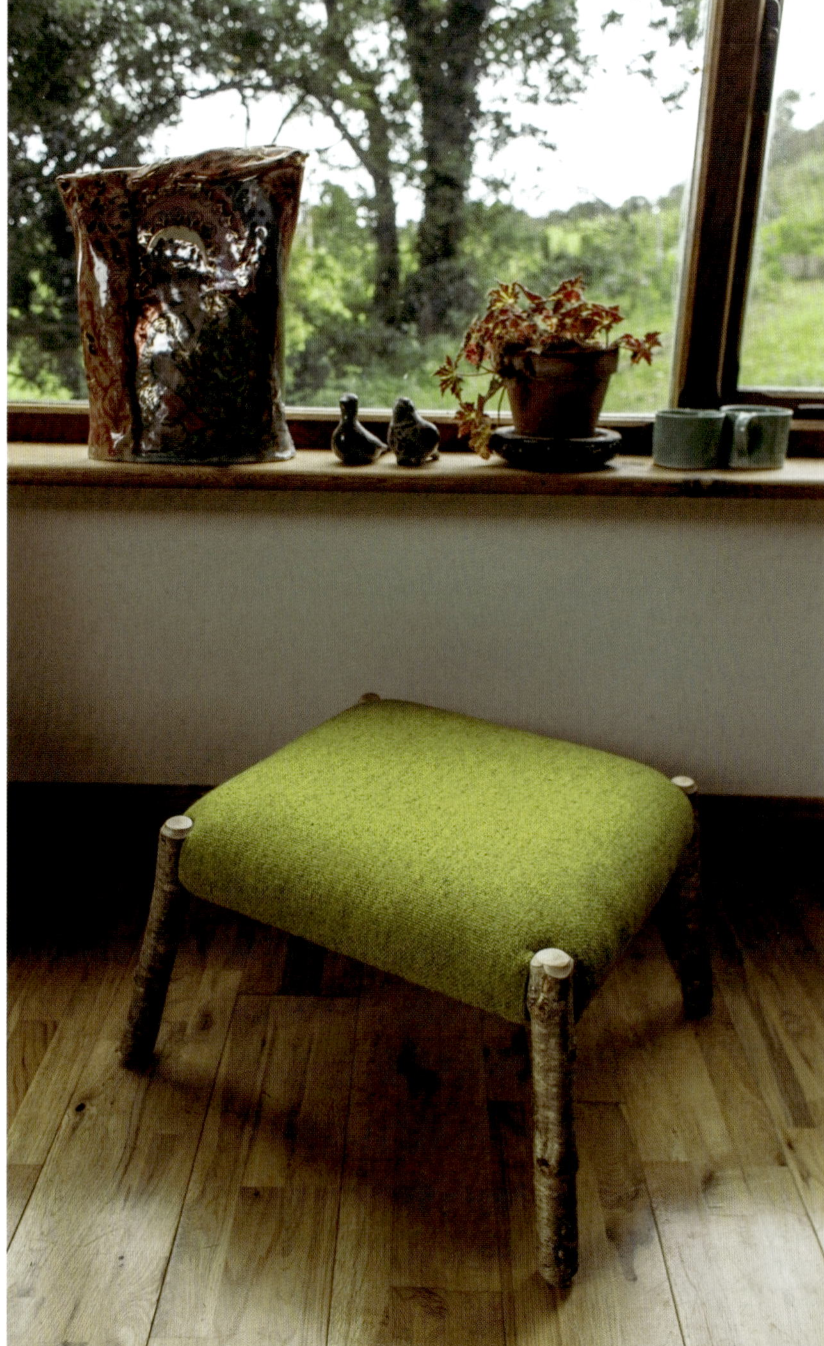

below: Single rail upholstered footstool with posts covered
right: Single rail upholstered footstool with posts exposed

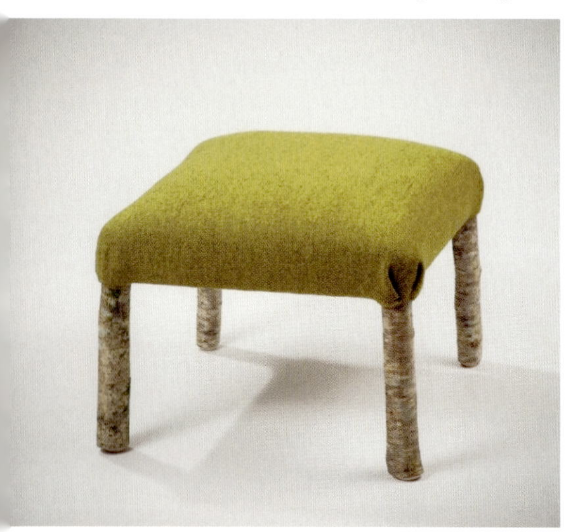

- 4 x 12" (300 mm) hazel posts approximately 1½" diameter at foot

- 4 x 15" (25 mm) square section ash 1" square

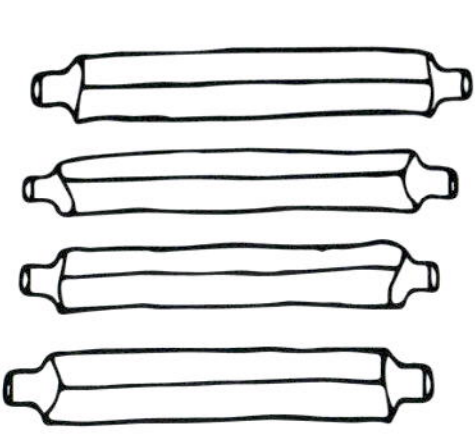

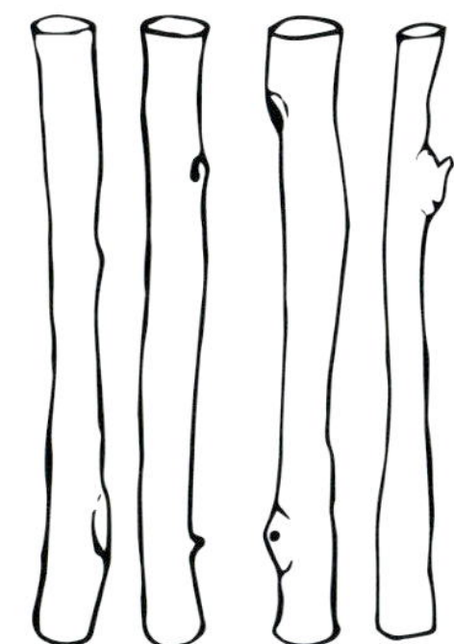

4 x square ash rails

4 x hazel posts

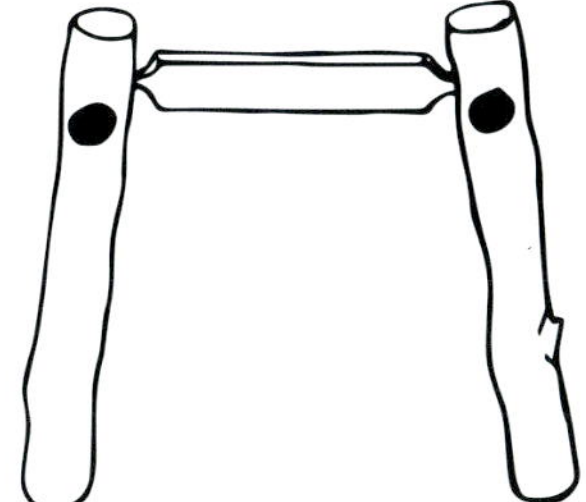

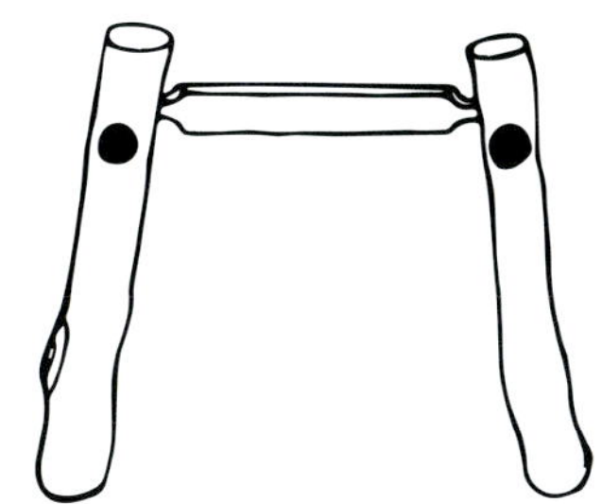

Offset frames

UPHOLSTERY

- Hessian strapping

- Wadding

- Sheepskin or upholstery fabric

INSTRUCTIONS

1. Make the stool in 2 stages.

2. Put a ¾" tenon on both ends of the 4 ash rails. Whittle to fit using a chairmaker's gauge.

3. Pair up the posts so that colour, shape and thickness are similar for each pair. Decide how they will face each other and which face you will be drilling into.

Ana testing the whittled tenon for size in the gauge

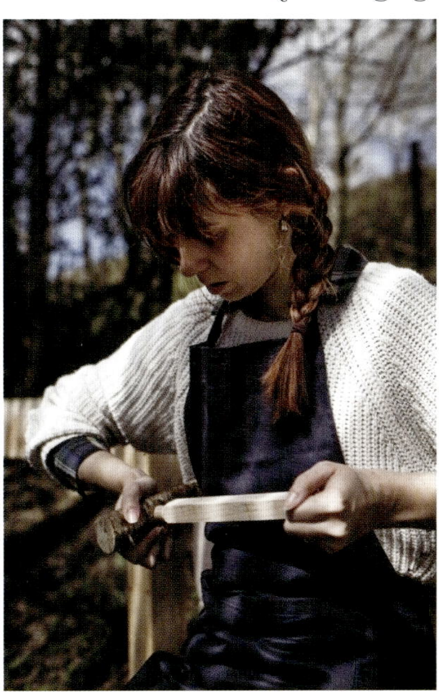

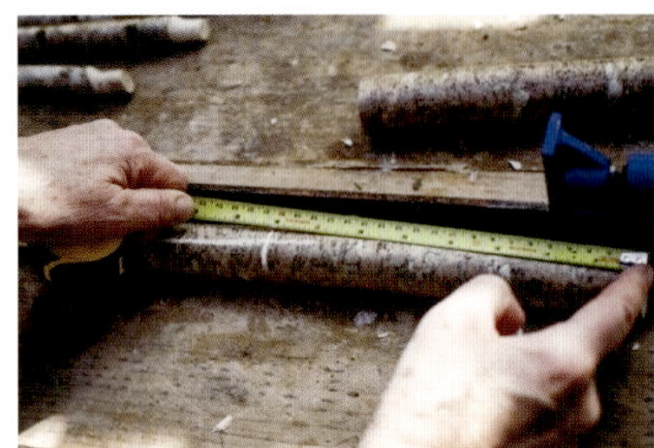

Using white chalk mark the centreline and then mark the mortice position with a cross

4. Using white chalk, mark a centre line all the way down the drilling face of each post.

5. Hook your tape measure onto top of post and measure 2" (250 mm) down, mark with chalk across centre line, forming a cross. Repeat this with all 4 posts.

6. Using a pillar drill and an 18 mm 3D drill bit, make a hole approximately 1" (25 mm) deep in each post (use dibbing stick to measure).

7. Apply glue to both mortices and tenons. Too much glue is better than not enough!

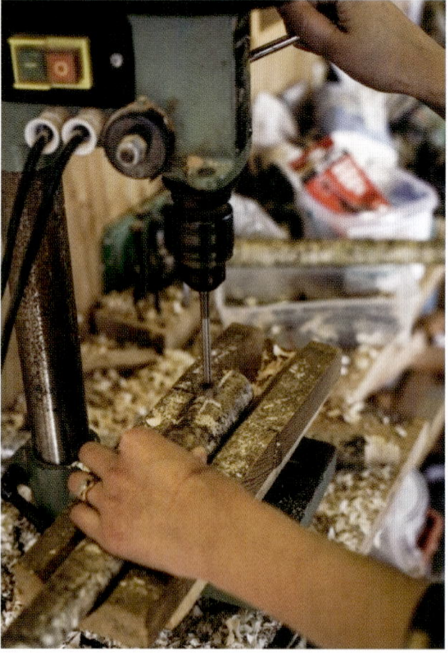

Using a pillar drill and holding post in a 'V' cradle drill mortice

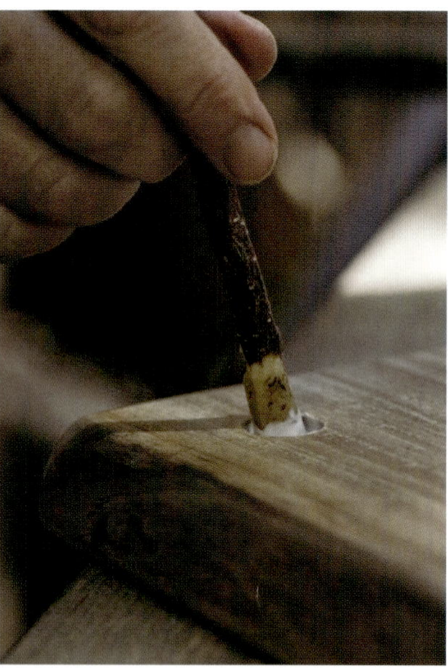

Apply glue to both mortice and tenon, spreading evenly using a twig

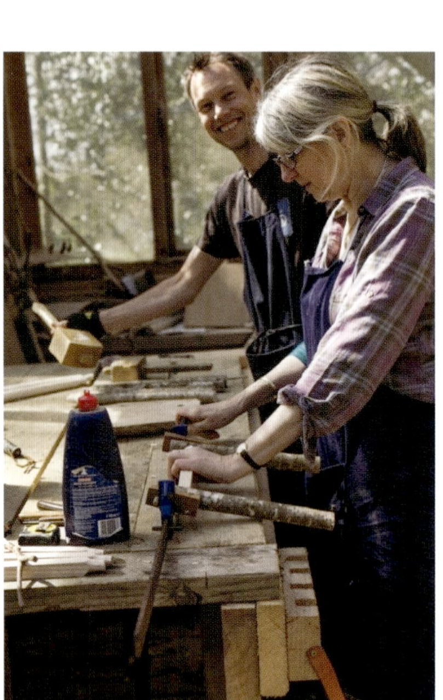

Use sash clamp to pull frame together

8. Tap joints into place using a rubber mallet so as not to damage the bark.

9. Before clamping, put a spacer i.e. a piece of scrap wood approximately 14¼" (362 mm) long between the posts at the bottom. This will ensure that the frame will dry with a slight outwards splay. You will remove it once the glue has set.

10. Clamp together using sash clamp with wooden glue blocks to prevent damage to the bark. Wipe off excess glue and remove clamp. Make sure the frame lies flat on the bench. If not, hold it in both hands and give it a twist, adjust it until it lies flat.

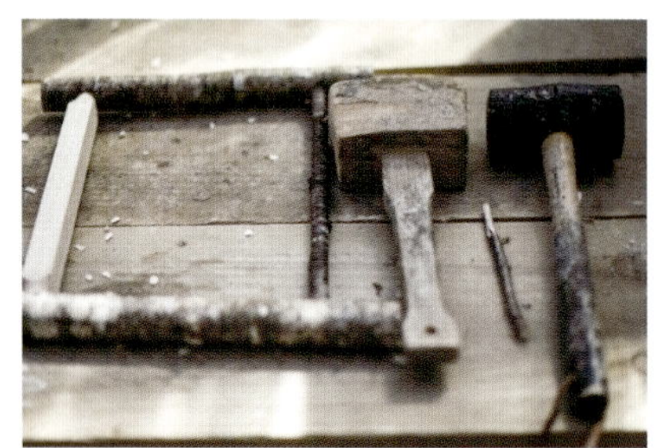

Put a scrap wood spacer between posts at bottom to ensure a slight splay

11. Once the glue has set on the 2 frames, choose which faces you want on the outside and which facing in. Draw a centre line with

white chalk and hook your tape measure on the top of each post and measure 2¾" (270 mm) down. Mark your measurement across the centre line forming a cross.

12. Using pillar drill and 18 mm 3D drill bit make holes in all 4 posts to a depth of approximately 1" (25 mm).

13. Coat tenons and mortices with glue and tap together using a rubber mallet then clamp using a sash clamp with glue blocks and with a 14¼" (362 mm) scrap wood spacer to give splay.

14. If all four feet are not touching the ground, try giving the whole structure a good twist. If that fails you can either sash clamp the stool to your bench and leave it for 24 hours or trim a small amount off one or two of the legs.

15. If you decide to trim, place the finished stool onto a flat surface (e.g. a kitchen counter or large ceramic tile) and get your eyes down to the same level. Note which leg is off the ground and by how much. Remove the corresponding amount off either of the legs beside the short one, never from the one diagonally opposite.

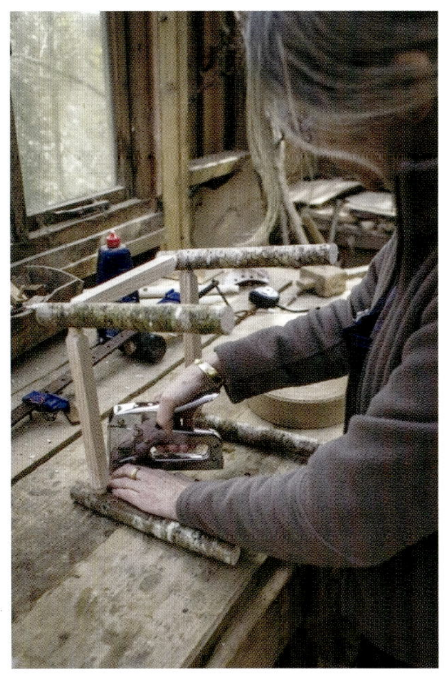
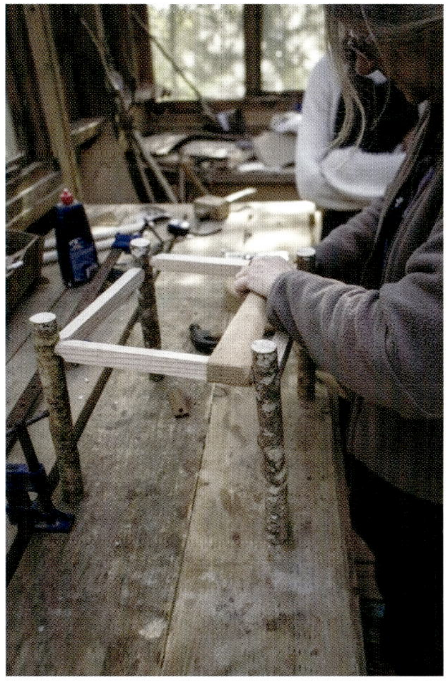

Use a staple gun to attach hessian straps, weaving them over and under to form a strong base for upholstery

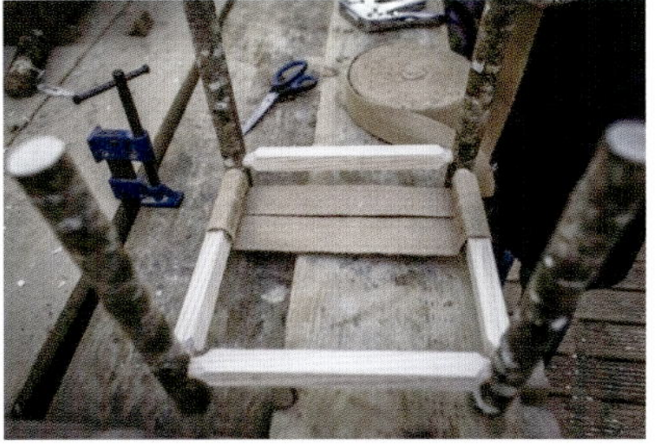
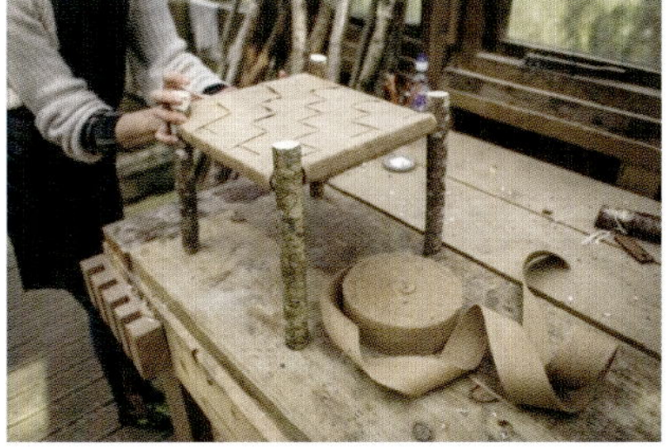
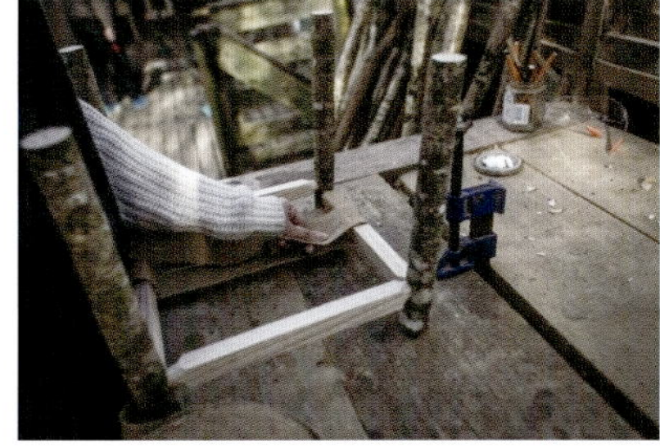

If one leg is off the ground by a large amount and it cannot be fixed by twisting, then take a small amount off both the long legs. I use a fine tooth Japanese pull saw for this job, it is the ideal tool for fine cutting.

It is best to allow the stool to season (dry out) indoors before trimming. Sometimes shrinkage can distort the structure slightly and you do not want to have to trim it twice.

right: Sheepskin upholstered Google Stool

Chapter Nine
The Google stool

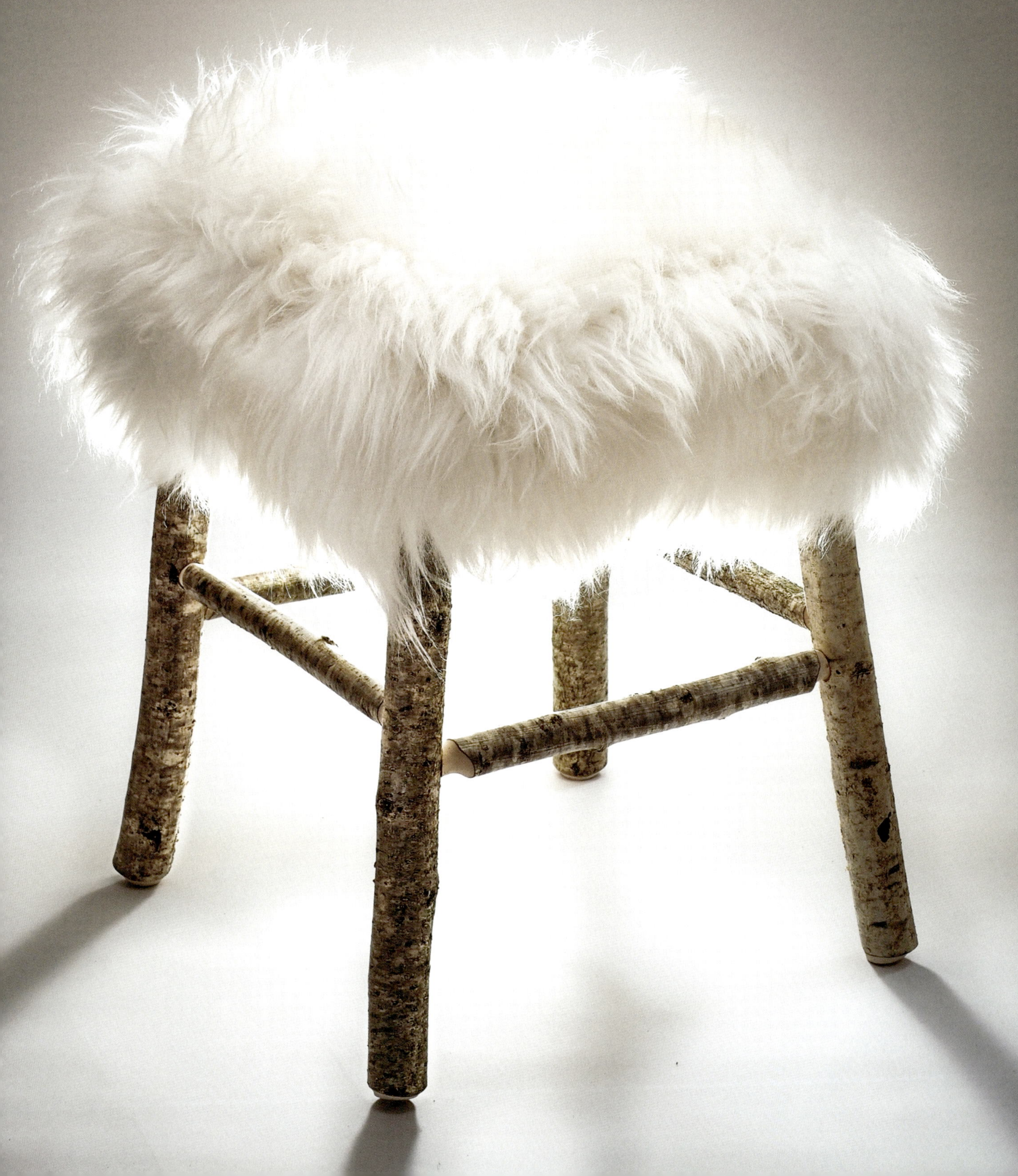

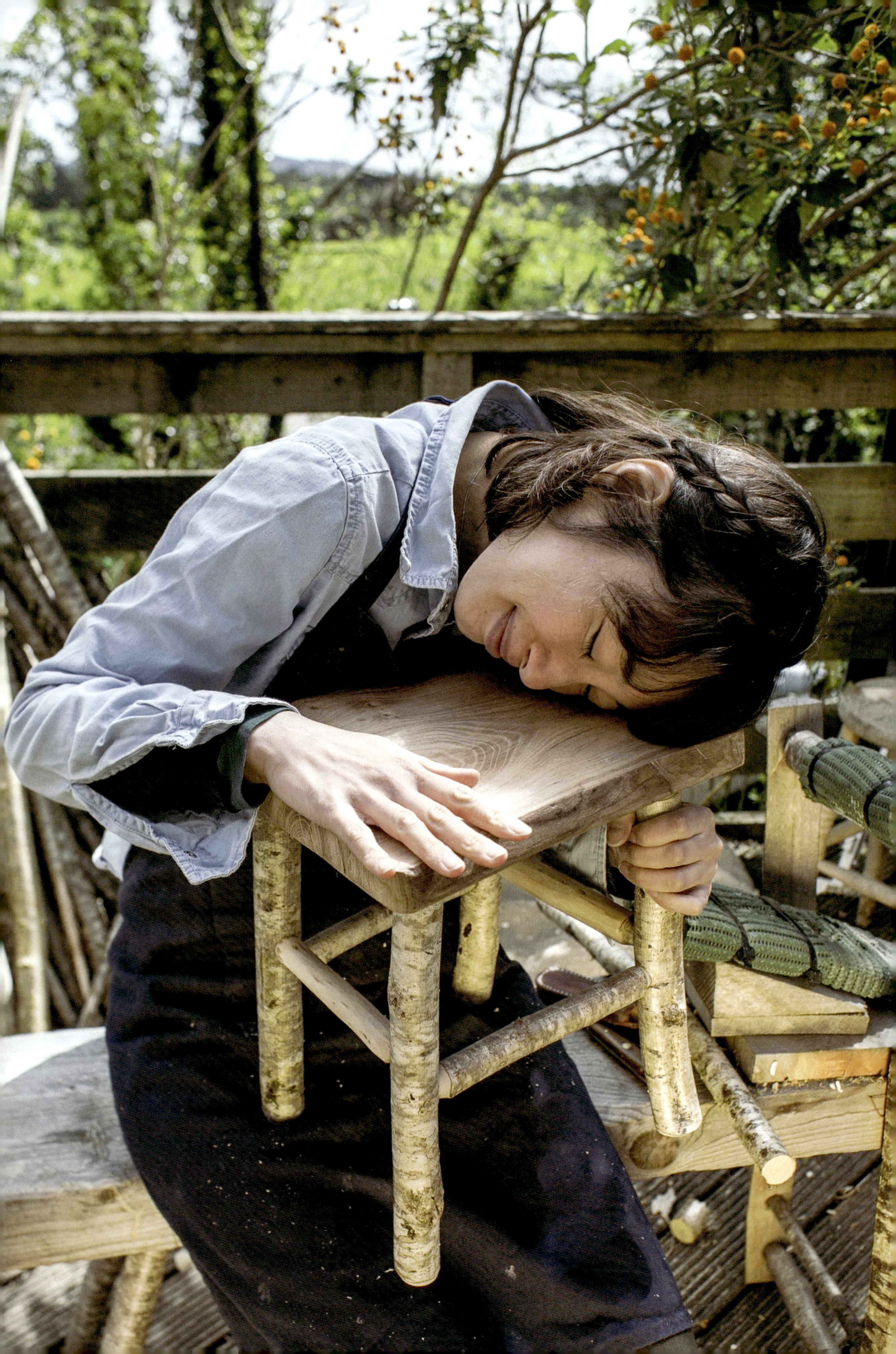

THE GOOGLE STOOL

It is hard to imagine a better material for seating than sheepskin. It is hardwearing, soft, beautiful and strong. I was therefore delighted in 2015 to be commissioned by Google to make four upholstered sheepskin stools, using all natural materials, for their new offices in Dublin. Google is famous for its inspirational work spaces and has made a commitment to build sustainably, using toxin-eliminating and eco-friendly materials throughout its office buildings in Ireland and across the world.

I was informed that these stools could be used by up to 200 people per week and therefore must be robust. I decided to look into it and was shocked to find (after a quick Google search) that office chairs are often neglected and mistreated. It is not unusual for office chairs to be kicked, tipped back, tipped sideways, dumped in corridors, thrown across the office, have their upholstery ripped or torn or be dumped in the street.

Once I had come to terms with the idea that people can treat chairs so badly, I decided to reinforce the structure of the stools by adding an extra rung, half way up the legs.

I earnestly hope that the soft, woolly sheepskin will have a calming influence and bring out the best in people who use them or work nearby. They are so appealing, I can only believe they will be stroked, hugged and adored.

Although the style is similar to the single-rung upholstered footstool (Chapter 8), Google wanted these stools to be higher, for use as seats at a table with a finished height of 18" or 45 cm.

It is not easy to measure the height of a stool which has a sheepskin seat. Depending on how thick you make your wadding and how long-haired your sheepskin is, the extra layers could add an extra 2-4" (50-100 mm) to the height.

Cutting list

- 4 x posts hazel approximately 1½" (30 mm) diameter and 16" (400 mm) long

- 4 x rails hazel approximately 1" (25 mm) diameter and 11½" (290 mm) long

- 4 x rails square section ash 1" x 1" (25 mm) diameter 10" (250 mm) long

Upholstery supplies

- Hessian straps 1½" (30 mm) wide

- Wool/cotton felt wadding 4 oz. approximately 10–11" (250-280 mm) square

- A large, long-haired sheepskin or similar

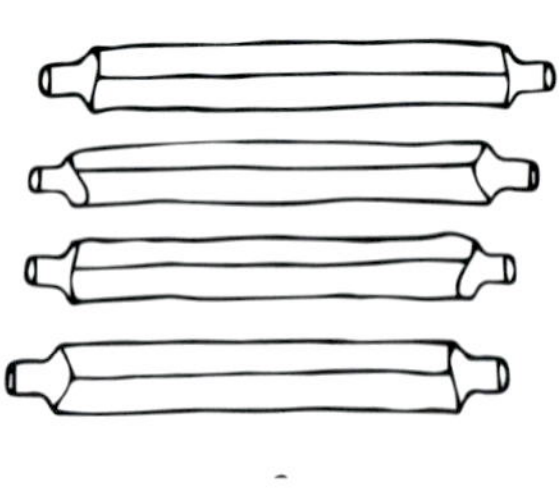

4 x square ash rails

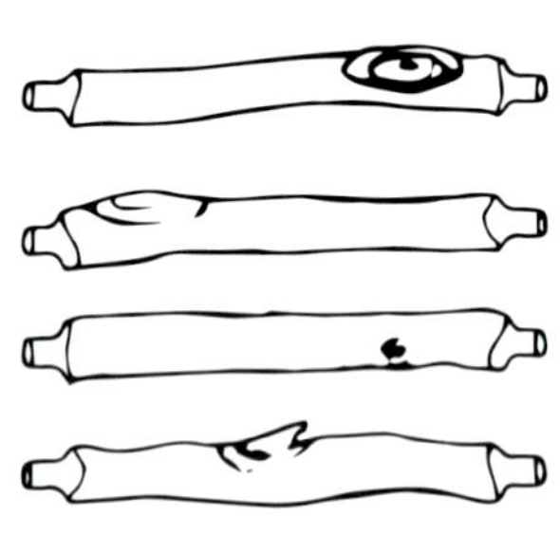

4 x hazel rails

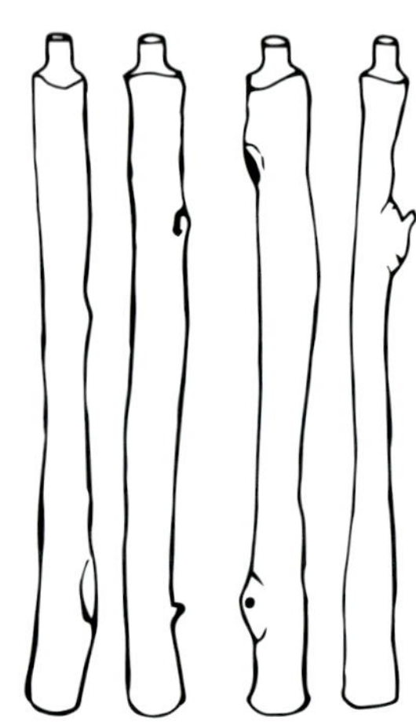

4 x hazel posts

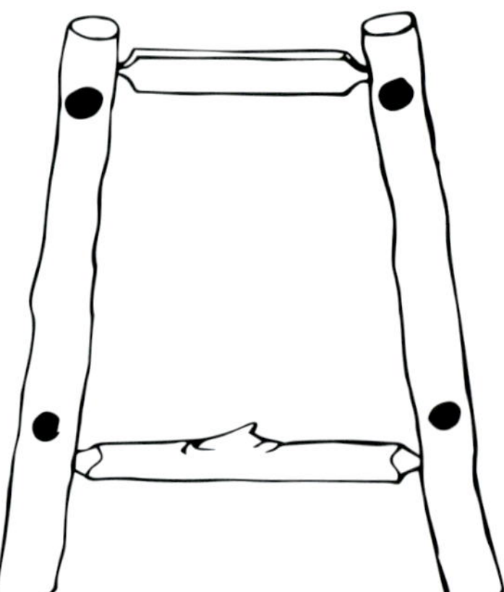

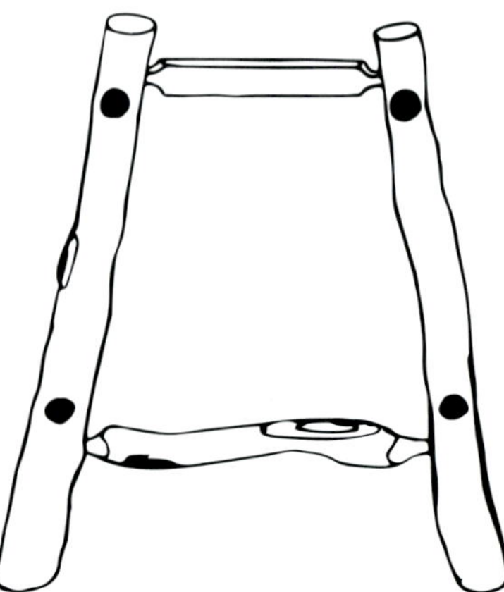

1. Select straight material approximately 2" (5 cm) at base. Cut four legs at just over 16" (40 cm) you will be trimming them down slightly after assembly and want them to finish at 16" (40 cm).

2. Cut the 4 x square rails 10" (250 mm) long. Take the sharp corners off at the ends using a fine-toothed Japanese hand saw or band saw (it helps the tenon cutter to do its job) before putting a ¾" tenon on each end of the rails. Whittle slightly.

3. Cut the 4 x hazel rails 11½" (290 mm) long. Put ¾" tenons on each end of the rails.

4. Whittle slightly, checking them for fit with your chairmaker's gauge.

5. This stool is made in two stages, first you make 2 x frames and then you join them together.

6. Pair up the four legs and on each one draw a centre line on the face you will be drilling into, using white chalk.

7. Take each leg and measure 2" (50 mm) and 9" (230 mm) down from the top, use a white chalk to mark two crosses with your measurement and centre lines.

8. Using an 18 mm MAD bit, drill both holes to a depth of approximately 1" (25 mm) including shoulder.

9. Apply glue, tap the square ash rail into the top hole and the hazel rail into the lower hole.

10. Assemble two frames. Tap the rails into place using a wooden mallet on the end of the rail and a rubber mallet when striking the bark.

11. Pull together tightly with a sash clamp, using glue blocks to prevent bark damage. Clamp the top rail first and then the lower rail.

12. If the frames do not lie flat on the bench then hold them, with a post in each hand and twist, adjust gradually until they lie flat. If they resist twisting, use your bench vice. Stand the frame up with one leg held in the vice and twist the other leg until the frame is flat.

13. Allow the glue to dry.

14. Meanwhile, whittle the tenons of the other two square rails and two hazel rails.

15. Decide how you are going to assemble. Choose which surface should face outwards.

16. On the inside face, mark your drill holes with crosses, ensuring you have offset them slightly. Measure 2½" (65 mm) not 2" (50 mm) as you did with the first holes, then 9½" (240 mm) not 9" (230 mm).

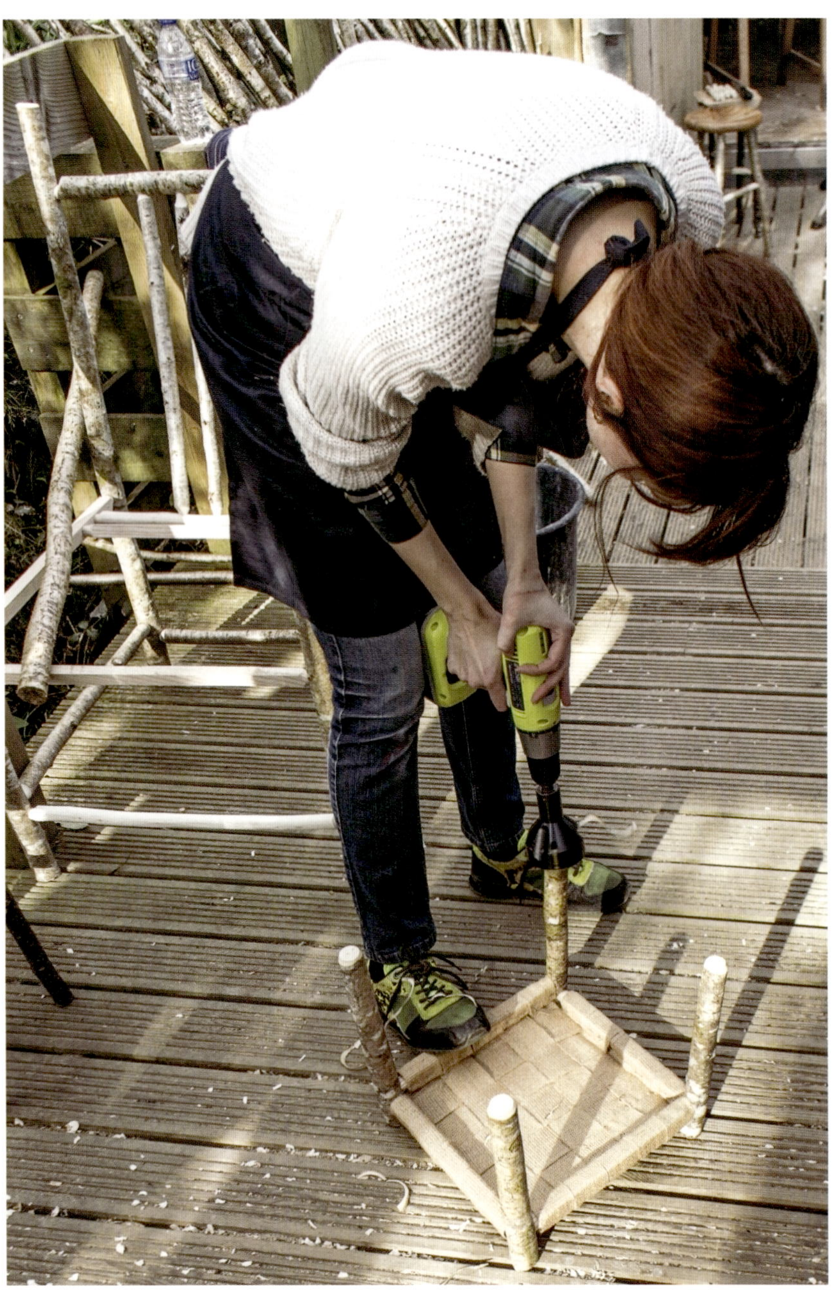

Ana uses a tenon cutter to neatly chamfer bottom edge

17. Using an 18 mm MAD bit, drill all 4 holes, glue and assemble. Use a sash clamp with glue blocks to ensure a snug fit.

18. Remove the clamp, wipe off excess glue.

19. If the stool does not sit flat, give it a twist or clamp it to the bench overnight. If necessary trim legs to sit flat.

20. Trim the top 1" (25 mm) off the top of each leg and soften the contours using a tenon cutter and/or sander. You do not want to feel that sharp edge through the sheepskin.

Upholstery

1. Weave hessian straps across in both directions, stapling the straps at each end, keep them taut.

2. Position the wadding square across the woven straps. Staple an extra layer of wadding on top of each leg in order to not be able to feel it through the sheepskin.

3. Place the sheepskin on top, pulling the sides tightly down and round, attach them to the rail on both sides using ¾" upholstery nails.

4. The long hairs of the sheepskin make it difficult to get close enough to hammer. I find it is easier to hold the nail with some pointy-nosed pliers until it has been virtually hammered down. In my experience, staples do not go in securely enough.

You will have to adjust and trim the sheepskin to make it fit. I am not an experienced upholsterer but I find that long haired sheepskin not only looks and feels great but the long hair hides a multitude of staples and nails. It is a very forgiving material!

next page: Detail kitchen stool decorated by Alison Ospina

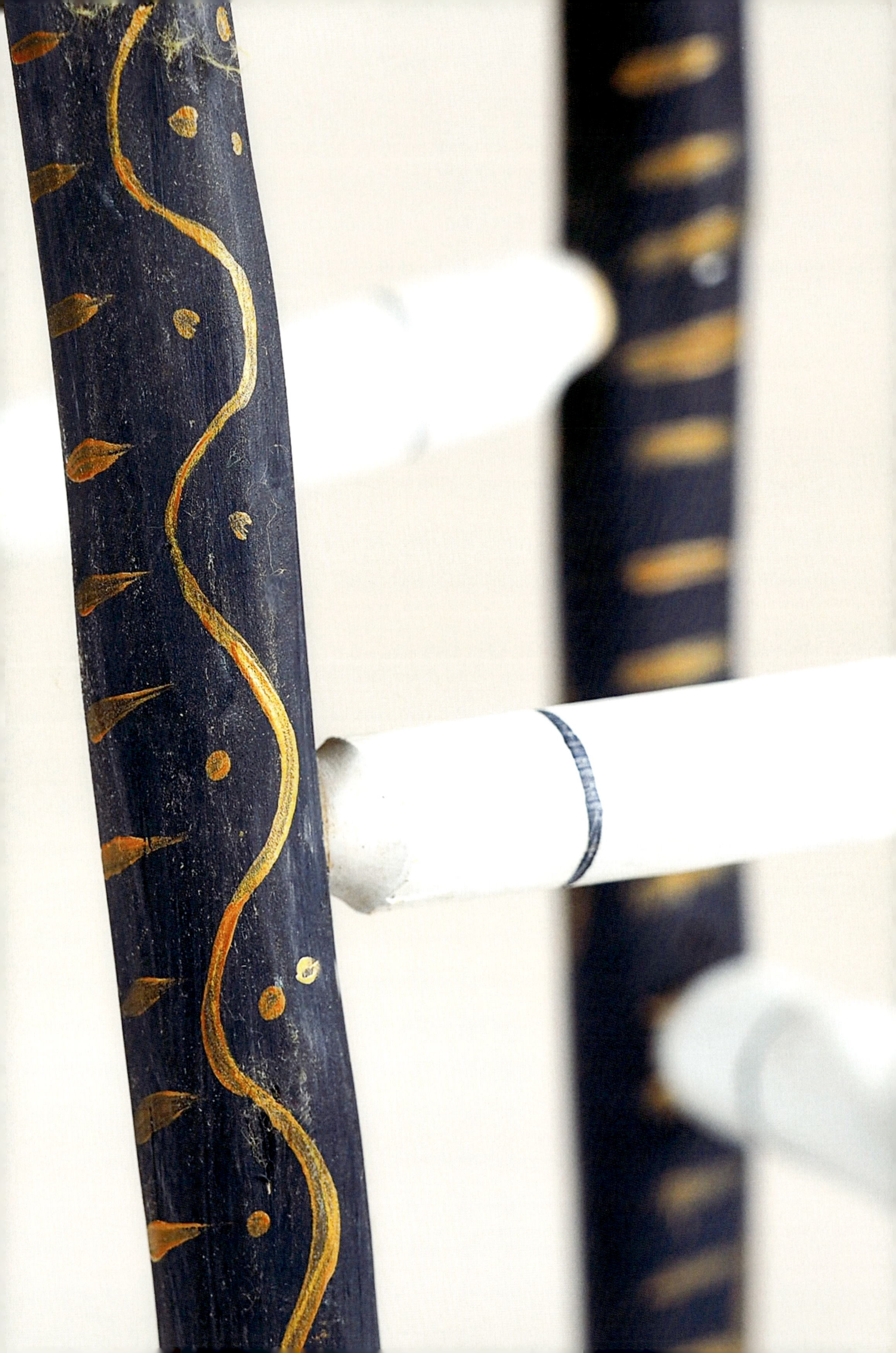

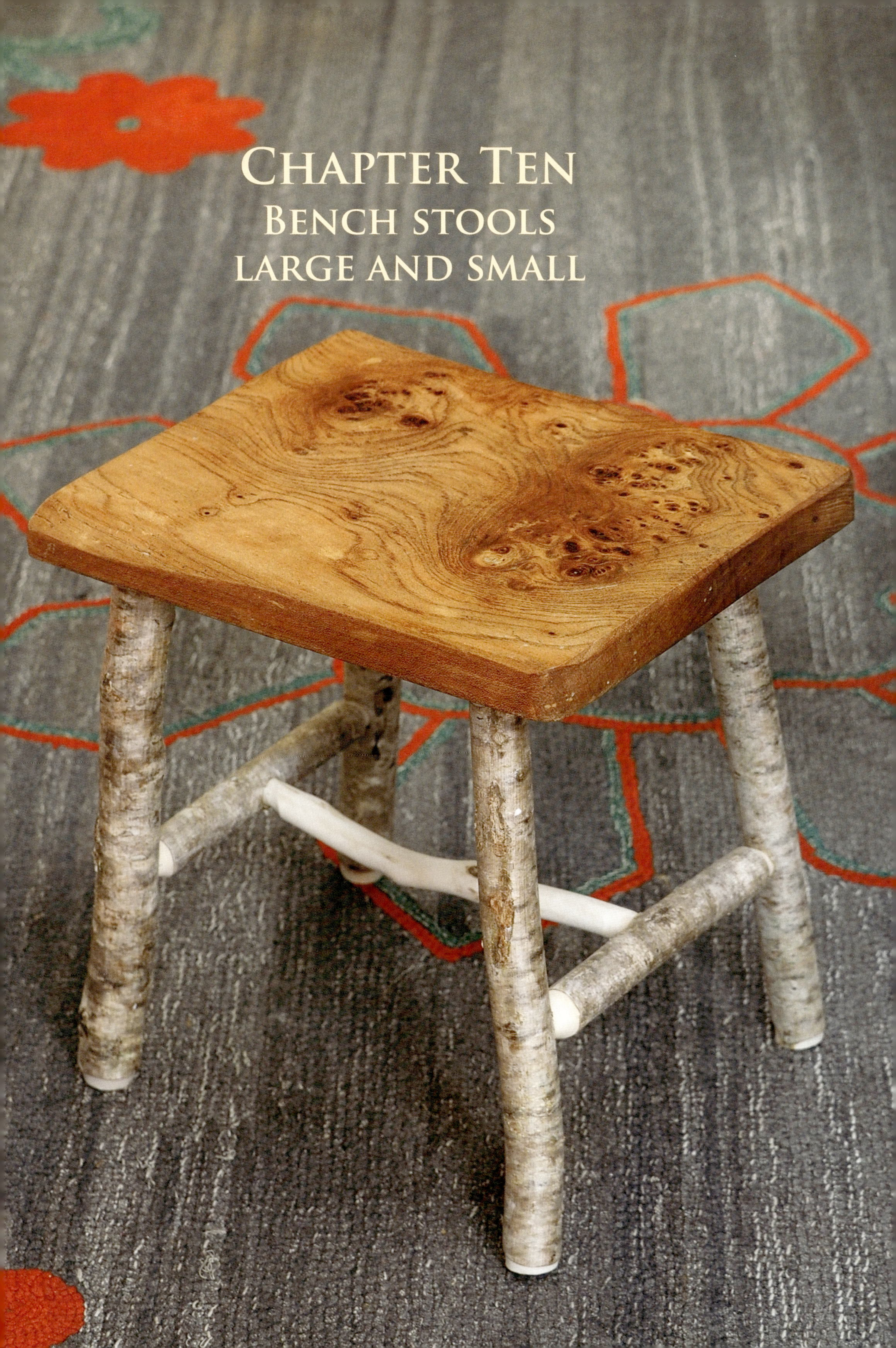
CHAPTER TEN
BENCH STOOLS
LARGE AND SMALL

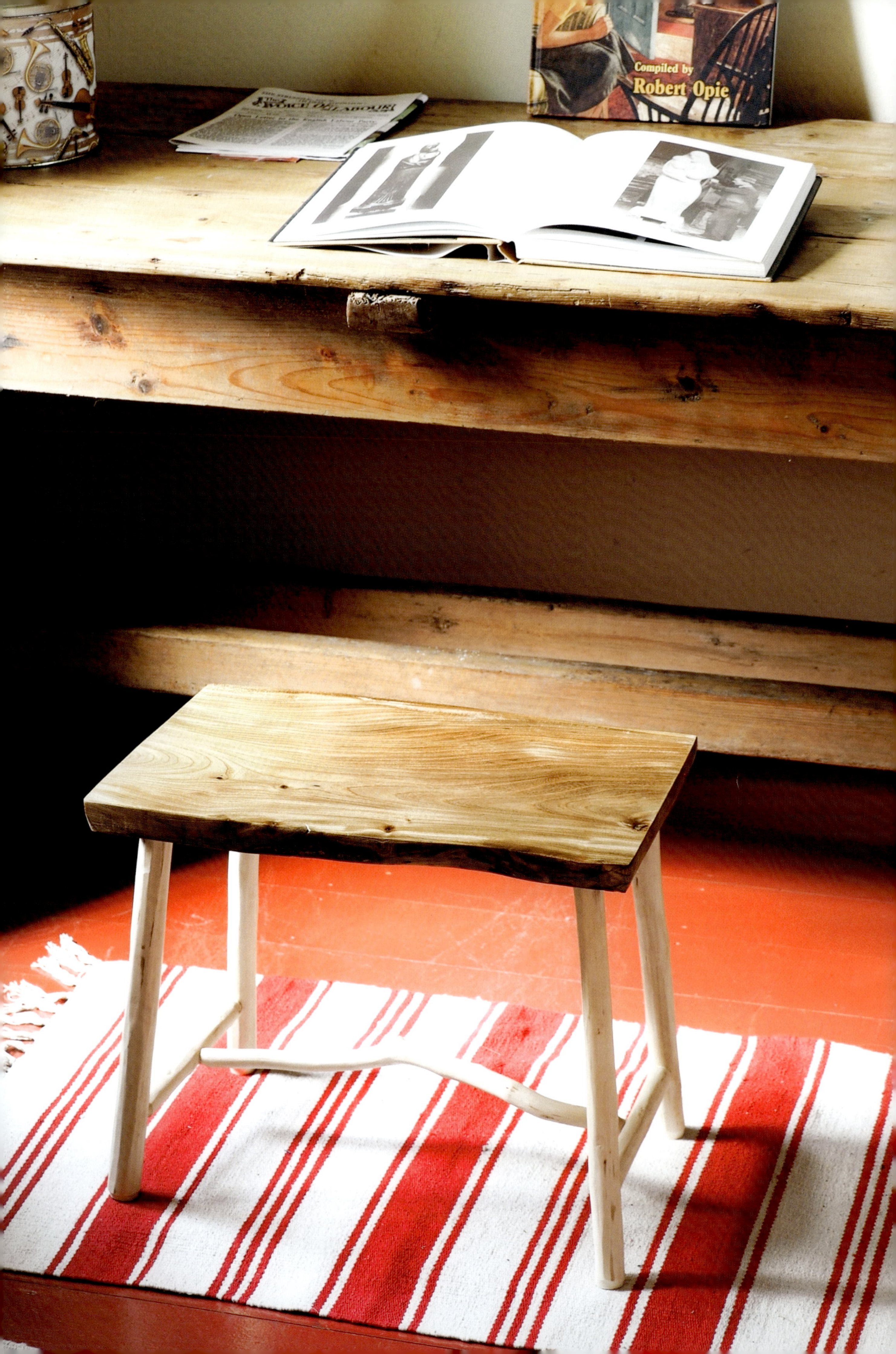

BENCH STOOLS LARGE AND SMALL

These handy bench stools can be made in a variety of shapes and sizes. The construction is very simple but still remains robust. At its smallest, this stool makes a useful seat for a child. At its largest, it has the potential to be a table or even a bench that could seat several adults. Naturally, the larger the bench, the heavier the materials you will need to use.

A single stretcher between the rails gives these benches a less cluttered appearance and gives the maker an opportunity to use interestingly-shaped branches, which look attractive and will not get in the way. A curvy, sinuous stretcher which has been stripped and polished will add a touch of elegance and character to this construction.

far right: Medium sized hazel bench stool with elm top
below: Large hazel bench with elm top

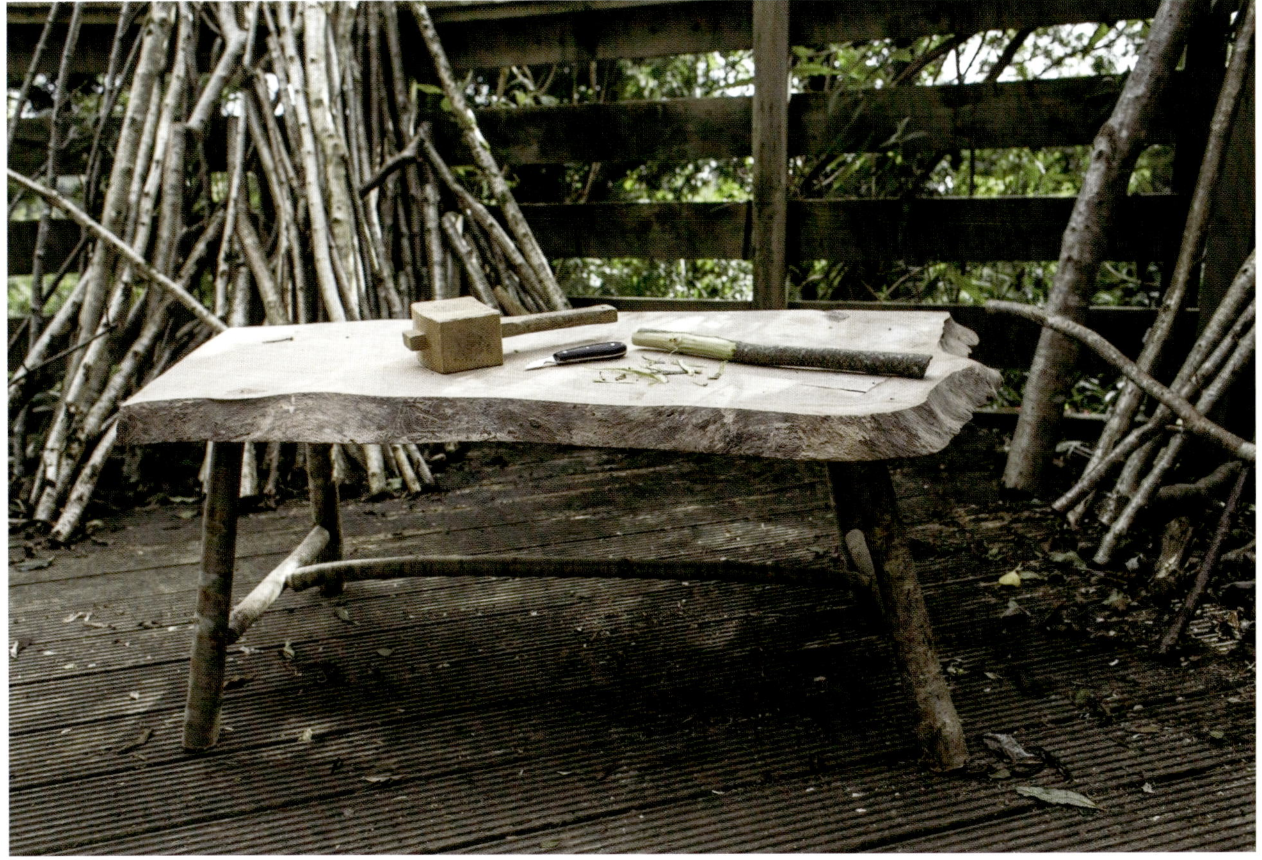

As with most of my chairs and stools, I have used elm boards for the tops of these stools. If you can purchase attractive, wide boards (10" (250 mm) is the optimum width) with natural (waney) edges, the materials complement each other and give a sculptural, freeform look to the piece.

When making larger items using green wood, I try to avoid the 'Lord of the Rings' look which tends to favour function over form. I try to avoid building anything too clumpy or over engineered. These materials are naturally strong and as long as your piece has well-made joints, it can be lightweight and elegant and still take the strain of everyday use.

Cutting list Large bench stool

- Overall dimensions 15" (40 cm) height

- 18½" (47 cm) long

- 11" (27 cm) wide

- Cut 4 x posts 15" (38 cm)

- Cut 2 x rails 9½" (24 cm)

- 1 x stretcher 17" or (43 cm) long (cut it over long and adjust as necessary when fitting)

- Elm board 18½" (47 cm) long and 11" (28 cm) wide

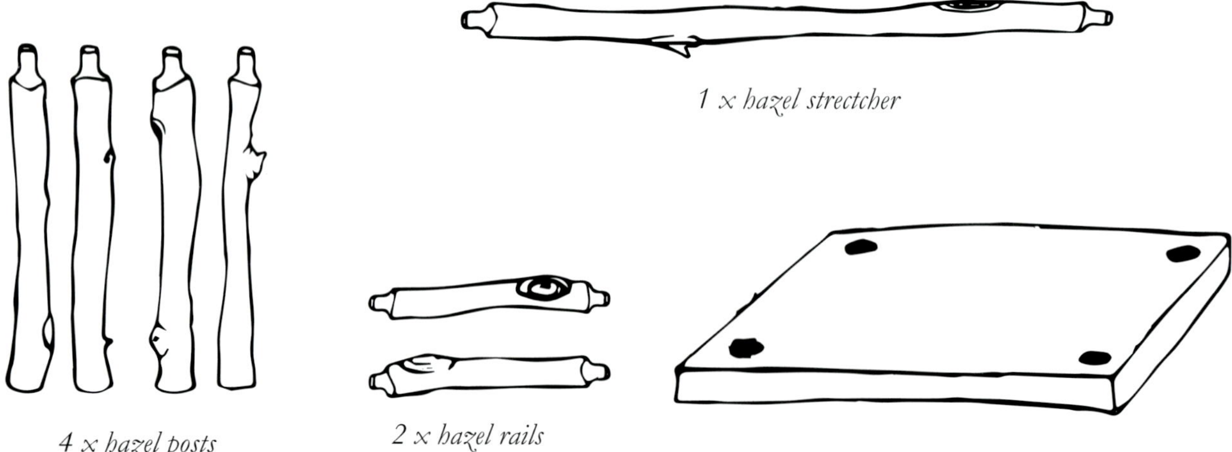

1 x hazel strectcher

4 x hazel posts

2 x hazel rails

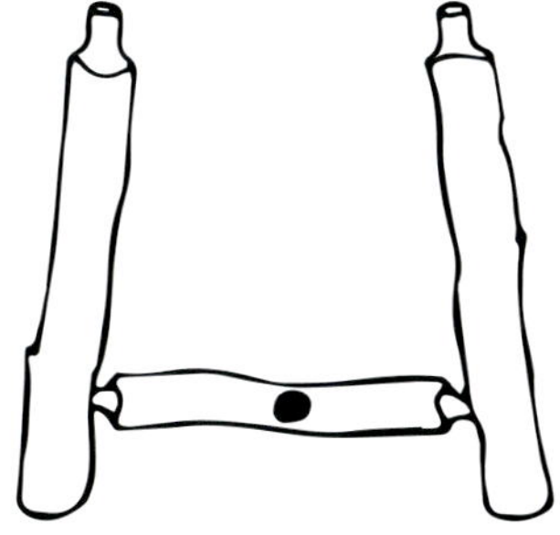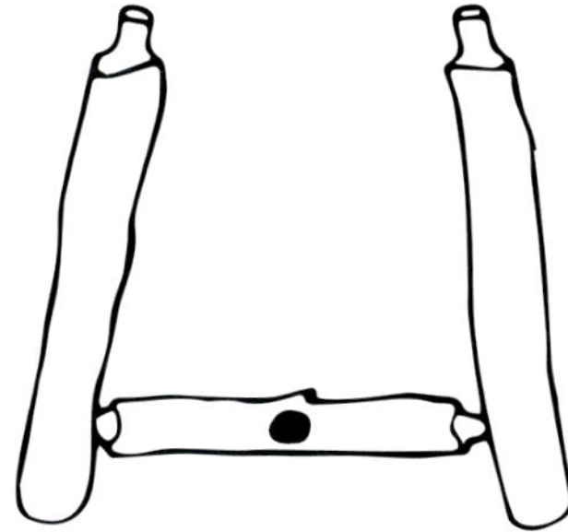

Splayed frames

INSTRUCTIONS

1. Cut the 4 posts and make ¾" tenons on top of each one.

2. Cut the 2 rails and make ⅝" tenons on both ends of each one.

3. Sand and shape the elm board, softening the edges and corners slightly.

4. Mark out the elm board and drill x 4 mortices using an 18 mm drill bit approximately 1½" (4 cm) from side and 2" (5 cm) from ends.

5. Mortices should measure approximately 8" (20 cm) apart across the board and 14½" (37 cm) lengthways.

6. Pair up the posts with kicking feet facing outwards, mark with white chalk the face you will be drilling into.

7. Whittle the tenons slightly and tap the posts into place using a wooden mallet. They should be in firmly enough to stay in place when you stand the stool up but not in to their full depth.

8. Turn the stool upright and stand it on the bench.

9. Adjust the legs by eye so that they splay slightly and measure each one up from the bench approximately 3" (8 cm) and mark with cross.

10. Drill mortices in 4 x posts using a 15 mm drill bit. If necessary, slightly whittle the leading edge of the tenons, apply glue and join together the 2 pairs of posts. Tap them together with a mallet and then use a sash clamp to pull them in nice and deep using glue blocks to protect the bark or wood. Once the rails joints are in snugly, remove the clamp and pull both posts in

towards the top. Place the tenons into the mortices in the elm top to hold everything in shape while the glue dries.

11. Once glue has set, measure for rail length. Pull posts outwards, causing them to splay and measure from the centre of each rail. In this case, the centre rail measures 17" (43 cm). It can be adjusted slightly longer or shorter. It is an aesthetic decision so please do what pleases your eye!

12. The centre rail is a nice one to peel, sand and polish. You could perhaps choose a slightly odd-shaped branch for this job. Once you have cut to length, make a ⅝" tenon on each end and glue

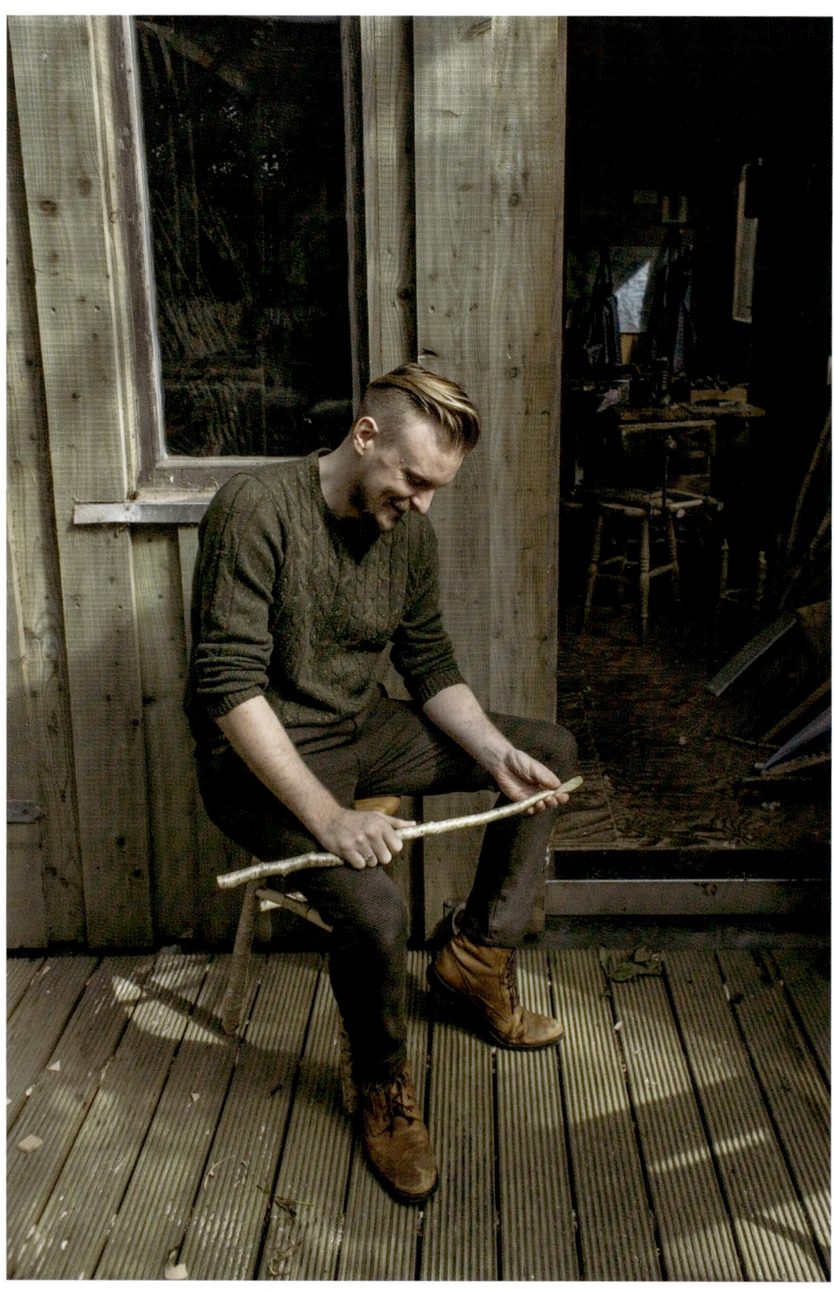

Stephen chooses a single stretcher for small bench

into position, glue the posts into the elm board at the same time
and pull them in using a sash clamp.

13. Sand the top of the elm board and finish with Liberon Finishing
     Oil or a similar product.

*The stretcher which runs from rail to rail and causes the legs to splay should
measure approximately 1½" (4 cm) longer than the measurement between
the mortice holes (lengthways) in the elm board. This measurement can be
adjusted slightly to create a wider or narrower splay if desired.*

CUTTING LIST Small bench stool

- Overall dimensions: 12" (30 cm) long x 12" (30 cm) high x 10"
  (25 cm) wide

- Posts x 4 sized 12" (30 cm) long

- Rails x 2 sized 8" (20 cm) long

- Stretcher x 1 sized 9½" (24 cm) long

Assembly instructions as for the large bench stool.

next page: Tall kitchen stool surface decorated by Alison Ospina
page 93: Fireside stool, hazel with sweet chestnut top

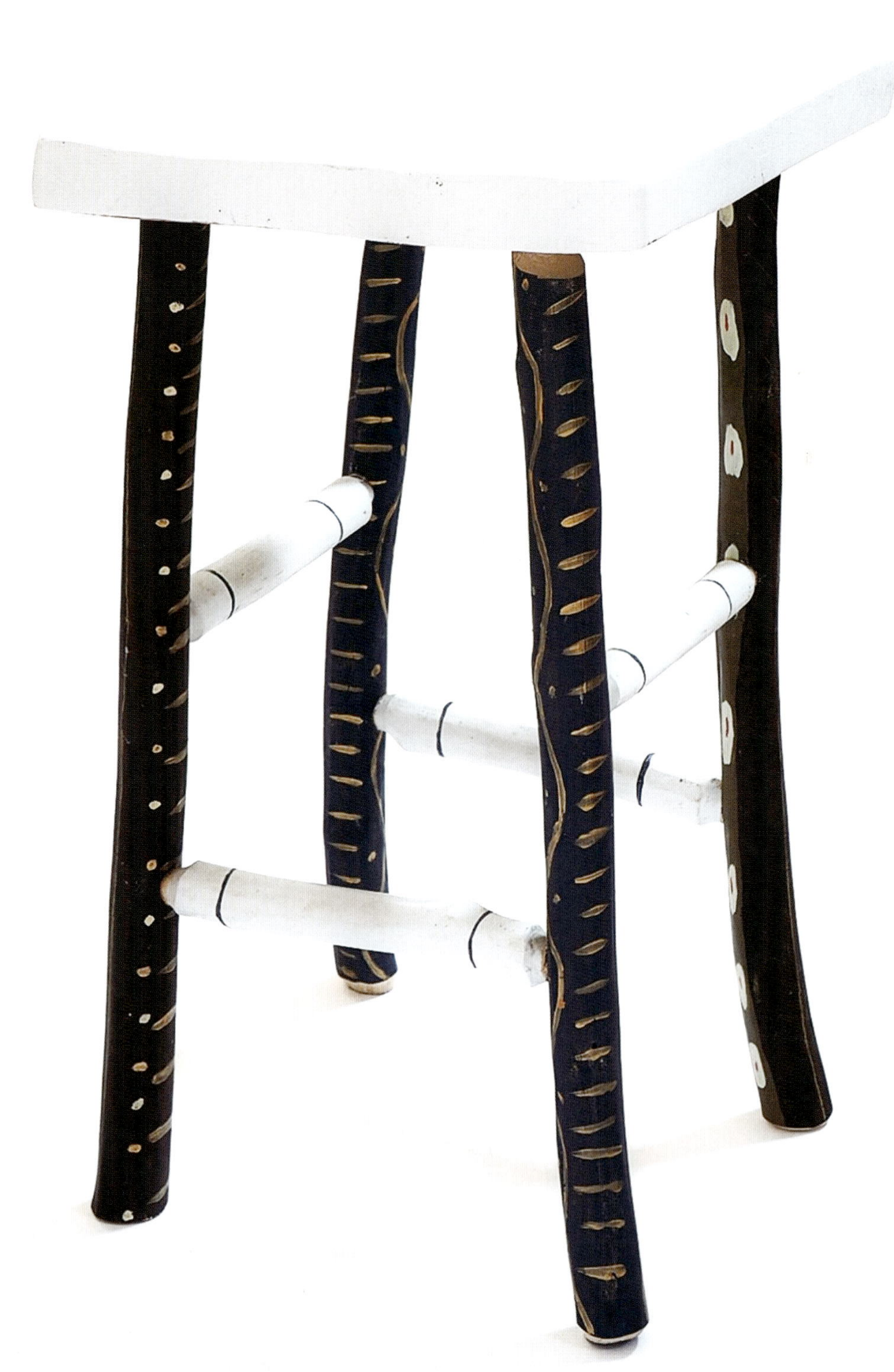

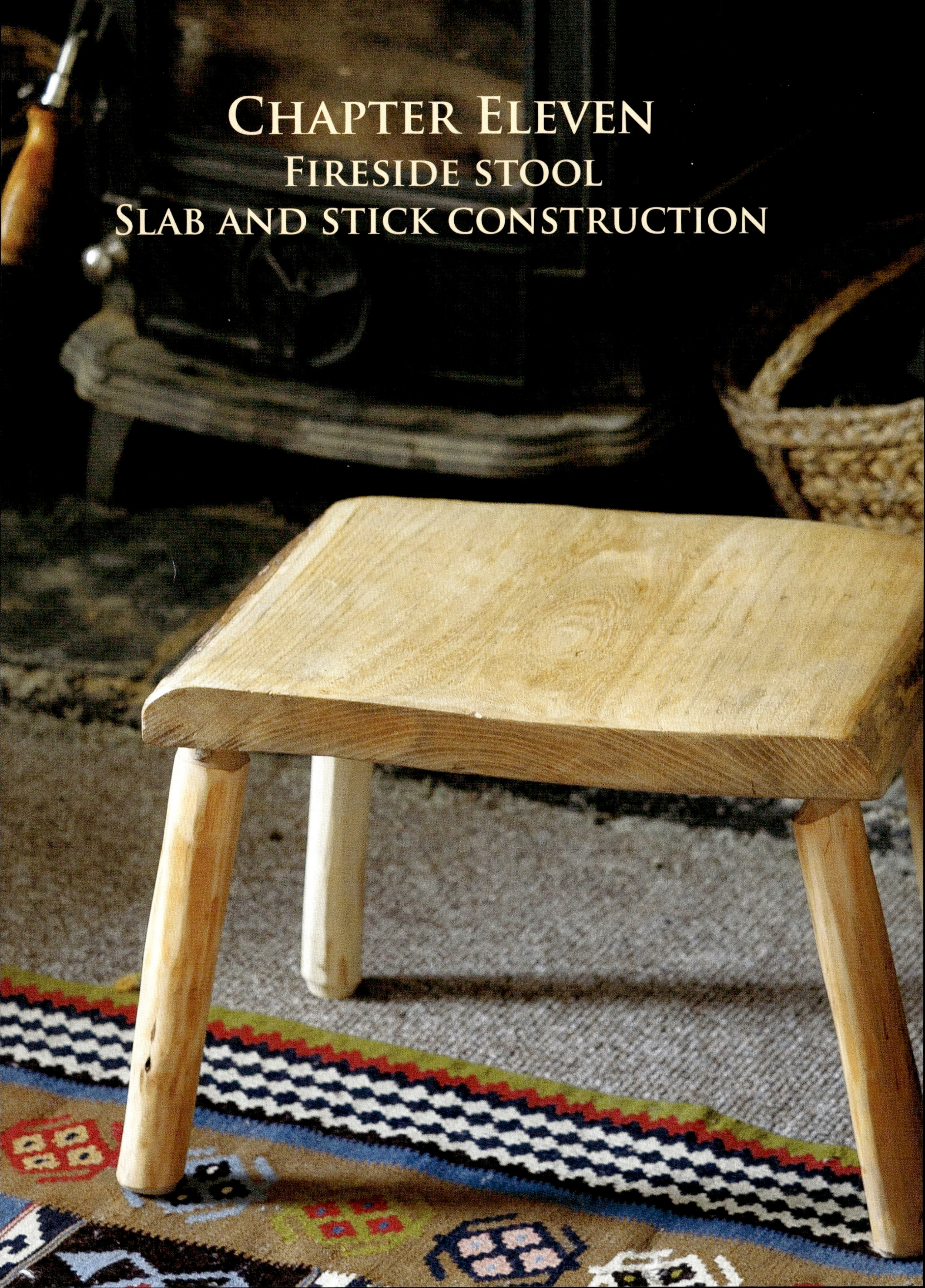

Chapter Eleven
Fireside stool
Slab and stick construction

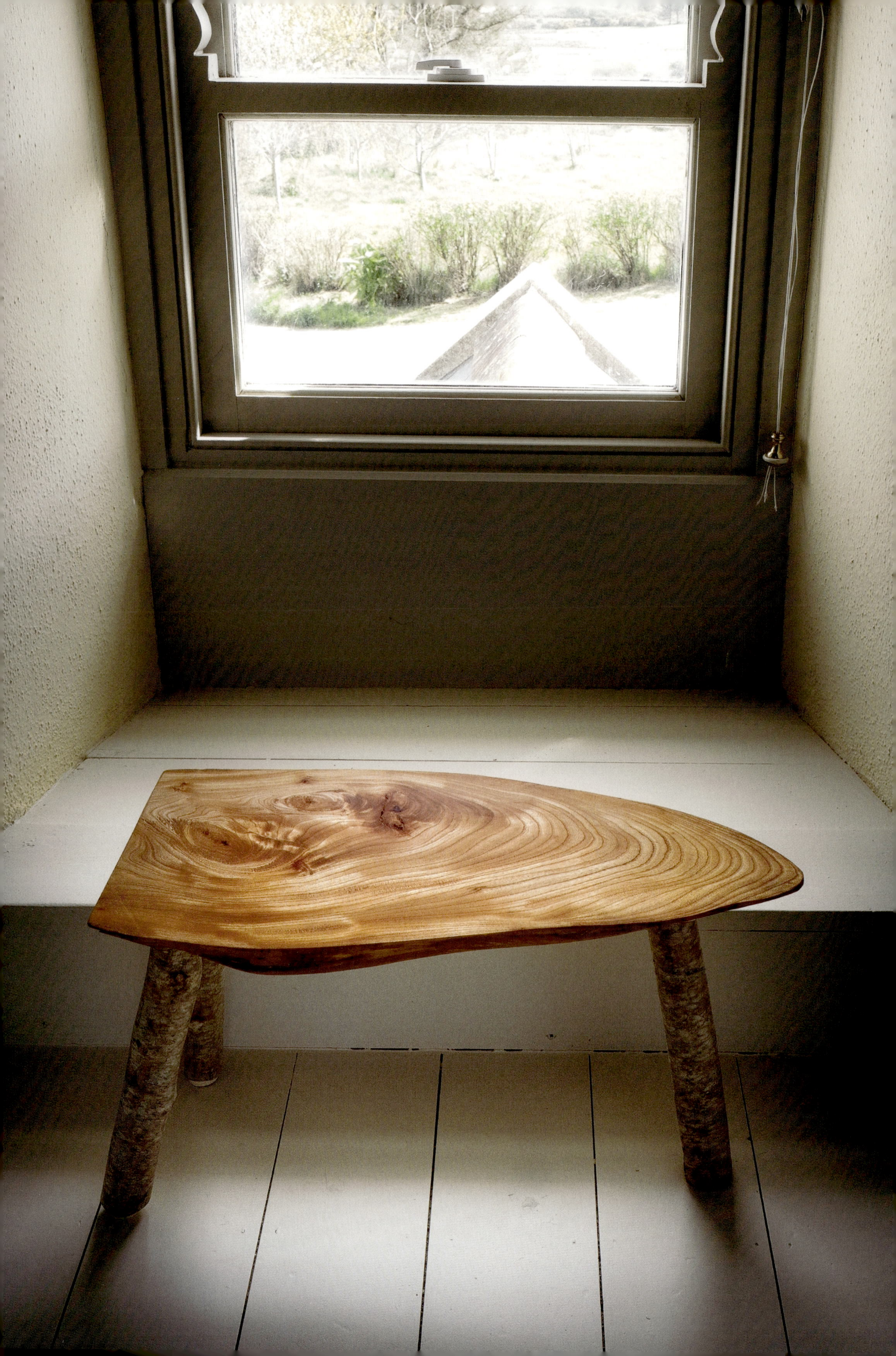

Fireside stool
Slab and stick construction

Anyone who has a fireplace or wood burning stove understands the need for a low stool that sits permanently in front of it. Without a stool you have to kneel to light the fire. John Oxenham in *The Sacrament of Fire* says you should "kneel always when you light a fire". While I take the point that we should be giving thanks to the trees for providing us with light and warmth, these days my knees can't take it!

*far left: Small hazel wedge-shaped
three legged stool with elm top
below: Small hazel fireside stool
with oak top*

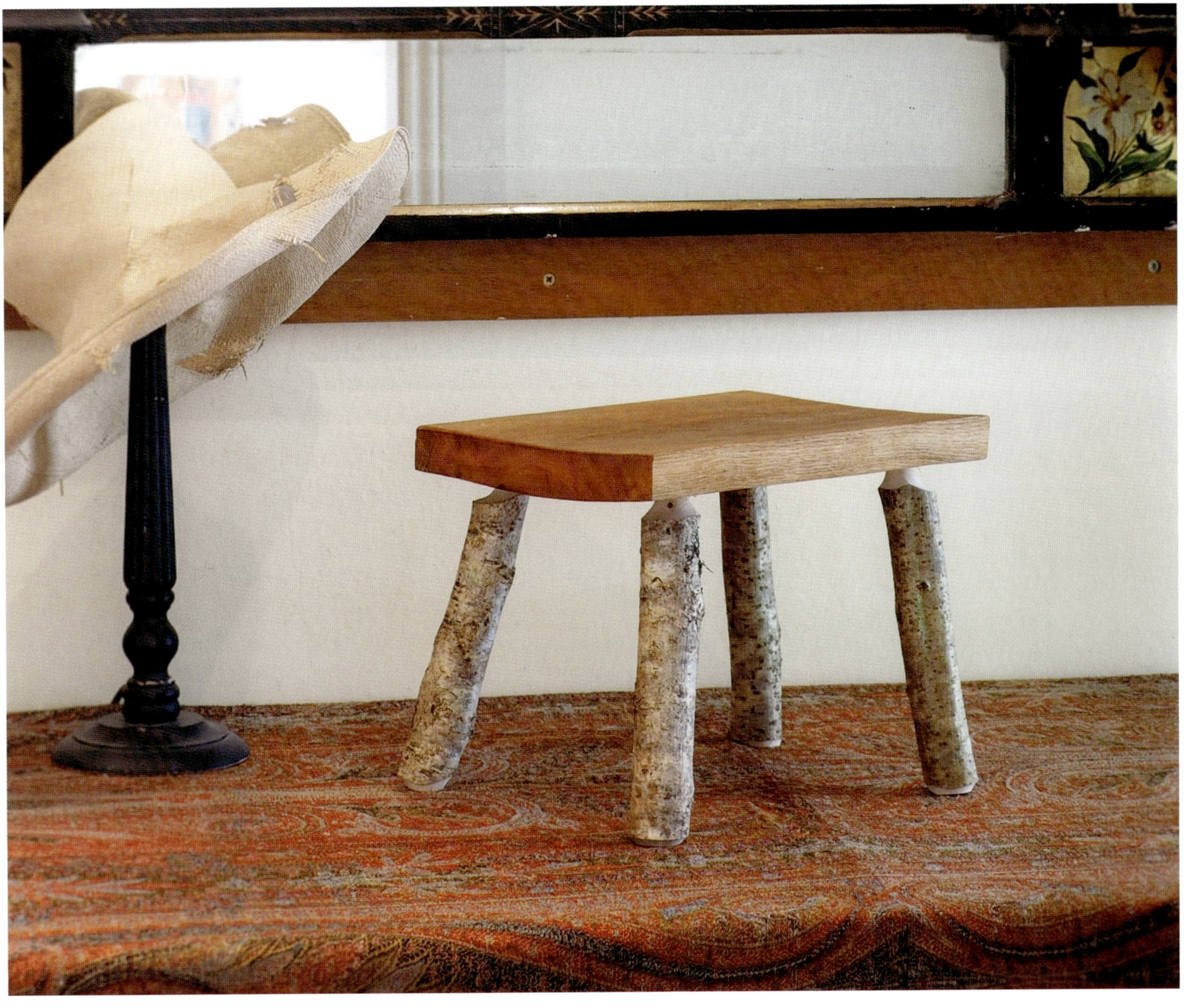

The same small stool, made of a sweet chestnut plank and hazel legs, has sat in front of our stove for almost twenty years. It is true to say the more we see things, the less we notice them. This little stool has become such a part of our surroundings that we barely give it a glance, although we all sit on it at least once a day, to light the fire, to warm our hands or to feed some logs and sticks into the stove.

When I started to write this book, I became a lot more aware of the number of stools we have in our house and what we use them for. I took pity on this particular stool because it had received little care or attention for a very long time and it has served us well. One leg had been replaced a few years back with a scrap I had grabbed out of the workshop — and you could tell it was a scrap!

When you join green wood to a dry plank there is a danger that the joints will become loose over time. The green wood tenons shrink but the dry plank mortices do not. The legs of this stool were all slightly wobbly and I decided to replace them but when I tried to remove them, I could not pull them out.

The lesson I learned is that if the legs are slightly loose, it does not necessarily matter. "If it's not broke don't fix it!" Gravity and your weight are always forcing the legs into place. Obviously, if the legs drop out when you lift up the stool, they are too loose and must be replaced. I settled for replacing one leg, sanding it all over and giving it a few new coats of clear Briwax.

With stools that have legs set at angles, it is usual practice to drill the mortices at a carefully measured angle. I have always found this problematic for a variety of reasons and when I drilled the holes for this particular stool I remembered doing it by eye, even though it was twenty years ago. The result being that the angles of the legs are not identical, but even so it does the job and looks perfectly fine!

Some might think this is shoddy woodwork but I urge people to develop the part of themselves that can measure intuitively and by eye. No green wood stick or stool or chair will ever be properly square or easily measurable. You must develop those skills. It takes time and practice but you will improve as you go along and the things that you do not get right first time, will still be perfectly functional and quirky and even beautiful in their own way.

NEW USE FOR VERITAS TENON CUTTERS

I have found a new way of creating the angled splay for stools made with this method. I drill the mortices at 90 degrees using the pillar drill but I make angled tenons on the tops of the legs. The tenon still goes into the mortice straight but the leg is slightly angled. Veritas tenon cutters work equally well cutting tenons at an angle as they do for cutting straight tenons, although the spirit level is not so useful!

CUTTING LIST FOUR-LEGGED FIRESIDE STOOL

- Cut 4 x posts 12" (30 cm) long

- Shape and sand a plank 10" (25 cm) wide and 12" (30 cm) long x 1¼" (25 mm) thick

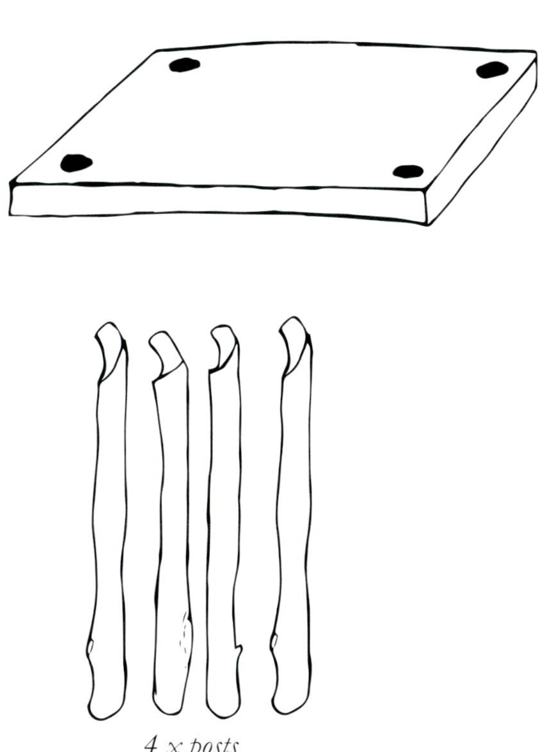

*4 x posts
raised tenons*

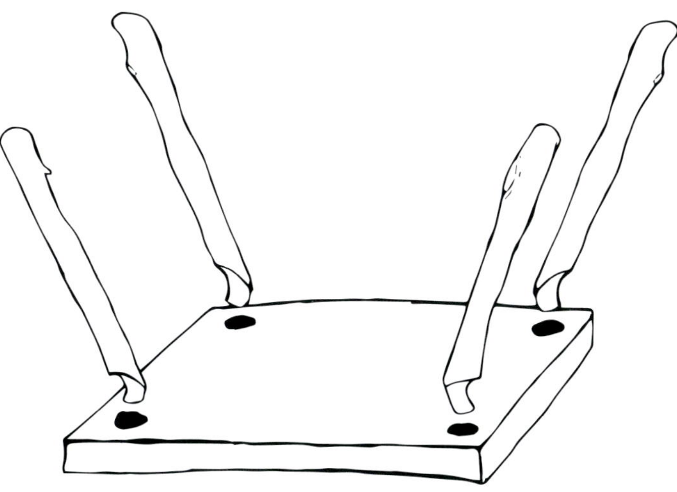

INSTRUCTIONS

1. Drill mortices approximately 1½" in from the sides and 2" in from the ends, using an 18 mm drill bit approximately 1" (25 mm) deep.

2. You can strip the bark off the legs or leave it on. Make ¾" tenons on top of each leg but instead of making them straight, lift the tenon cutter slightly so that the spirit level bubble is right at the end (nearest the drill). Make the tenons approximately 1" long including shoulders.

3. As you will be joining green wood to a dry plank, it is advisable to leave the tenons to dry for a couple of days before assembly, or take them into your house overnight. Do not put them close to a

Making angled tenons

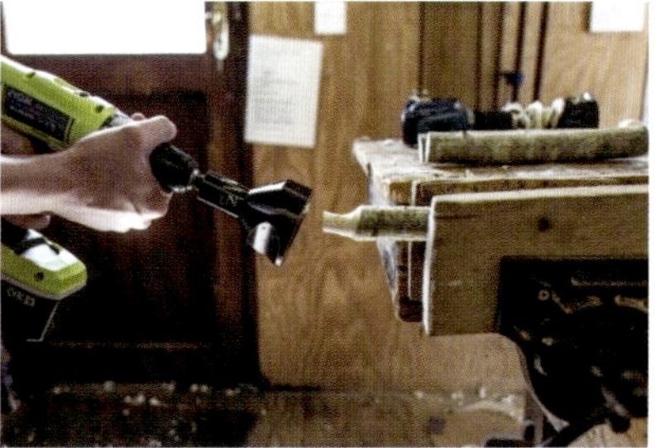

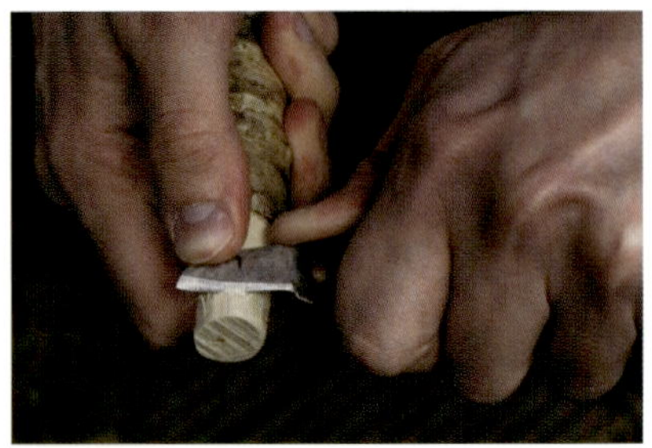

Carefully whittling tenons

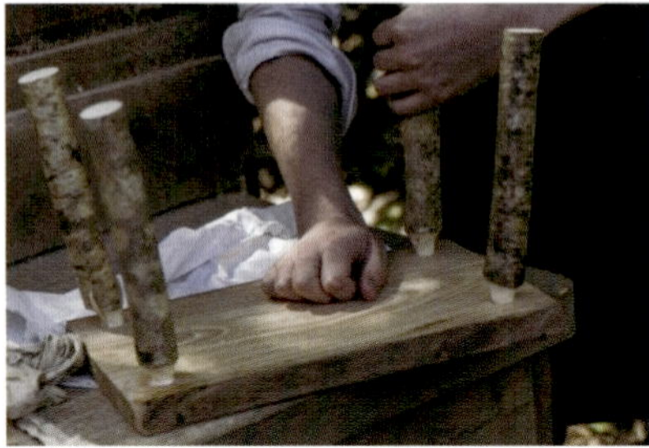

Adjust posts so they are all kicking out

heat source as they might crack and split as they dry. If you want to assemble straight away and your tenons are quite green, whittle them only a tiny bit, just enough to ease them into the mortices under pressure.

4. Apply glue to mortices and tenons, position the legs so that they are kicking outwards. If you want to increase the splay of the legs, insert scrap wood spacers between the legs, forcing the legs outwards and remove them when the glue dries.

The three-legged wedge-shaped stool is made using the same method.

CUTTING LIST THREE-LEGGED STOOL

* Cut 3 x legs 12" (30 cm) long

* Select a plank with a naturally rounded end, shape and sand thoroughly

* Make ¾" tenons on top of all 3 legs, angling the tenons upwards slightly as with previous instructions. Assemble and adjust in the same way as the fireside stool.

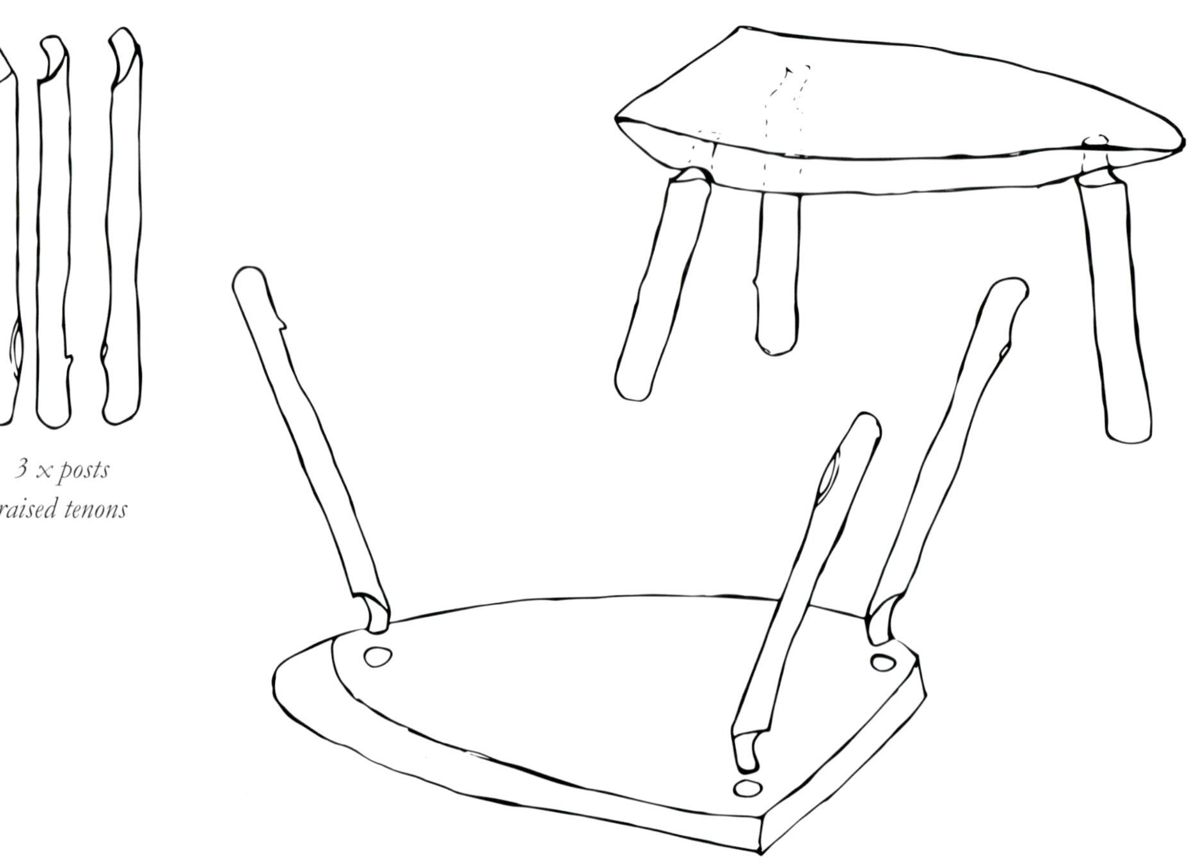

3 x posts raised tenons

right: Eddy with finished fireside stool

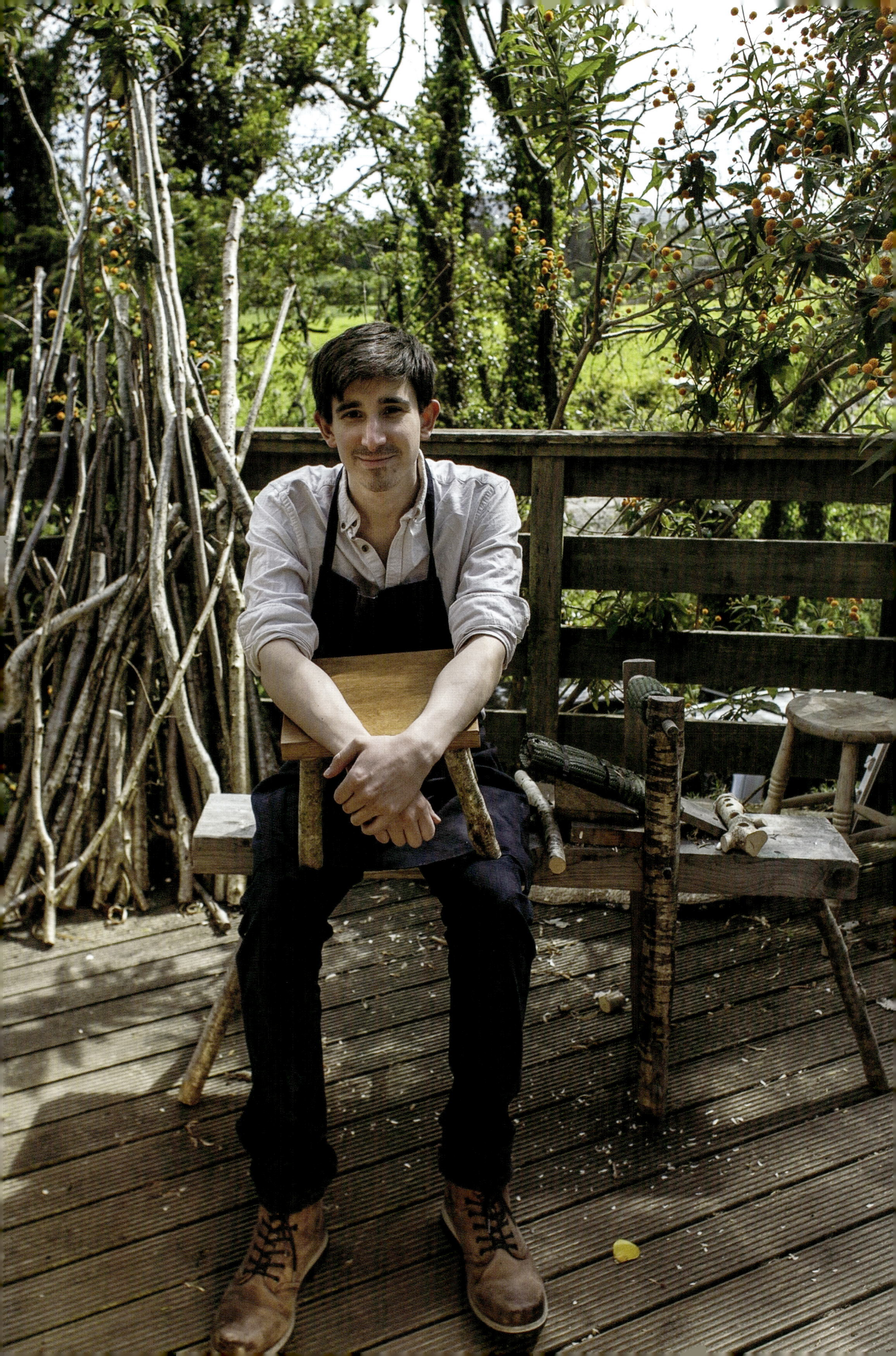

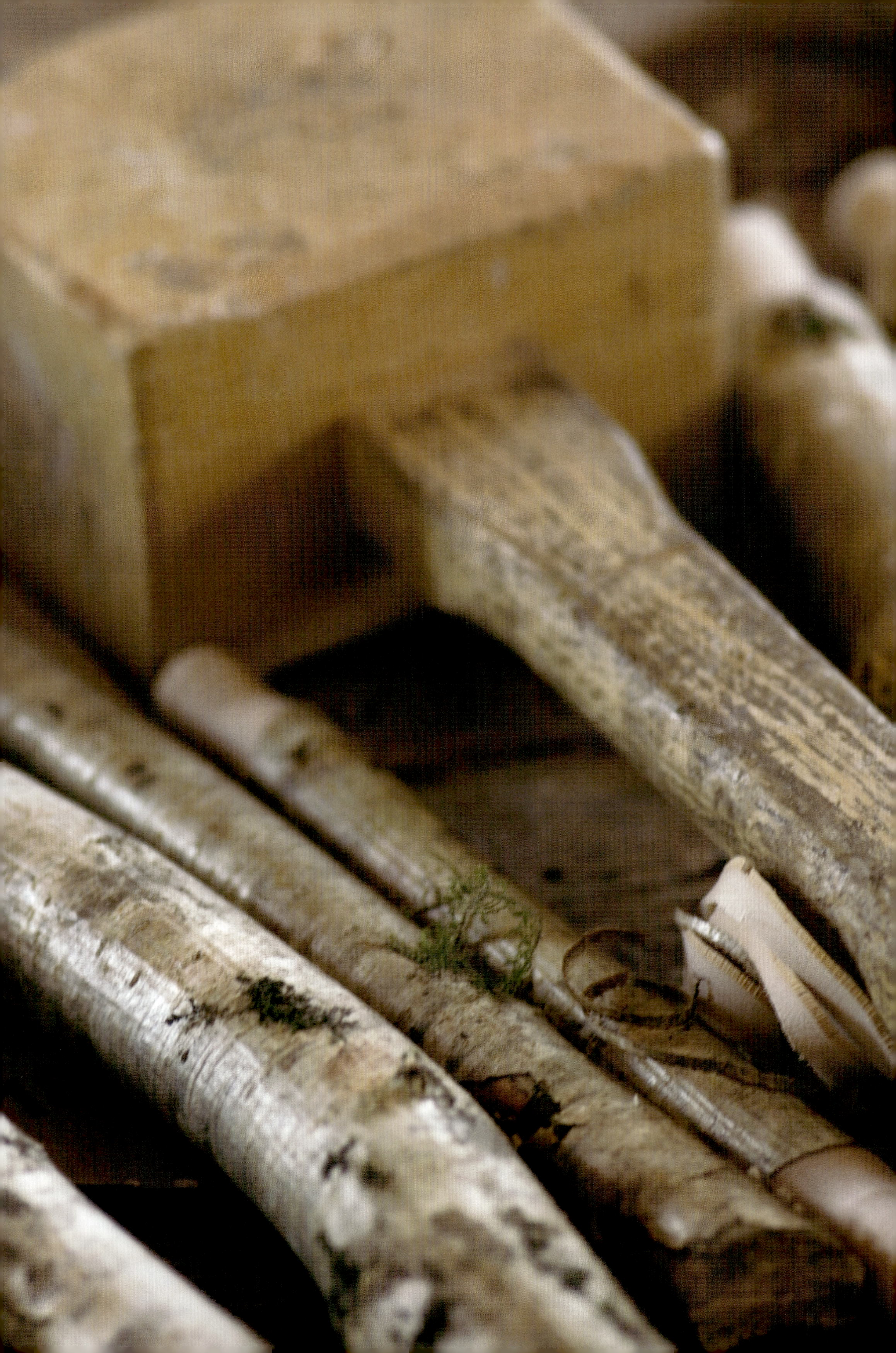

CHAPTER TWELVE
TRIPODS

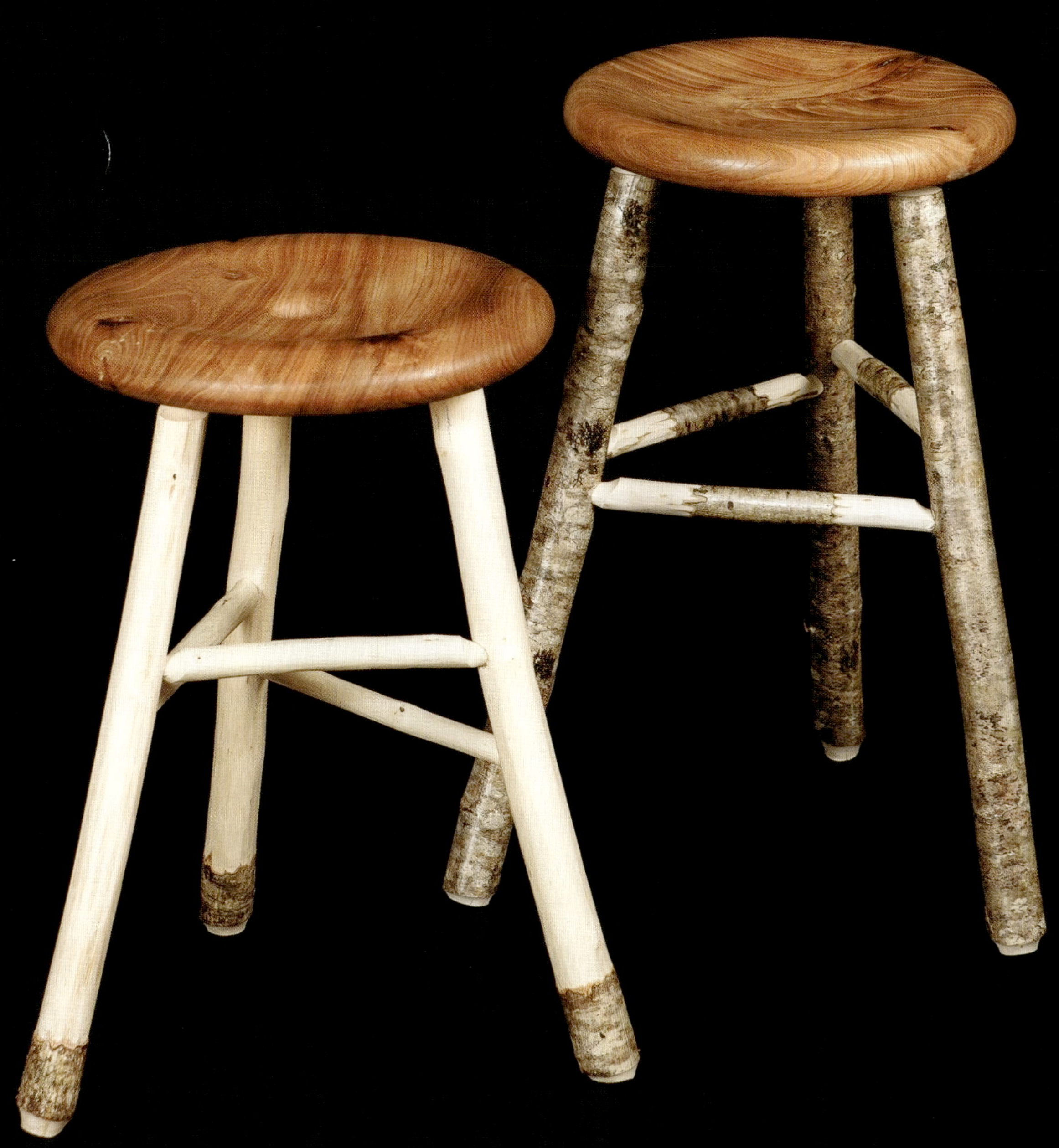

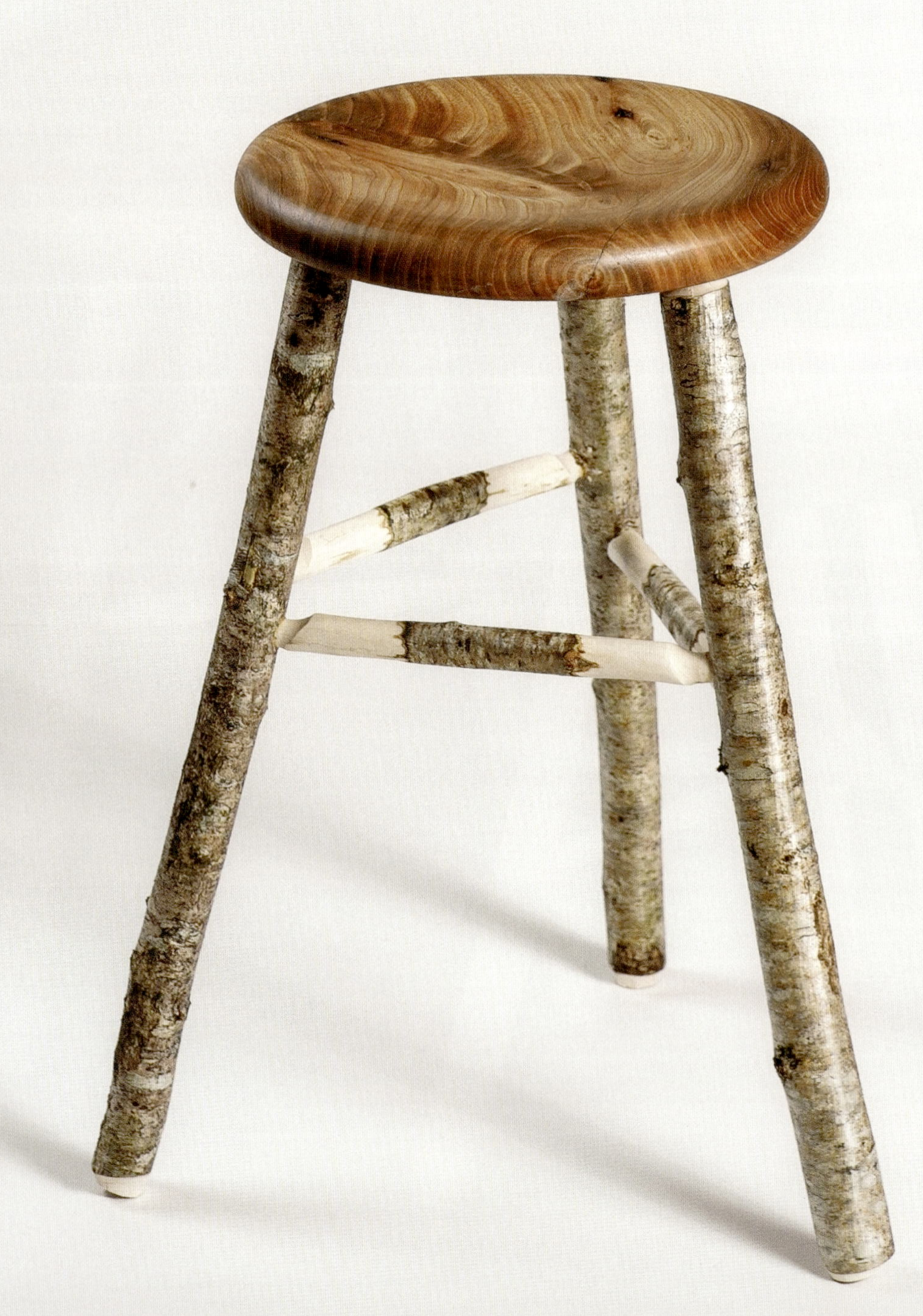

TRIPODS

Wharton Escherick (1887-1970), best known for his sculptural work in wood and the manner in which he applied the principles of sculpture to functional pieces, has inspired my green wood version of his tall, elegant, three-legged stools. I am not sure how he shaped the stool tops but I quickly discovered that simple design is not necessarily easy, so I asked my friend, wood turner Kieran Higgins, to make me some nice, elegant, discs of wood as stool tops.

I am not used to working with regular shapes but I was excited when Kieran delivered these perfect discs of elm and oak, each with a different shaped edge. I had asked him to play around with the idea and so I ended up with two that were thinner at the edges, one that was dished in the centre and another with a hole in the middle.

Round discs, perfectly sanded and oiled are very pleasing both to the eye and to the touch. I hardly dared drill into them.

I had only ever made one tripod stool before, it was very small and intended for a child. I never have got round to finding a toddler to try it out but I suspect the splay is not wide enough. However, it is an attractive piece and I enjoy having it in the workshop where it is frequently admired.

Three-legged stools are useful in places where floors are uneven, a good example being the milking stool for use in a barn or field. Historically, in Ireland, cottages were made with beaten earth floors and four-legged chairs or stools were of limited use because one foot would always be off the ground. A three-legged stool or chair will always accommodate itself to the uneven surface and although the angle of the seat might not be altogether comfortable, the stool remains stable.

To find the positions for the three legs, you need to mark an equilateral triangle on the underside of the stool top. I started out in my usual way, using a white chalk and positioning the crosses by eye. It took

far right: Tall hazel tripod stool with elm seat

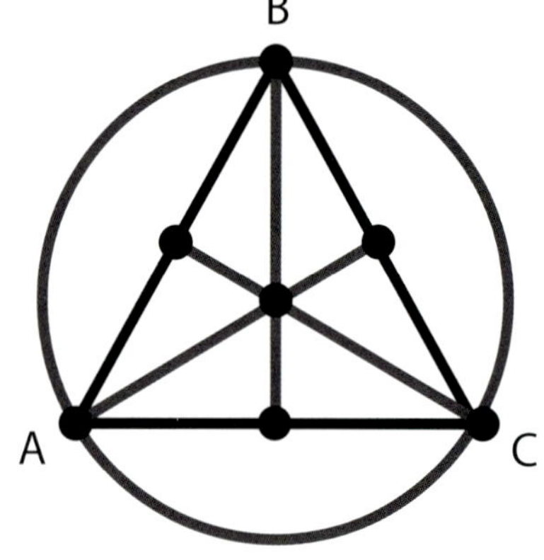

me a few goes to get it right and I concluded that once you have worked it out, it is best to make a triangular cardboard template so you do not have to keep starting from scratch.

On my large stool top (diameter 14") the sides of the equilateral triangle measure 13¾" (35½ cm) and the angle is 120 degrees. For the 12" (30 cm) top, the sides of the equilateral triangle measure 6¼" (16 cm) and the angles are all 120 degrees. I know this generally contradicts my green wood approach but the difference is that the stool top is perfectly circular and therefore different rules apply. The stool will look odd and could be unstable, if the legs are not positioned the same distance apart.

CUTTING LIST FOR TRIPOD STOOLS

- 12" (300 mm) diameter disc min. 1¼" (30 mm) thick

- 3 x posts 18" (450 mm) long

- 1 x rail 9" (230 mm)

- 1 x rail 9½" (240 mm)

- 1 x rail 10" (250 mm) long

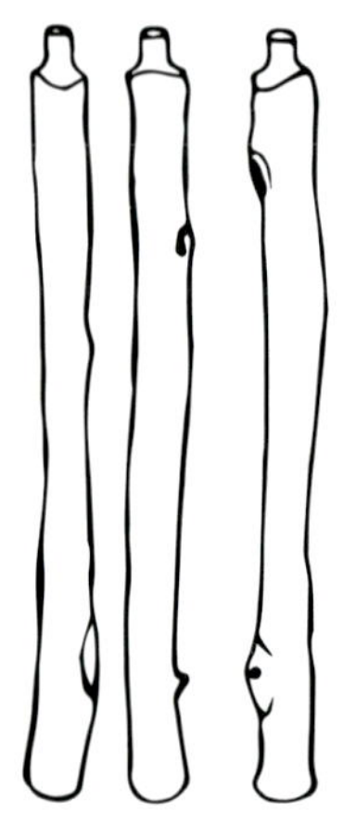

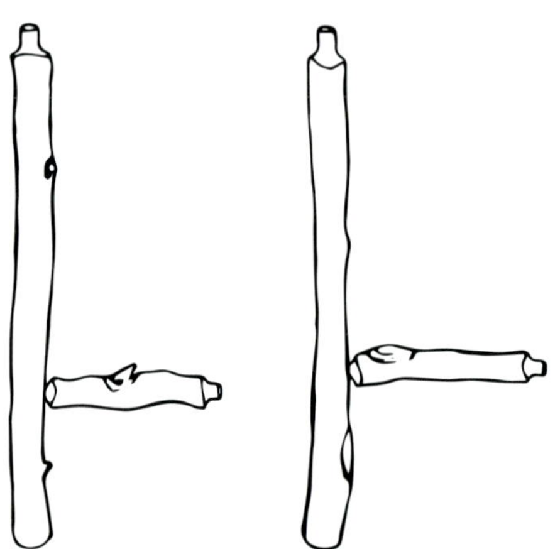

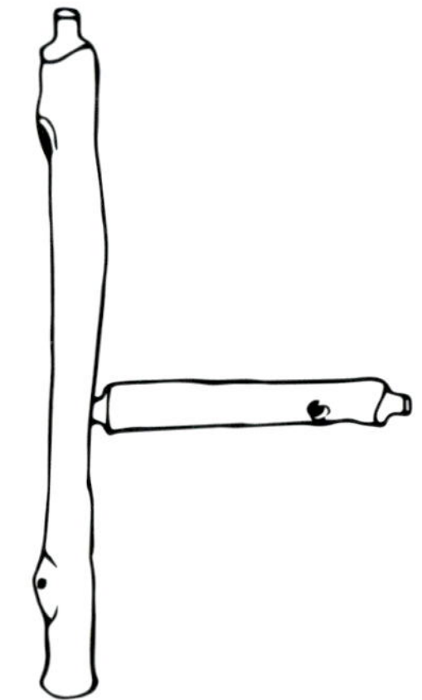

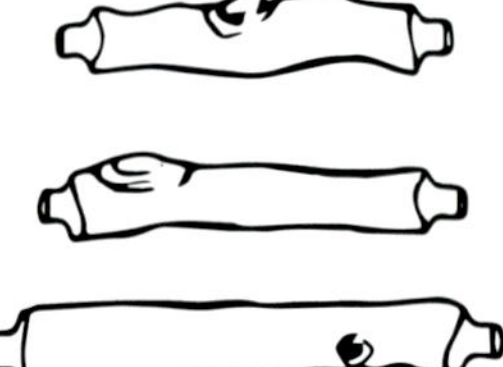

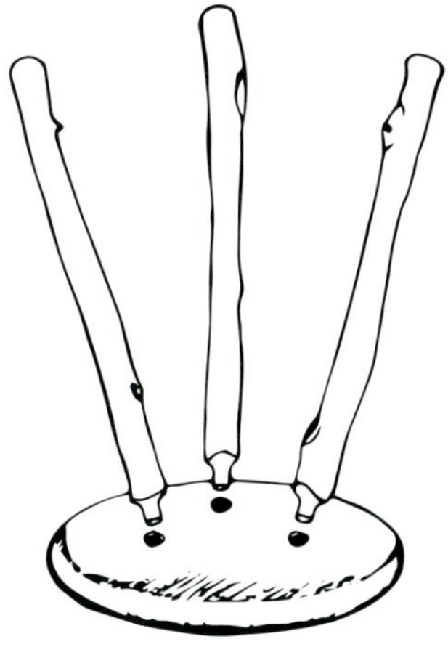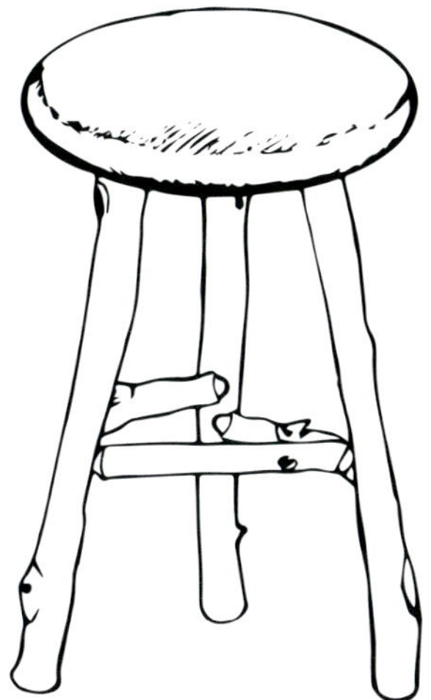

1. Once you have your triangular template made, place it in the centre of your circle and draw around it, then measure half-way along each side and mark with a cross. These 3 crosses mark the positions of the 3 legs.

2. Use the 18 mm MAD bit drill mortices on those points to a depth of approximately 1" (25 mm).

3. Now make a ¾" (18 mm) tenon on top of each leg. Whittle them very slightly and tap them firmly into position, so they will stay in the holes when you turn the stool upright, but not in as deep as they will go.

4. Once you have the stool standing upright on the bench, twist and turn the legs so that they are in their 'best' positions — this is of course an aesthetic decision! I generally prefer them to kick out slightly if the legs have a curve in them. Pull the legs outwards, so that they are well splayed and the stool is stable. Keep checking by eye, see how it looks from all sides and keep adjusting until you are happy with it.

5. To mark the faces you are going to drill into for the rails, turn the stool upside down with the legs still in position. Place it on a surface that is low enough for you to look straight down on the legs from above.

6. With a pencil, mark arrows on the bottom of each leg showing the angle of the rail as it hits the opposite leg. When drilling, check to make sure these arrows are pointing upwards. They ensure you get the angle right.

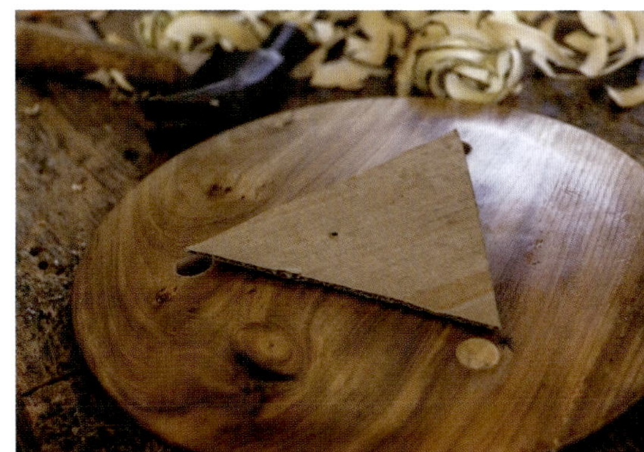

Make an equilateral triangle out of cardboard and use it as a template to work out post positions — note wrongly drilled mortice repaired with scrap tenon (Chapter 5 Tools and Techniques)

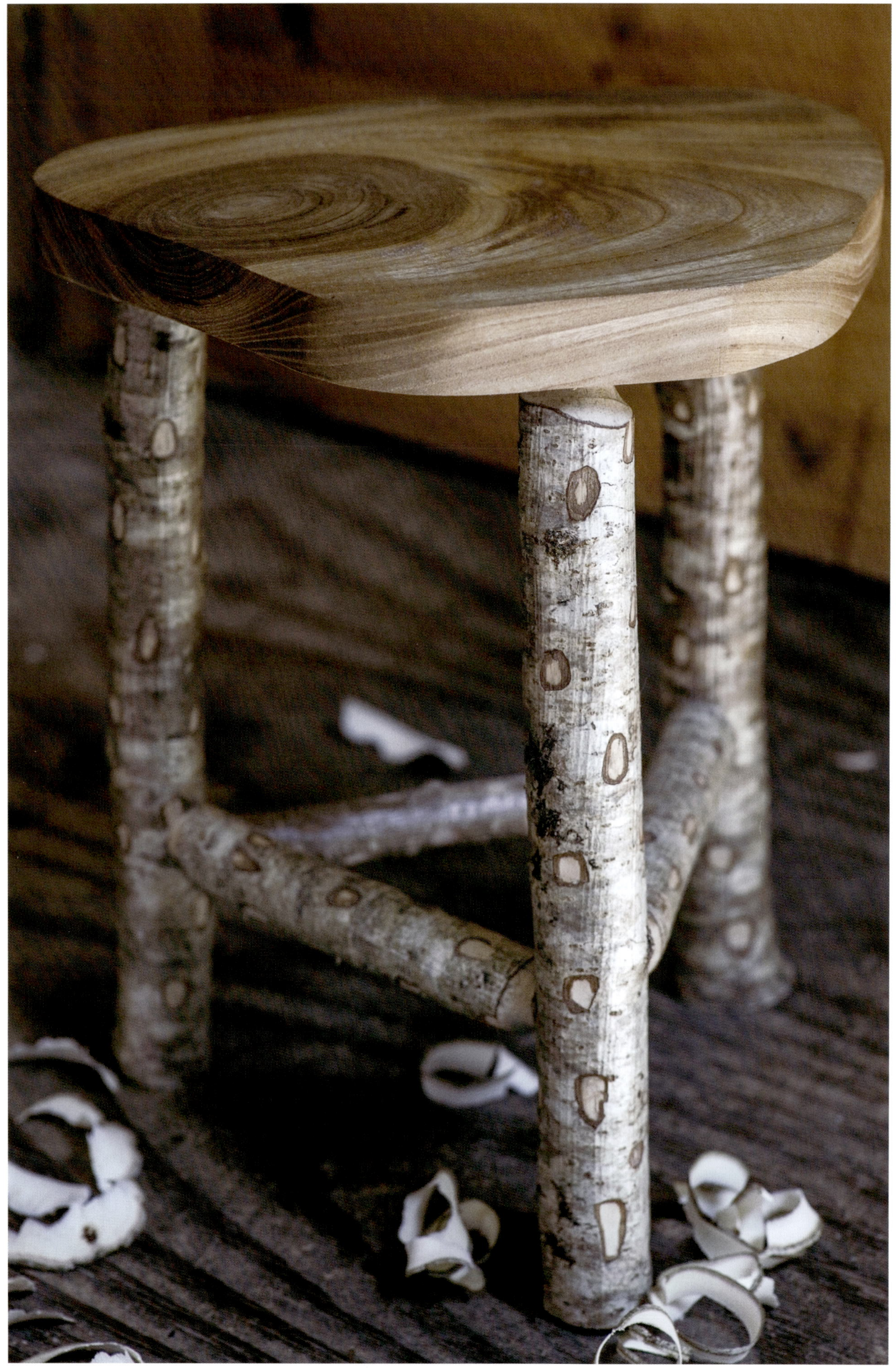

7. Use a white chalk and mark a line down the face that is directly
    opposite the next leg.

    Use one of the rails, offer it up against the legs and see where it
    makes contact. Measure down from the bottom of each leg,
    slightly offsetting each mortice.

Your rails can be measured with the three legs in place. Otherwise,
the first time you make a three-legged stool, use my dimensions and
experiment from there.

This stool looks great either with bark on or stripped and polished. I
left bark around the bottoms of the legs on this one because although
stripped legs are attractive, they can get a bit grey and dirty from being
so close to the floor. In this manner, the bark continues to protect the
wood.

right: Baby tripod stool with decorative bark
page 109: Small kitchen stool — surface decoration by Etain Hickey

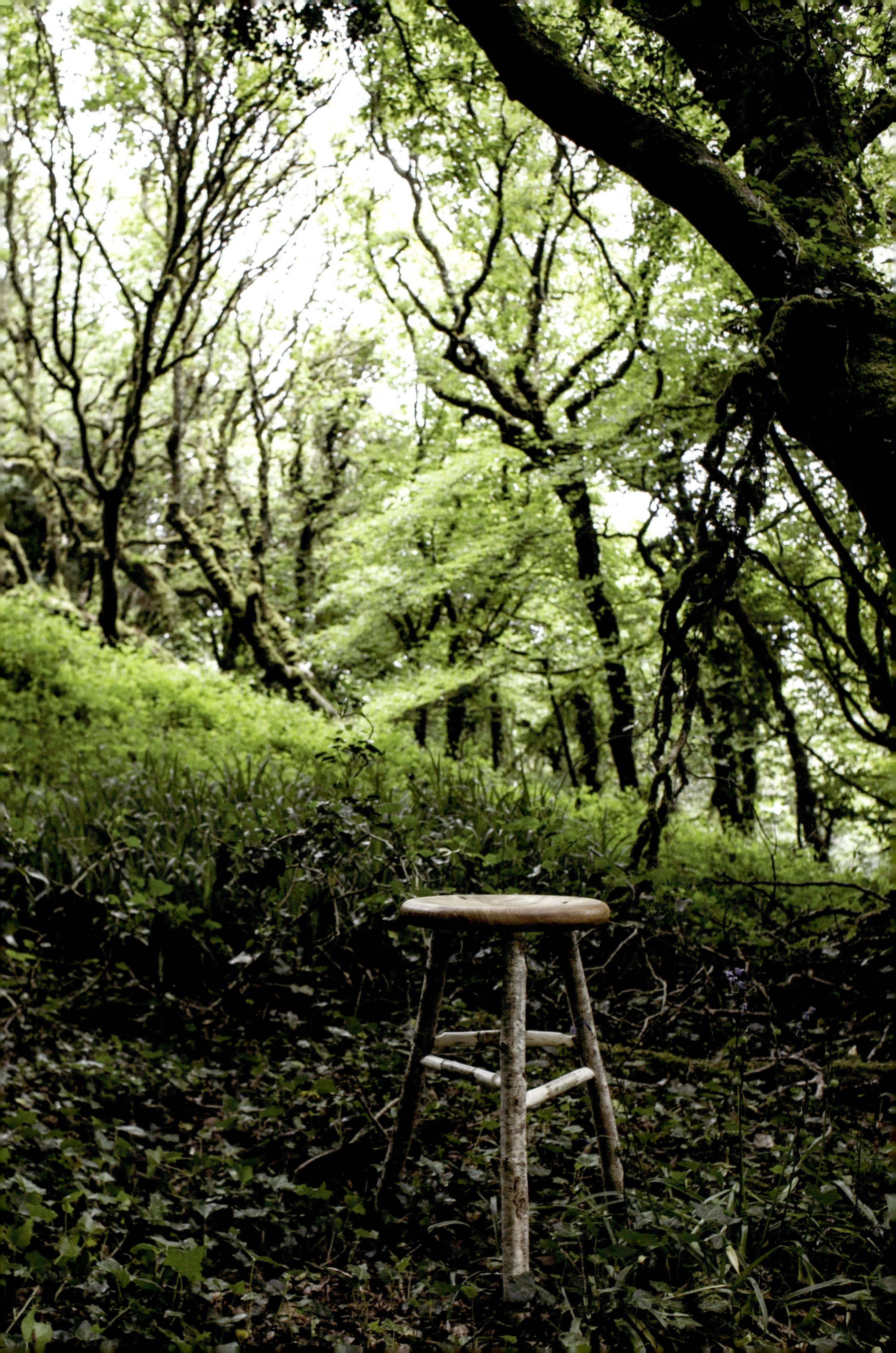

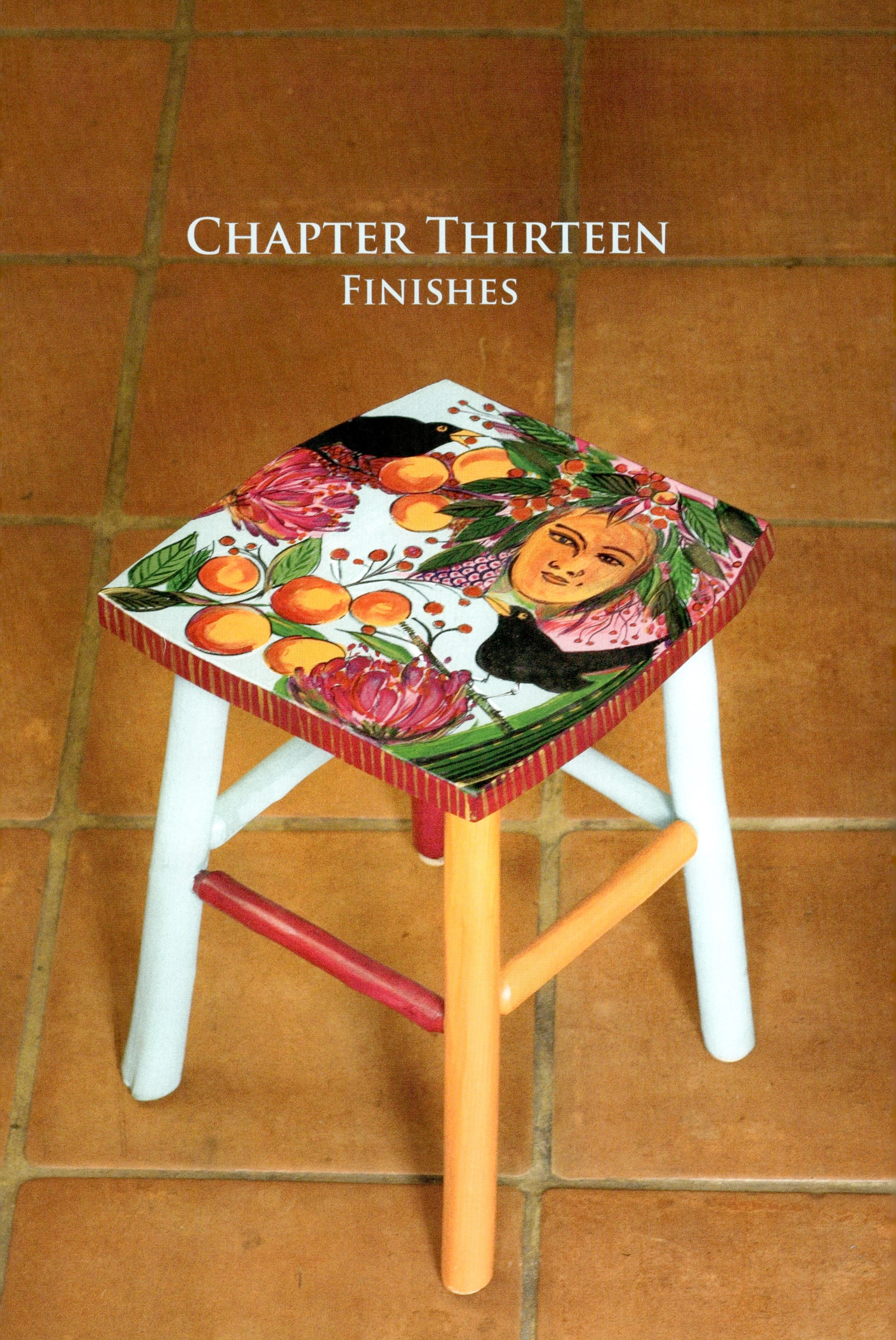

CHAPTER THIRTEEN
FINISHES

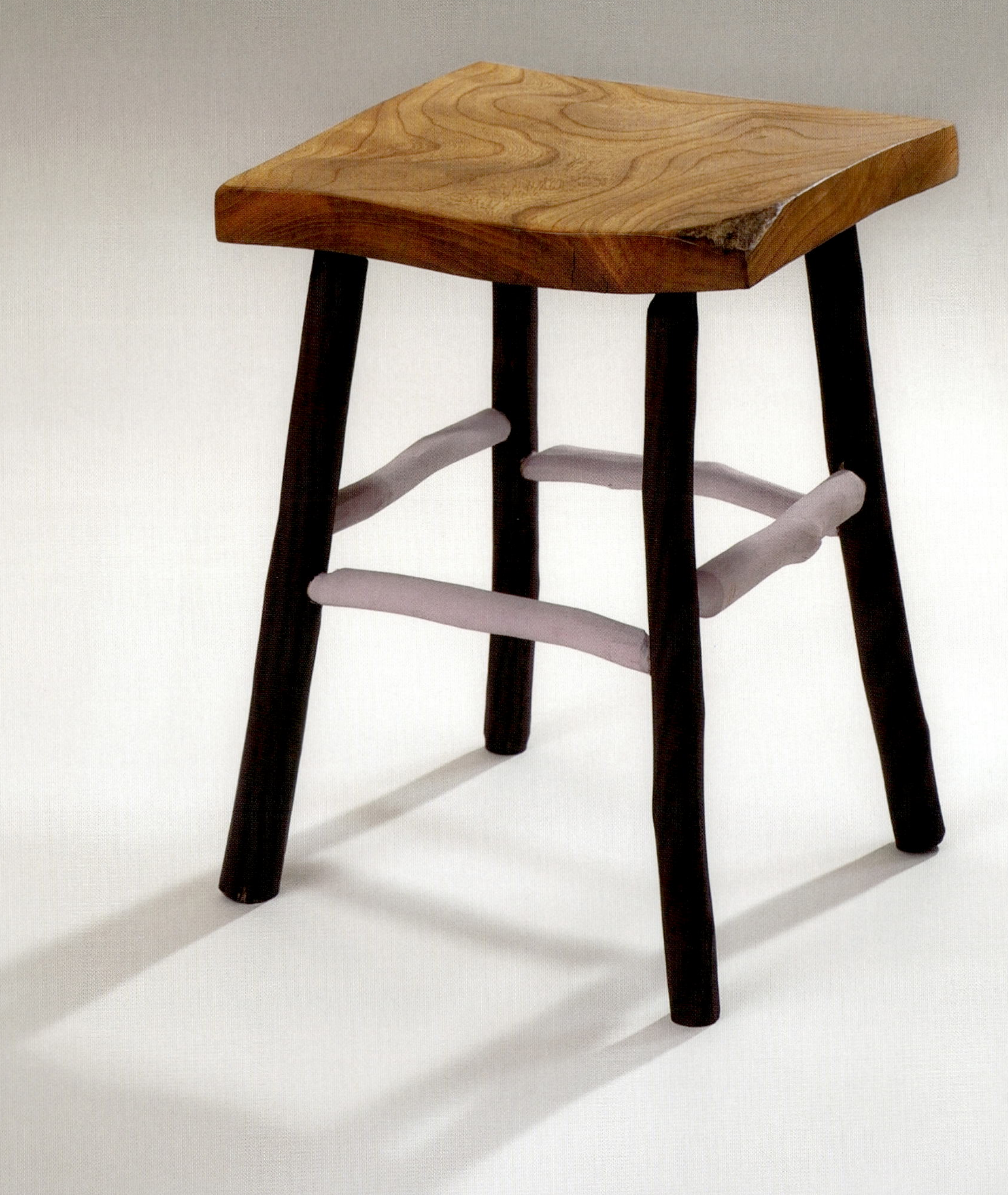

Finishes

The way a stool looks is determined by the design, the material it is made of and by its finish.

I love the grain, the texture and natural appearance of wood and I generally finish my pieces by either leaving the bark on, or peeling the bark off and sanding and polishing the bare wood.

A few years ago I decided to try something different and introduce colour to my work. I had little experience in surface decoration and was uncertain how to go about it. I began experimenting with some small-scale children's chairs I had made, removing the bark, lightly sanding the wood, then painting and decorating the hazel frame.

I soon discovered that hand painting is time-consuming and requires a very steady hand. It is also quite difficult to paint on rounded surfaces. I tried two different methods: i) painting the components before assembly and ii) painting the whole thing once it had been put together.

Both methods have their pros and cons. If you paint the components first, you will almost certainly damage the paintwork when assembling but equally, once assembled, it is quite hard to get the paint onto the rough wood shoulders of the tenons.

I purchased several sample bottles of acrylic paint for interior woodwork. There was a huge variety of colours available and they worked quite well on the sanded hazel. I used a 1" (25 mm) paintbrush for the larger surfaces and some very small artists' brushes for finer decoration.

I began to wonder if artists, skilled in surface decoration, might make a better job of it. I asked some local artists if they would undertake the experiment and they agreed to have a go.

far left: Small kitchen stool with elm top, painted with acrylic wood paints

I was delighted when Alison gave me one of her greenwood stools to decorate and relished the challenge. The stools were sanded and painted a base colour, using an indoor woodwork, water-based paint. I then used acrylic artists' colours to paint a fine outline of the design. It was good to have such a great palette of colour available. As a ceramic artist, I am used to decorating on clay with raw glazes and stains, the colours of which look completely different before and after they are fired. For example, you can have two 'greys' sitting side by side, one will come out of the kiln a strong dark blue and the other ochre yellow, so as you work, you have to imagine the results.

I found it much more difficult to paint fine lines on the wood as the fine brush did not flow as well as on clay. The thickness of the paint was crucial and the brush dried up too quickly before I had finished my flowing line. While the paint was still slightly wet, I sgraffitoed (scratched) a fine line to create added texture, definition and depth to the pattern. As well as brushes, I also used my fingers to mix and work in the paint directly onto the surface, building up layers. It is wonderfully liberating to be able to improve on my first attempt and to continue making fine adjustments to the design. In ceramics, you have one chance to get it right. Once the glaze makes contact with the clay it is there forever, there is no going back.

Etain Hickey, Ceramic Artist, Rossmore Pottery, Clonakilty, Co Cork

right: Small kitchen stool — surface decoration by Etain Hickey

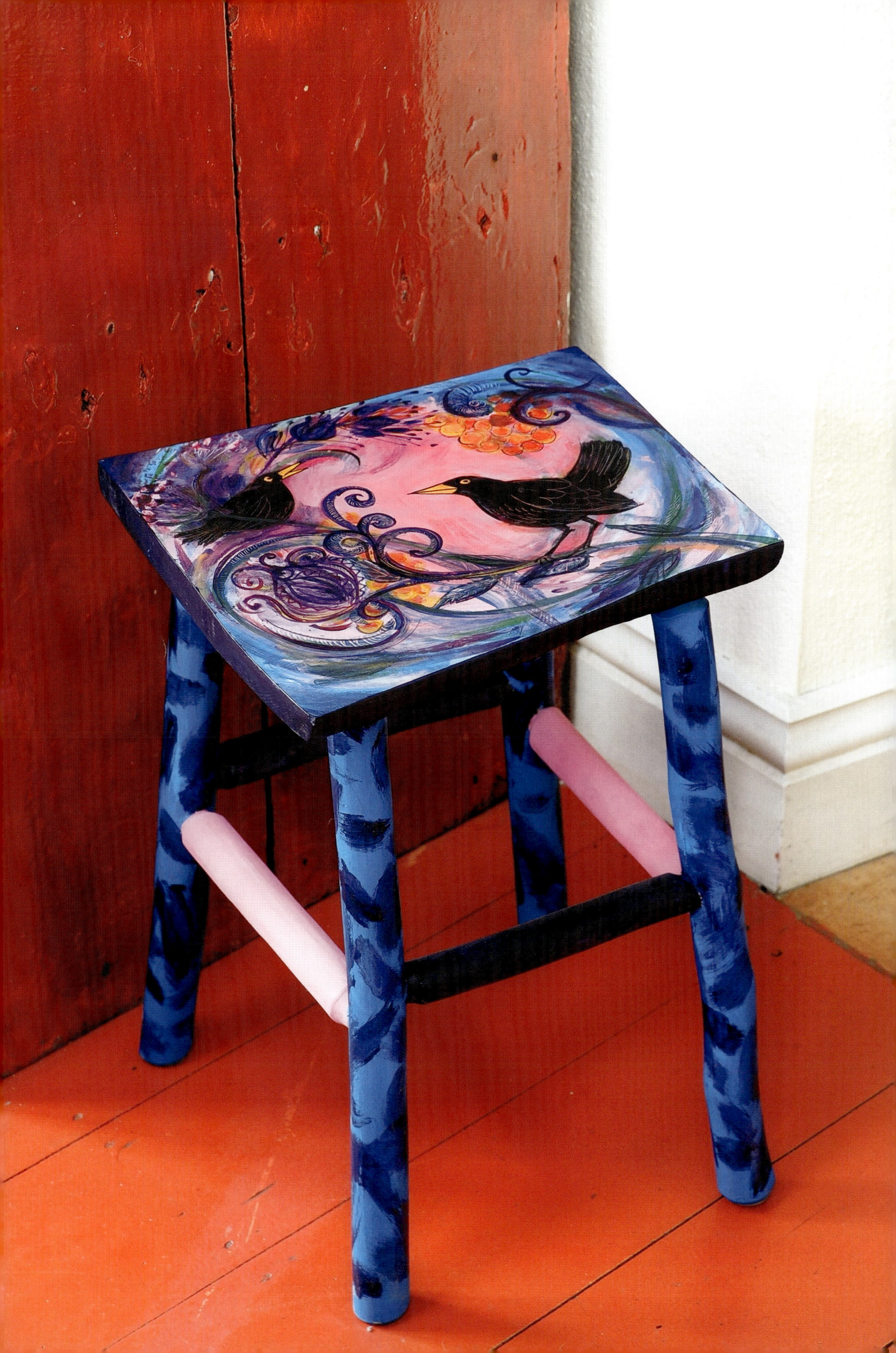

PAT CONNOR

When Alison invited me to decorate two of her greenwood stools, I spent some time wondering what my approach should be. The stools stood around my studio for some time until the muse reared its tattooed head and suggested working with stencils.

I decided to work with a variety of stencils and acrylic spray paints (Liquitex professional spray paint has a low odour, is durable and lightfast) building a multilayered surface of pattern and colour. This approach is fluid, producing chance effects, much like the abstract expressionism of Jackson Pollock and the end result becomes personal.

When the paint has dried, the stools are sprayed with a transparent glaze.

Pat Connor, Ceramic Artist, Painter, Print Maker, Schull, Co. Cork

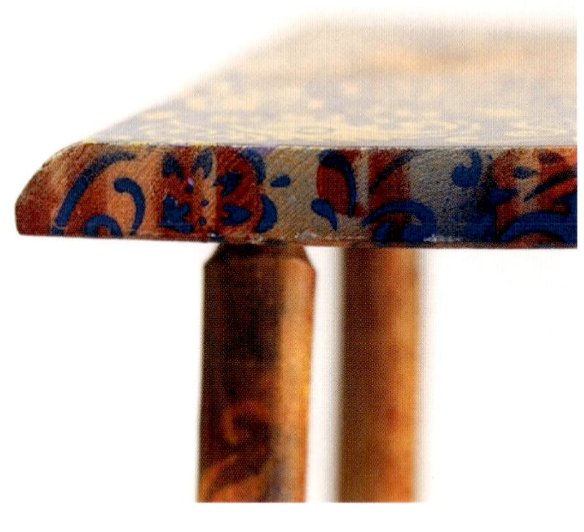

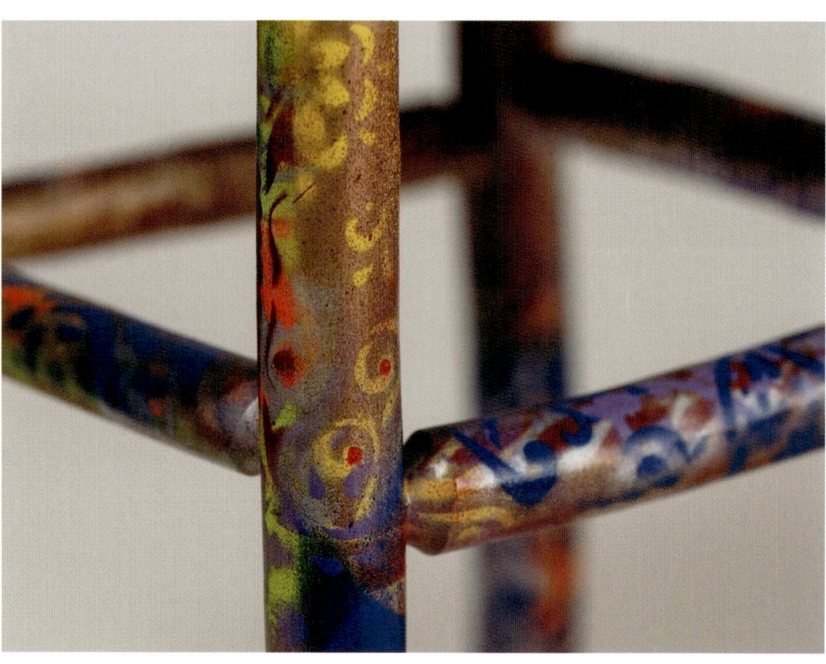

left, above and right: Kitchen stool — surface decoration by Pat Connor

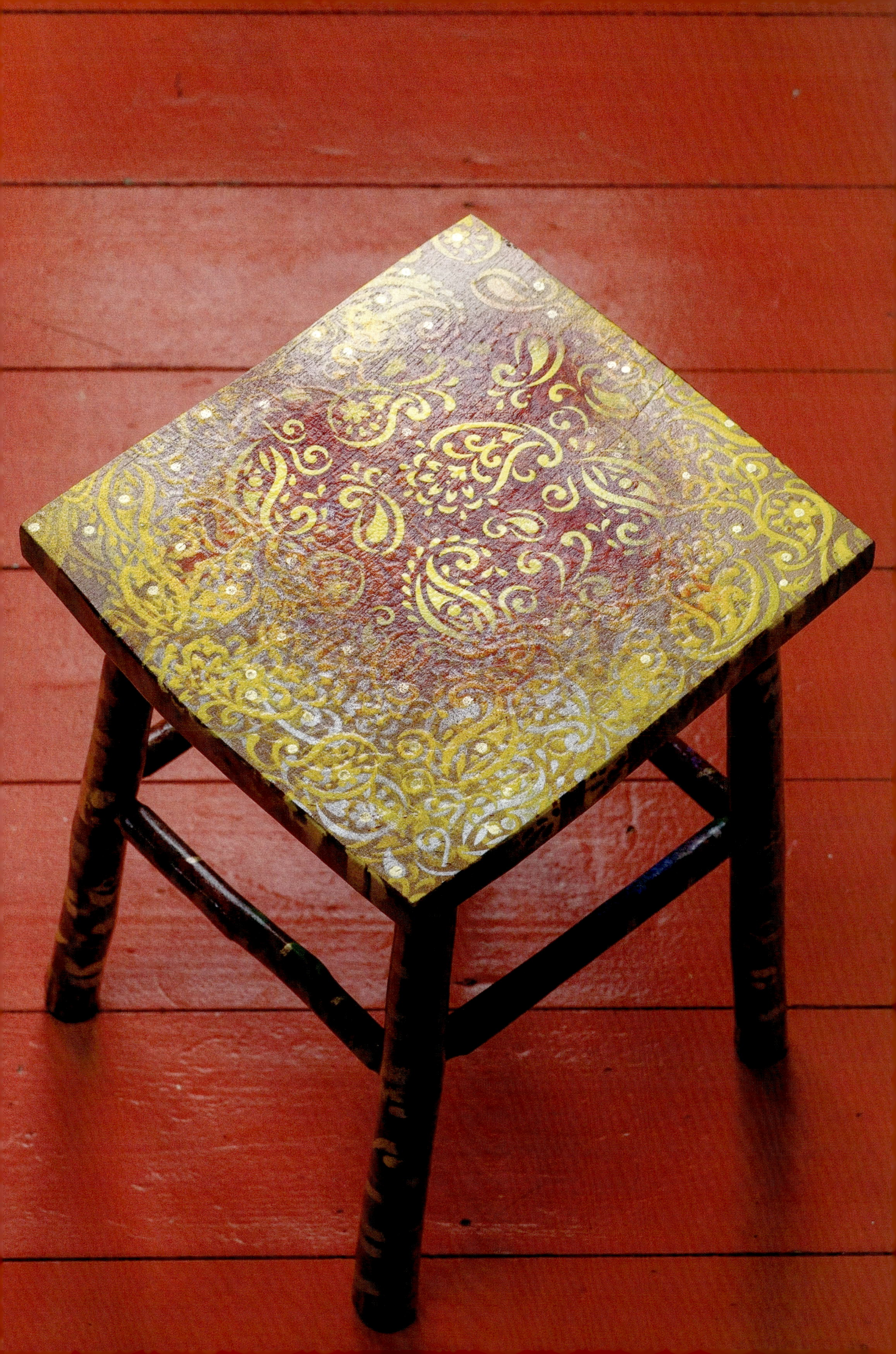

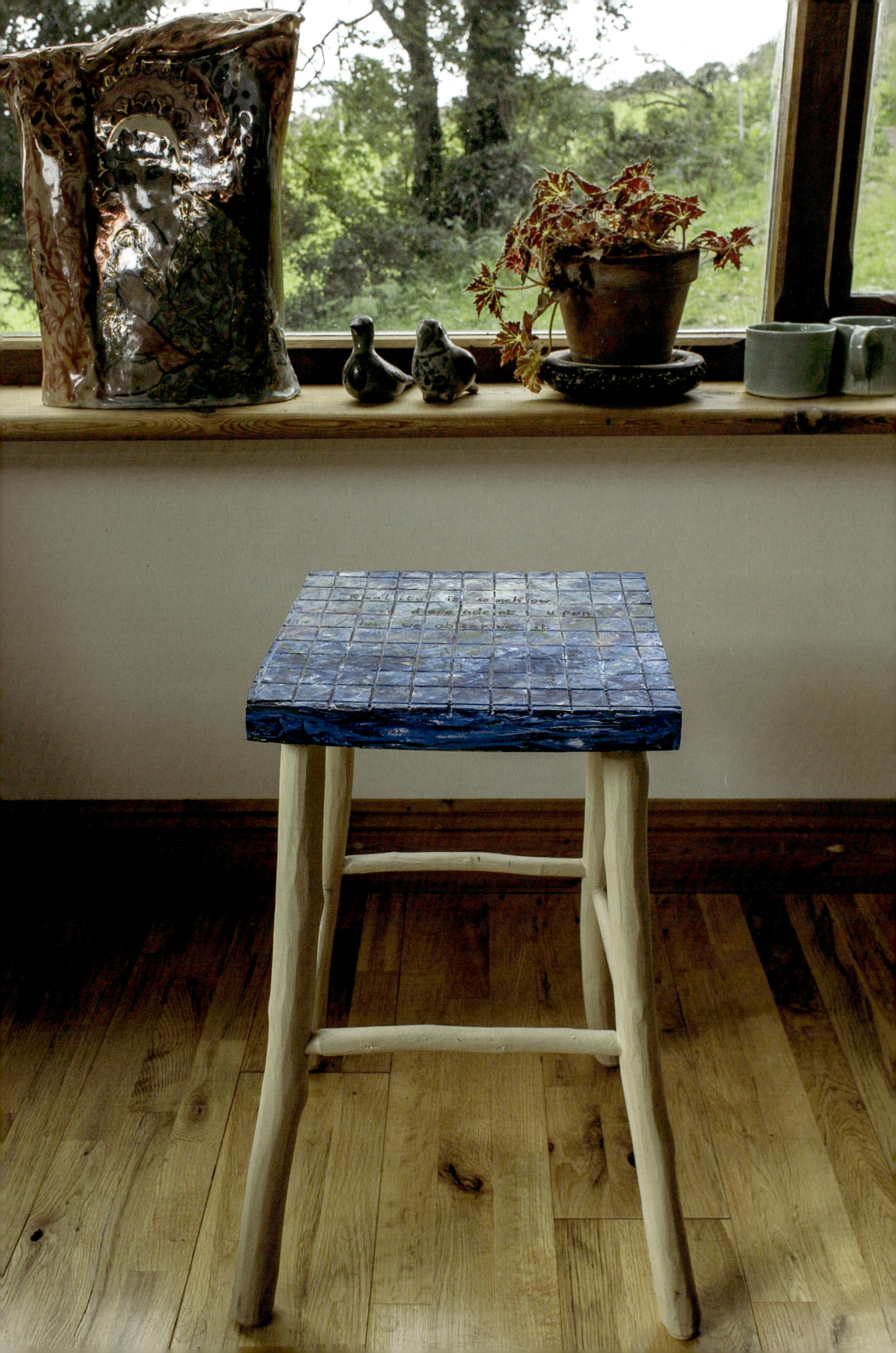

Reality is somehow dependent upon how we observe it

JIM TURNER'S EXPERIENCE OF PAINTING A GREENWOOD STOOL

The concept for this piece is based on Irish physicist's John Stewart Bell's "Inequality experiments". Bell's experiments explored Einstein's dilemma of how his theory of relativity does not completely describe quantum mechanics. Bell's Theorem (1965) is important in how we see and perceive all about us — "reality is somehow dependent upon how we observe it".

The treatment of the seat of this stool is in the form of a grid incised by a disc cutter. The acrylic paint is applied with a credit card cut up into various widths to work the surface texture.

Look at this stool and question how you observe it.

Jim Turner, Ceramic Artist, Rossmore Pottery, Clonakilty, Co Cork

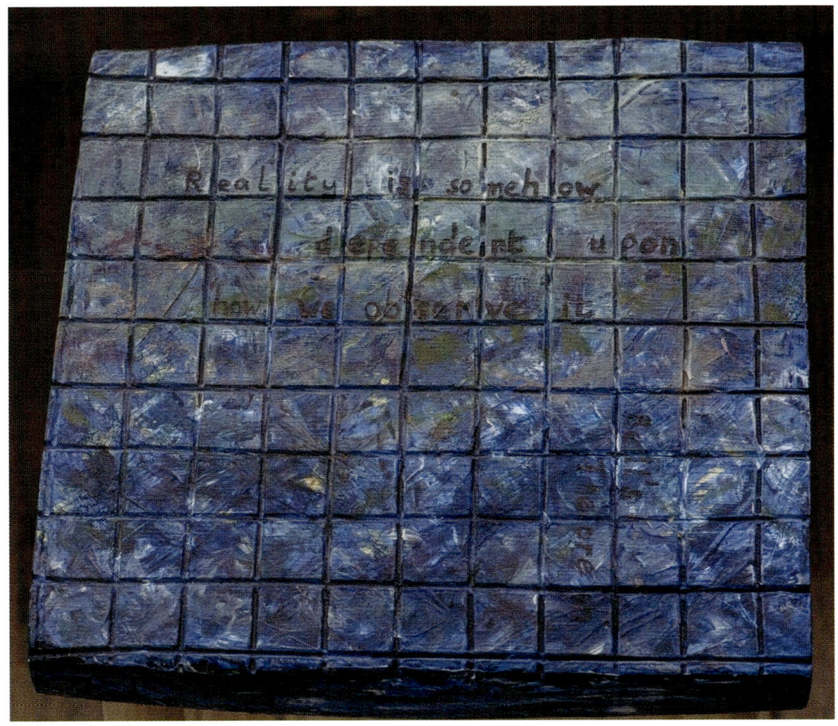

left and above: Kitchen stool — surface decoration by Jim Turner

Removing the bark, sanding and polishing

The basic finish for green wood stools is simply to leave the bark on. As long as you have not damaged the bark in the making process it will stay in place. Hazel bark behaves like a skin and does not easily separate from the wood. Those who find the bark somewhat rough and abrasive might choose to lightly sand it down and polish it.

If you plan to paint your stool or wish to have a stripped wood finish, remove the bark using either a whittling knife or drawknife as detailed in *Chapter Five — Tools and Techniques*.

You will have to spend some time sanding the hazel until it feels really smooth. If you begin using coarse sandpaper (grit 80) and work down through medium and fine papers (grit 240), eventually the finish will be super smooth and feel like polished bone.

Once your surface feels like this, you are ready to either apply the first coat of paint or Liberon oil or clear Briwax. My preference is for Briwax as it gives a mellow sheen once the surface has been buffed up but the problem is it marks if it gets wet or if a drink is put down on it. Liberon finishing oil is a safer alternative, once dry it can be wiped with a wet cloth and drinks can be put on it with no damage to the surface.

Painting

If you choose the painting option, while working on the frame, turn the stool upside down and keep turning it as you go. It is surprisingly easy to miss small areas if you approach from just one direction.

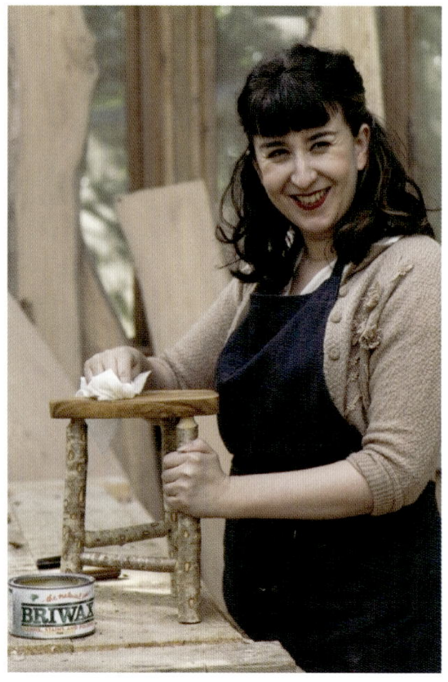
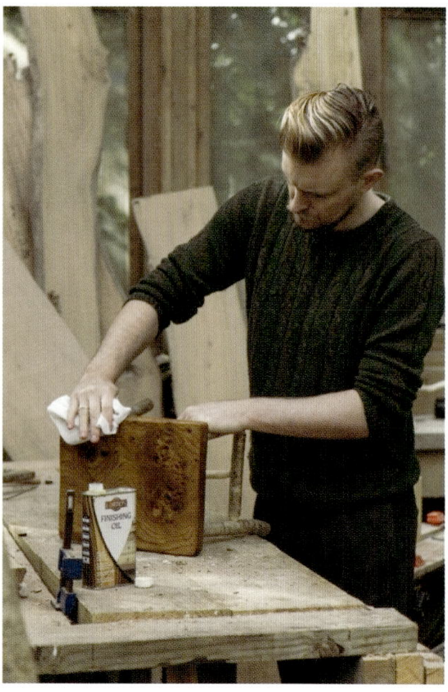

Rosa applies clear Briwax finish and Stephen applies Liberon finishing oil

If you choose not to paint or strip off the bark, there are other decorative effects which can be achieved by removing parts of the bark using a whittling knife or microplanes with a variety of profiles.

Decorative effects

- Spotty animal pelt effect

- Spirals using the microplane

- Stool with 'socks'

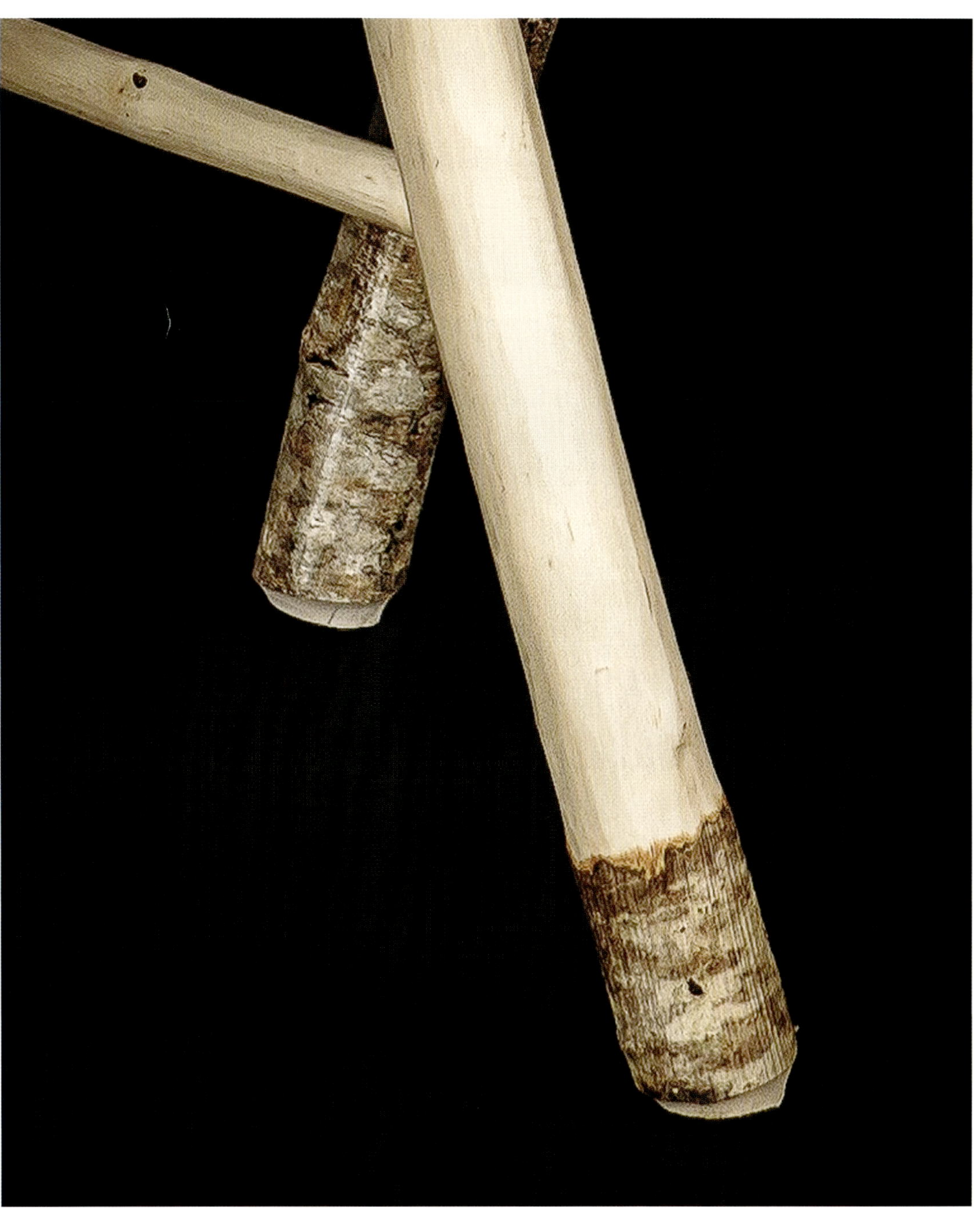

- Sanding and polishing the bark

- Stripping off part of the bark and leaving a shape on the surface

There are likely to be many more ingenious methods for surface finishing green wood stools but I have not seen them yet!

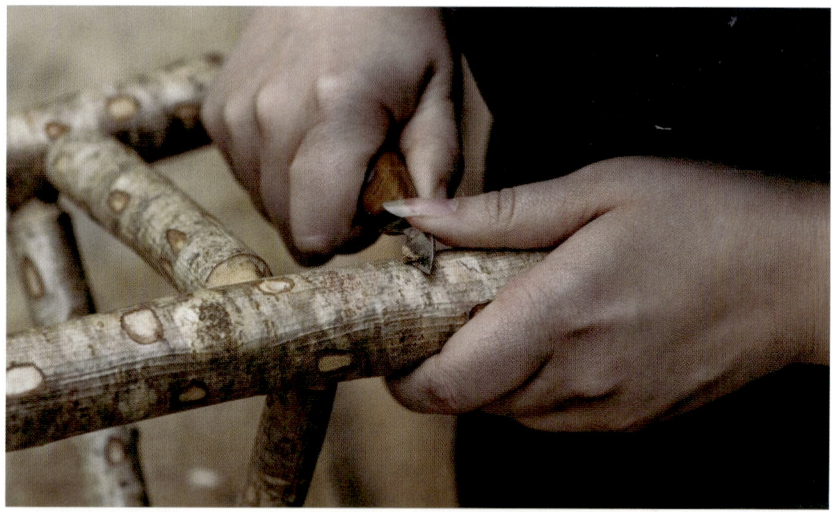

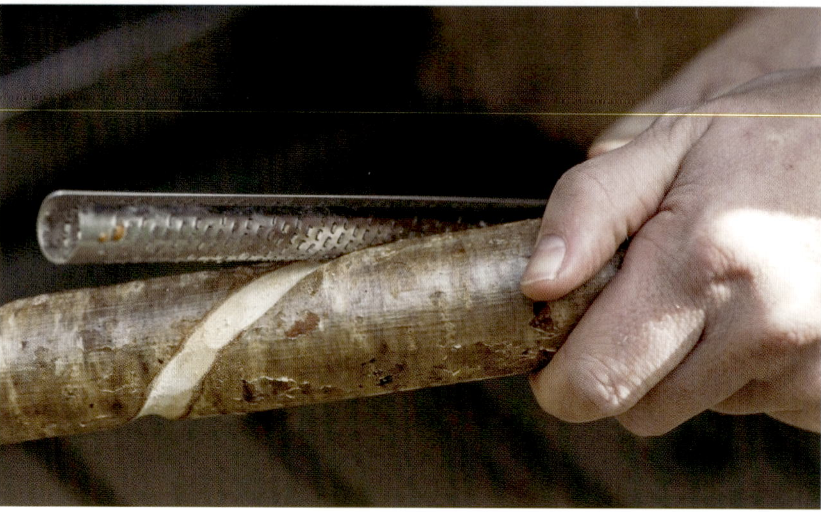

above: detail decorative bark finish
following page: Removing some of the
bark leaving a shape on the surface,
design by Irene Paradisi
page 122: Tall kitchen stool,
surface decorated by Pat Connor

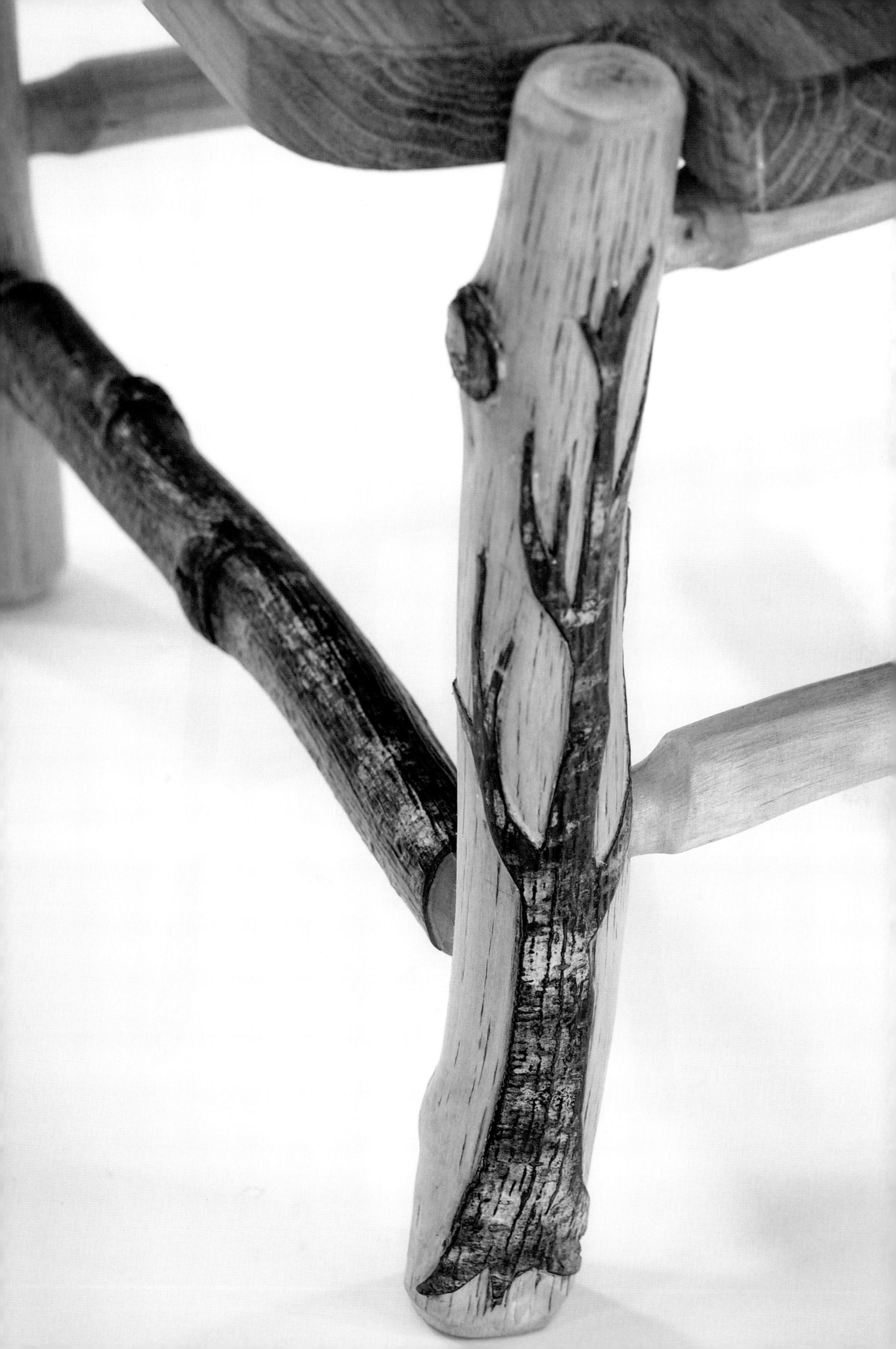

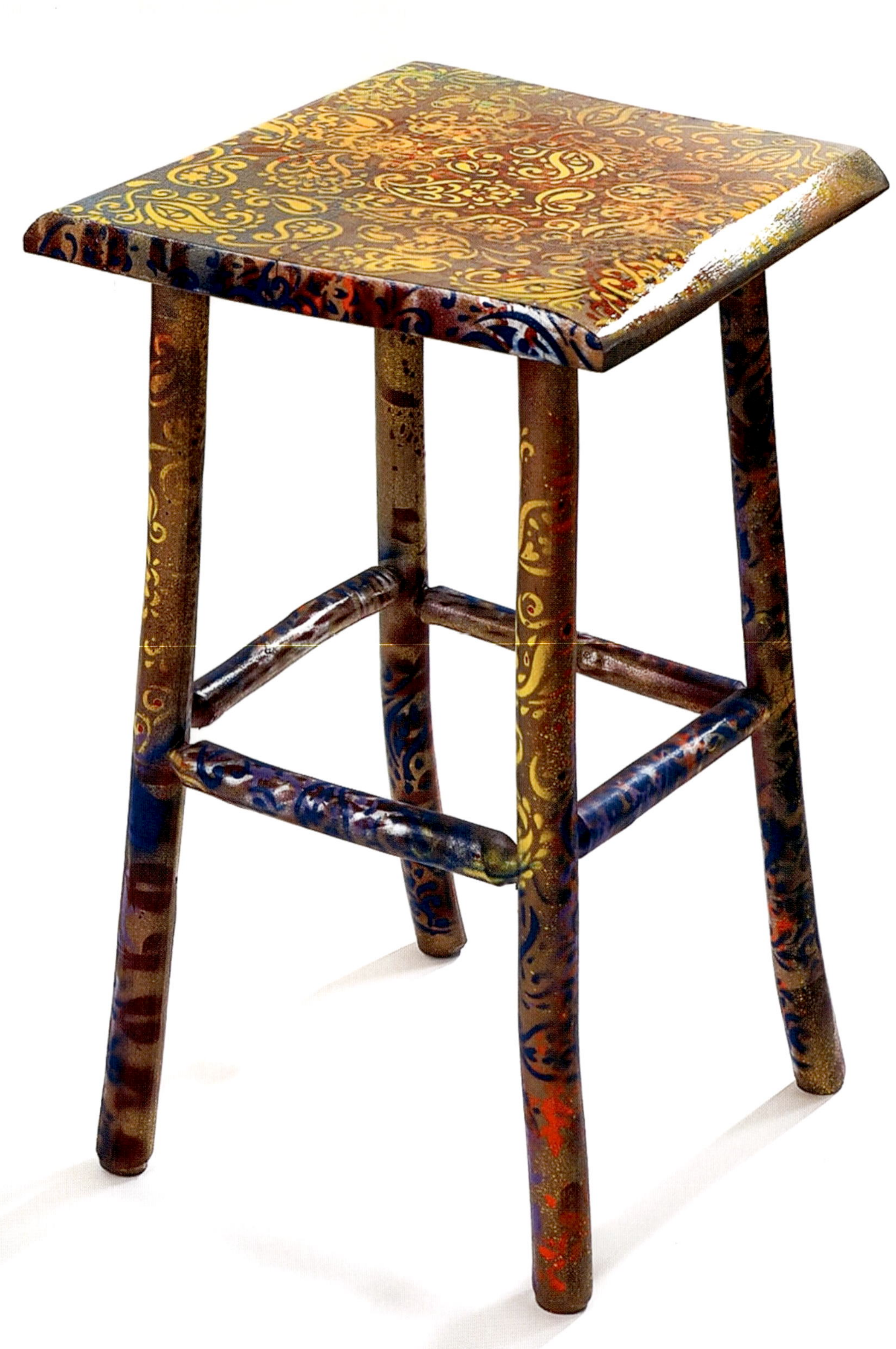

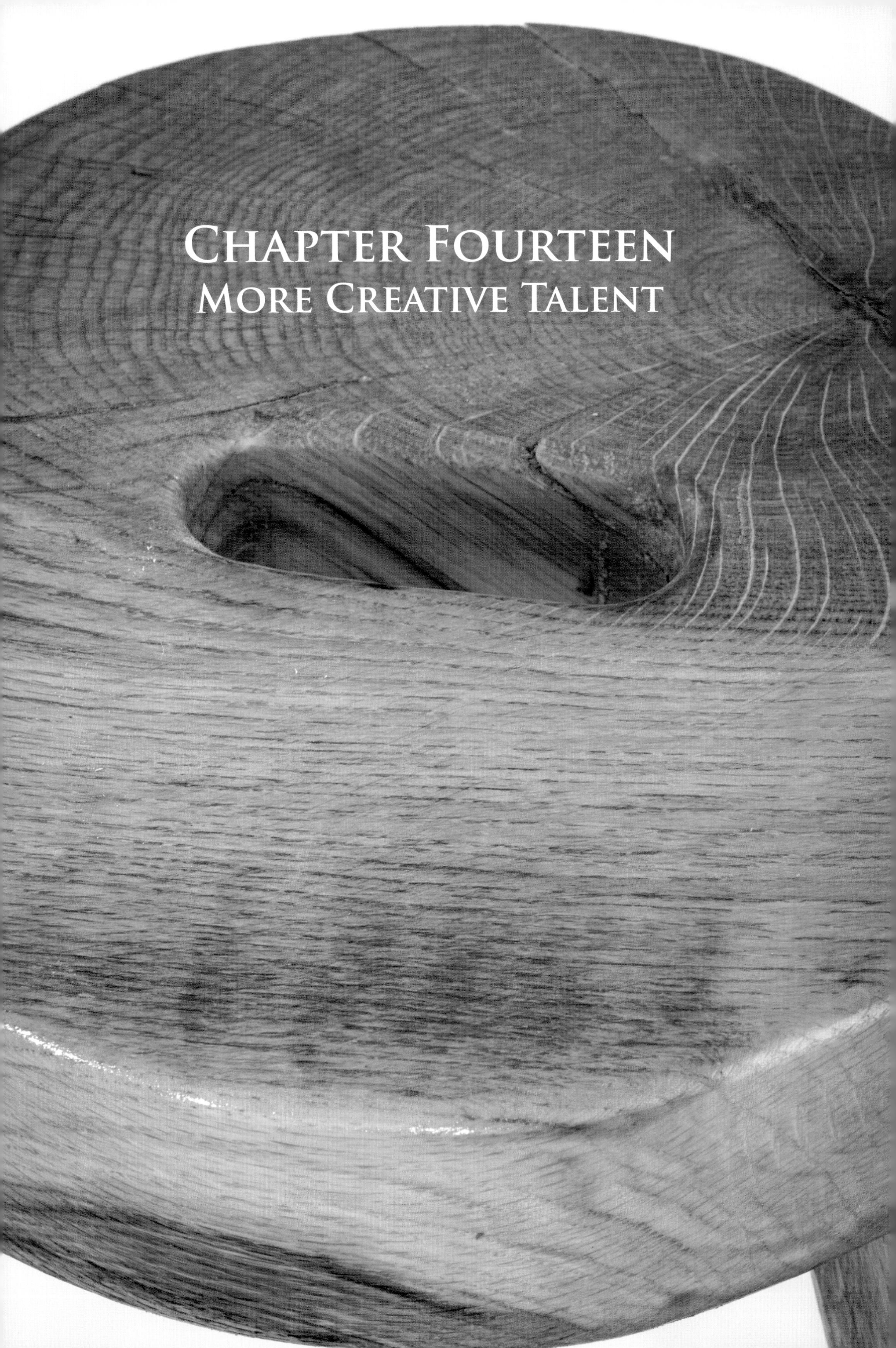
CHAPTER FOURTEEN
MORE CREATIVE TALENT

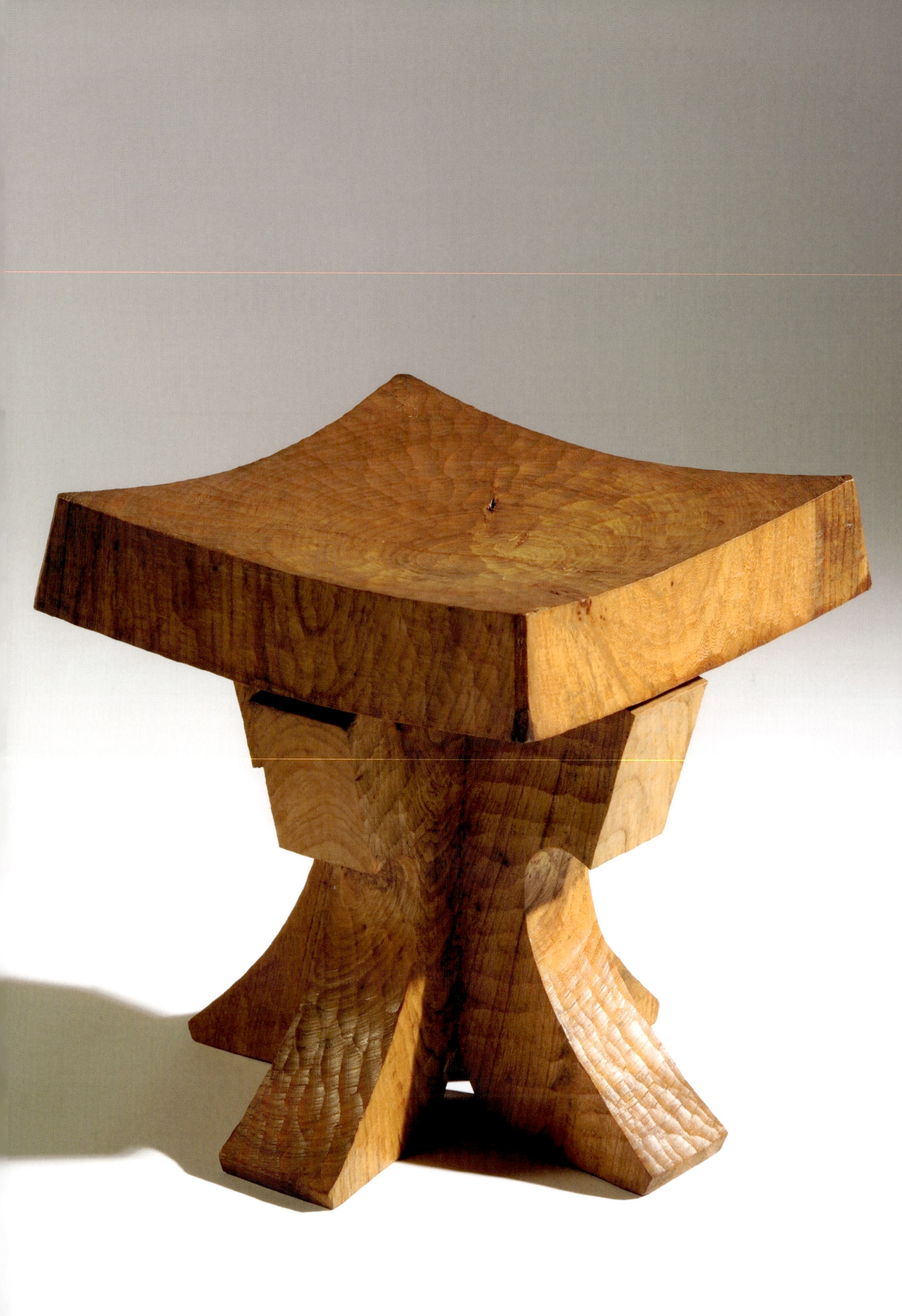

MORE CREATIVE TALENT

There is a vast number of creative people in this country, working away in their studios designing and making chairs and stools using native timber. I was curious to discover how other makers go about their process, so I decided to invite four stool makers to contribute three designs each to the book. In addition to images, they have each written briefly on how they approach stool making and given some information about their inspiration and their techniques. I find it an interesting addition, partly because it gives a context to my work and because it demonstrates the wide range of stool design happening in Ireland today.

Here Thomas Kay, James Carroll, Charlie Huffer and Eamon Quinn describe their background and their particular approach, in their own words.

Thomas Kay

The practice of carving wood is very time-consuming. It requires an accurate awareness of the finished object within the trunk and a careful, gradual approach. Material once removed cannot be replaced. Continuous work on paper and models usually accompanies this process. My preferred tools are chainsaws or a hammer and chisel.

East stool square

This is an early piece which aimed to combine West African tradition with the elegance associated with eastern art and architecture.

It is carved with a hammer and chisel from a single piece of elm.

Curves & loops

This is a series of sculpted chairs and stools

It crosses the borders of sculpture and functionality and couples an archaic production method with playful design.

left: East stool square, Height 33 cm

Each chair and stool is carved by hand out of a large spalted elm tree trunk. This is a slow process.

The two stools chart the progression from arc to spiral and are created with ecological considerations throughout: from sourcing locally grown trees, a low-tech manufacturing process, to using natural finishes.

The irregular chain-marks create a subtly textured, sensual surface that gently contrasts the sleek, streamlined shapes.

The knots, cracks and the seamless grain render each piece a living and unique functional sculpture.

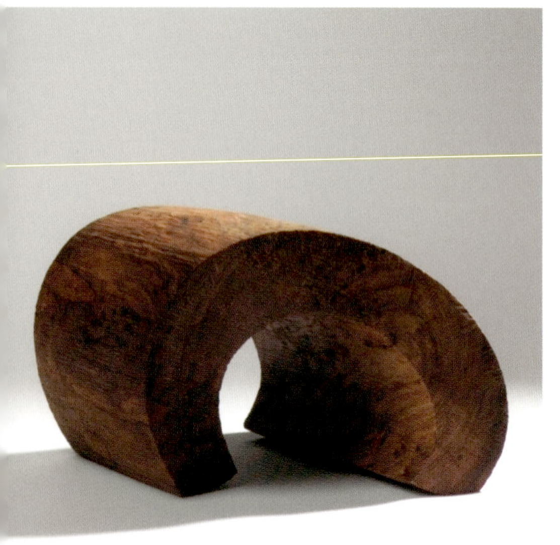

below:
Curves & loops, curl 2
Size: 45 / 35 / 28 cm

right:
Curves & loops, curl 4
Size: 48 / 35 / 28 cm

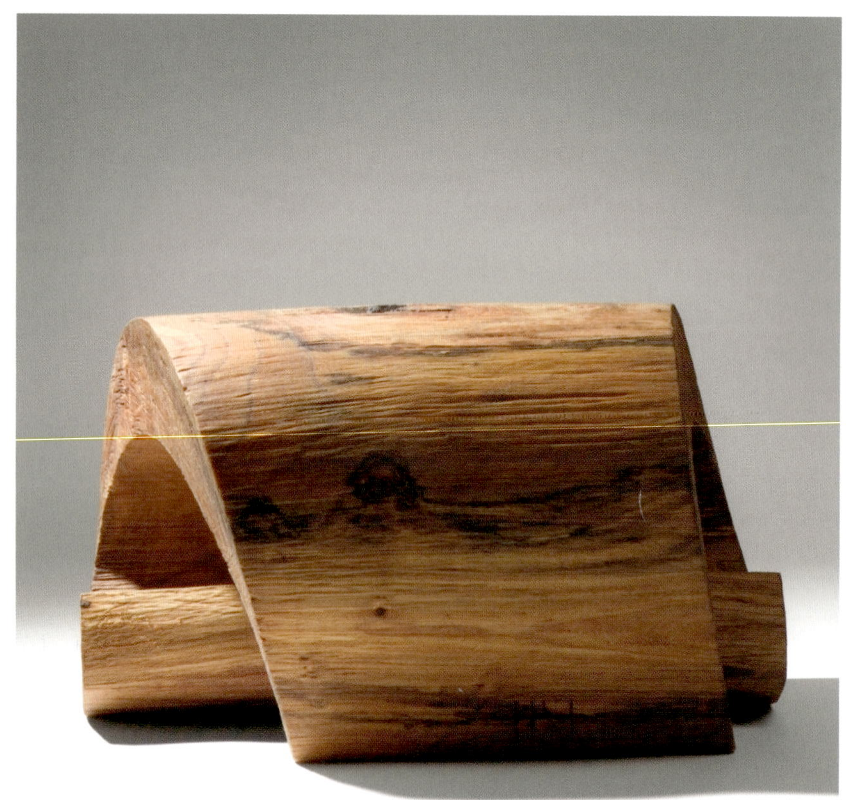

JAMES CARROLL

This little stool is as easy and simple as I could manage. I split a green ash log in half and finished the inside surface with just an axe and drawknife.

I love the quality of a surface finished with an edge tool as opposed to a sanded finish. It's very smooth without necessarily being very flat. I had intended to use the other half of the log to make three cleft legs but changed my mind halfway through. Instead, I used a branch from the same tree for the legs. I then dried and tenoned the legs into the base.

ELM ENTRY STOOL

In the late 80s, fifty golden elm trees landed in Ireland. These were resistant to the Dutch elm disease that decimated elm in Ireland and around the world. One of the plants was given to us by a family friend and was planted at around the time I started to get interested in working with wood.

The tree grew well but part of it fell down last Christmas and it was just large enough to mill into useable planks. On revealing the beautiful grain, I decided to make a small batch of stools and benches

Elm Entry Stool

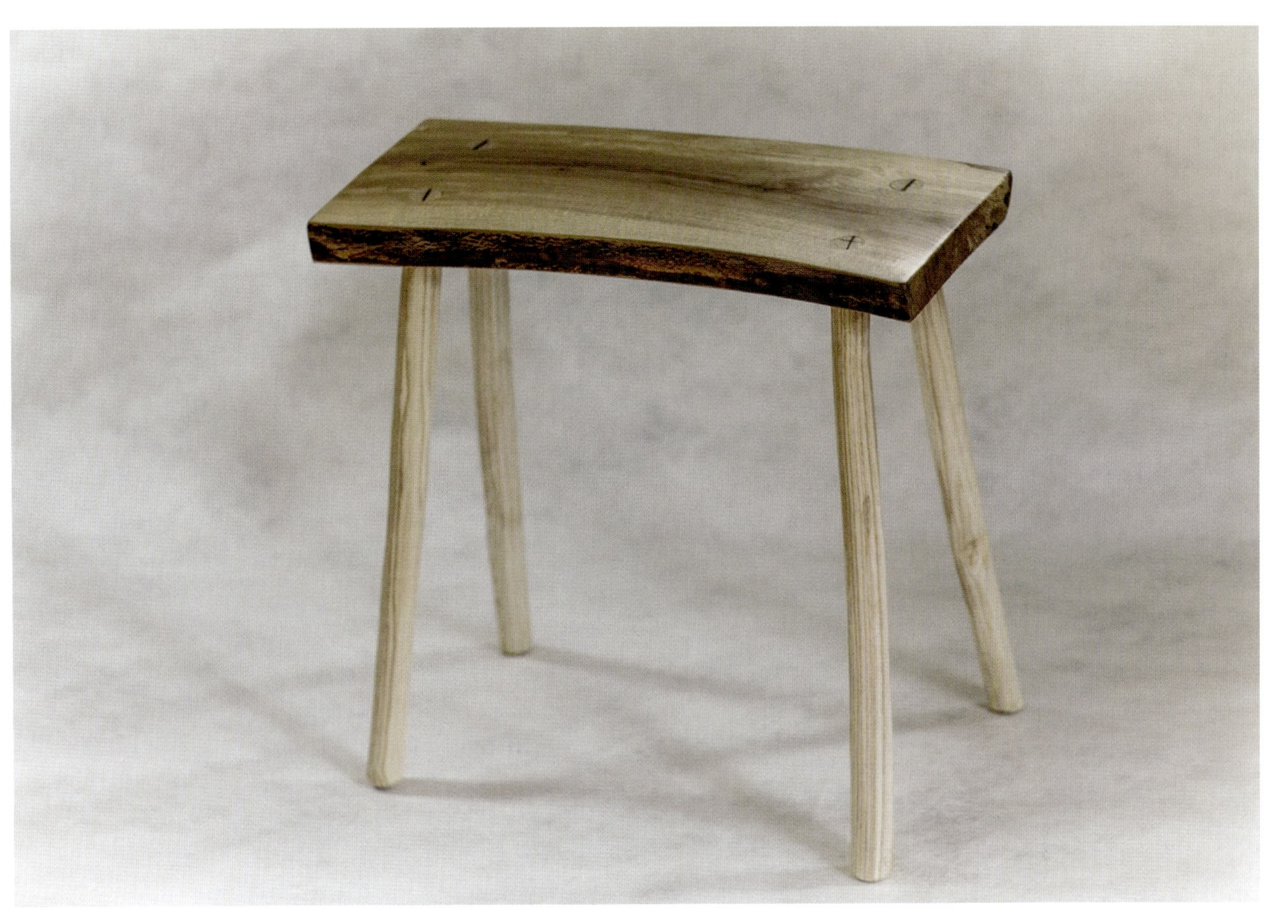

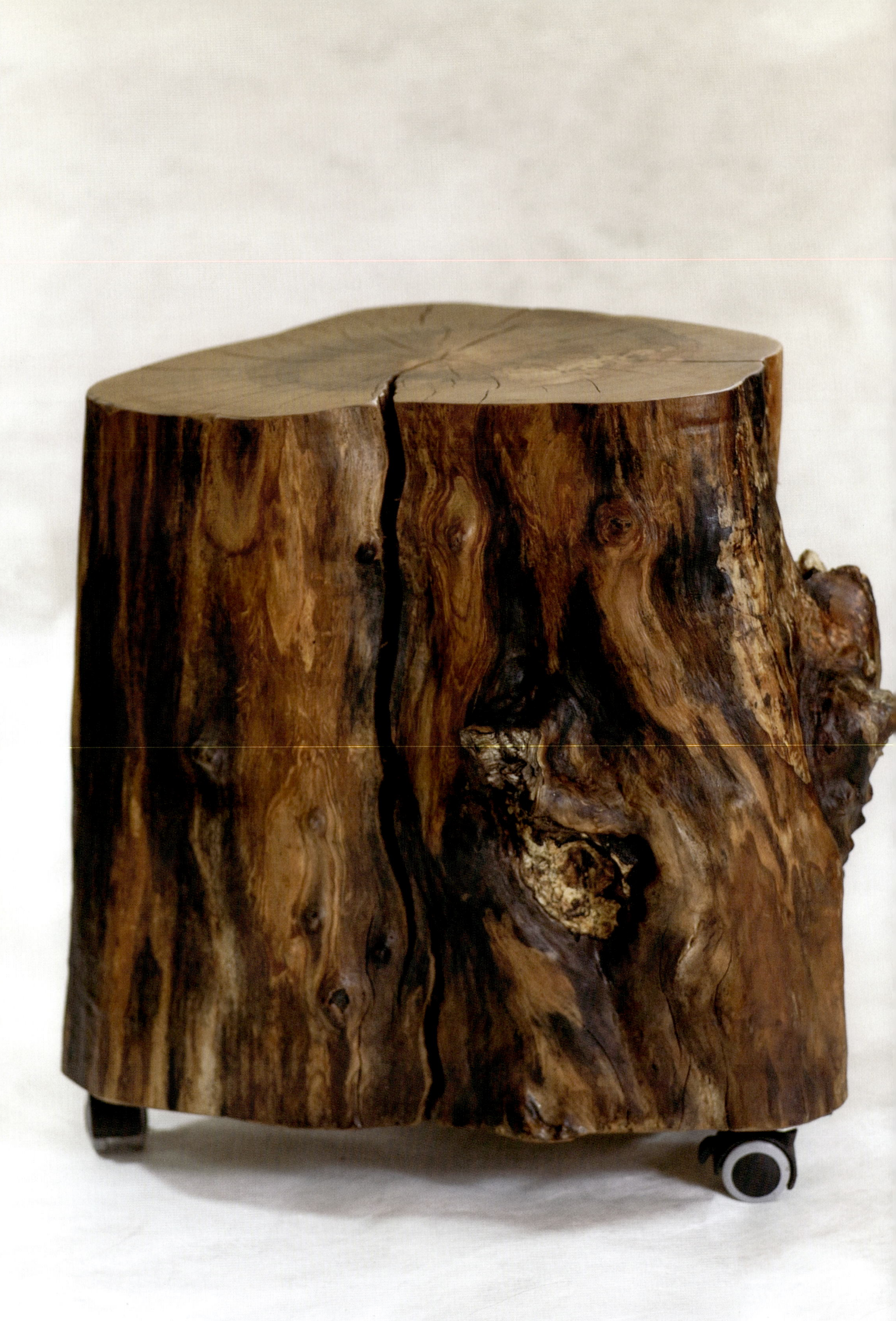

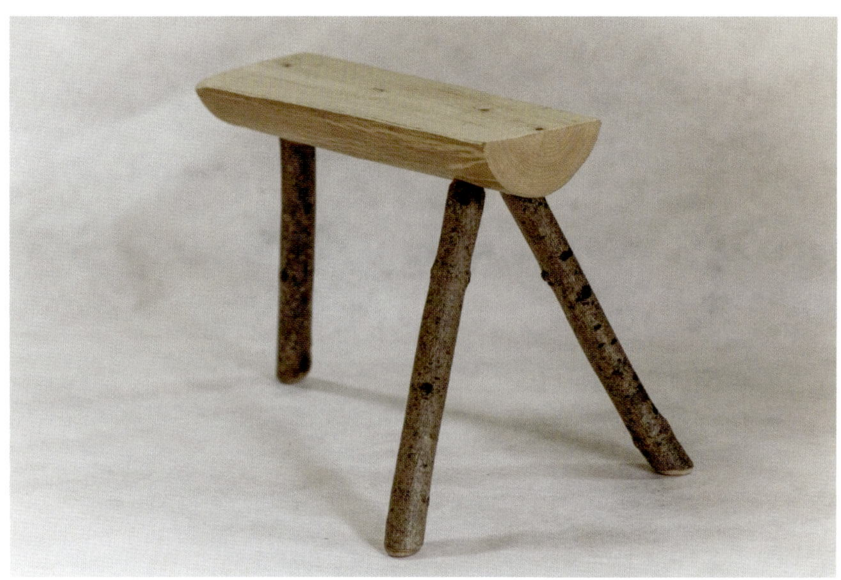

from the log. It was quite a short turn-around. I finished the top with a gouge to give a dappled texture and secured the ash legs with a walnut, wedged-through tenon.

SCEACH STOOL

Hawthorn (sceach as it is known in Irish) is a ubiquitous plant in Irish hedgerows and deeply connected to the folklore and fauna around the country. However, it rarely grows to a large size. A really large one blew down in a hedge nearby and I had planned to mill it to hopefully reveal some unusual planks.

I scratched my head for a few days on how to move it as access was a problem. In the meantime a friendly person with a chainsaw had crosscut it to 'do me a favour'.

It seemed fitting to at least keep intact the rare and heavy, large pieces that were left. Merely cleaning up the sides and squaring, sanding and polishing the top, felt like sufficient intervention. The cracks will expand and contract a little with the relative humidity of its environment. But that's ok.

The wheels? They are just to solve any future transport issues.

left: Sceach Stool, hawthorn

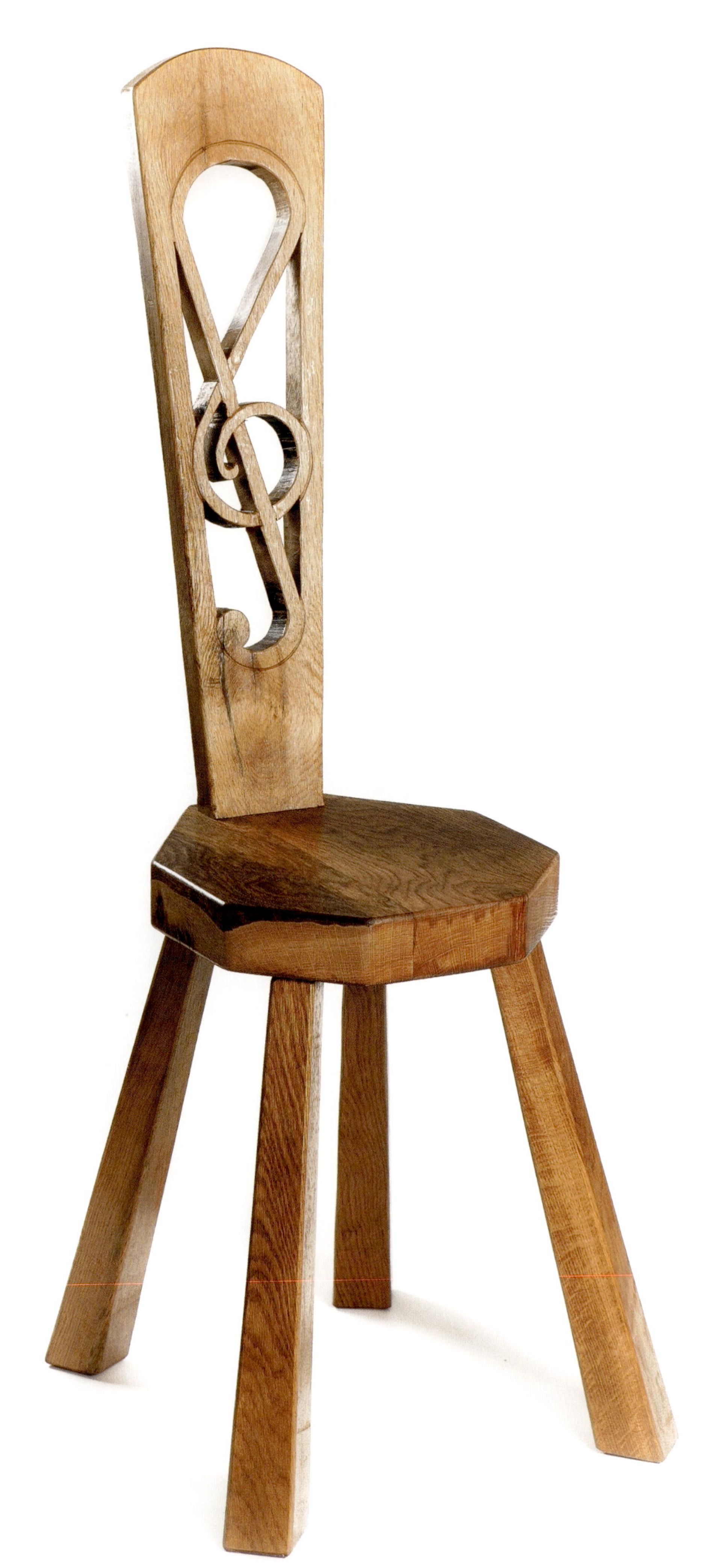

Charlie Huffer

I moved to Ireland 1996 and started making furniture in 2001. I am a self-confessed rock music freak and try to incorporate something musical into most pieces whenever possible, hence guitar-shaped stools and tables, or musical motifs cut or carved into stool backs. I am not averse to putting the odd violin or oboe in, if customer requests it.

I try to make each piece unique and sometimes personalize pieces if required such as carving names, mottos or messages.

I only use locally sourced hardwoods, usually from the sustainable woodland at Manch, Co Cork although it's amazing what I am offered from boatyards, farmers' barns and people's garages.

High-back stool

The high-back stool is made of Irish oak, the design is loosely based on the Welsh spinning stool. The main component pieces are cut by machine and the design in the back is carefully cut by a jigsaw. Carving chisels are used to create the over and under effect, then hand sanded to achieve a smooth finish.

Traditional milking stool

The traditional milking stool is made of elm and oak, the seat being elm. The legs are turned on the lathe to fit snugly into the three holes that are drilled at 14 degrees to give the stool stability on uneven floors. This design has been tried and tested for many hundreds of years.

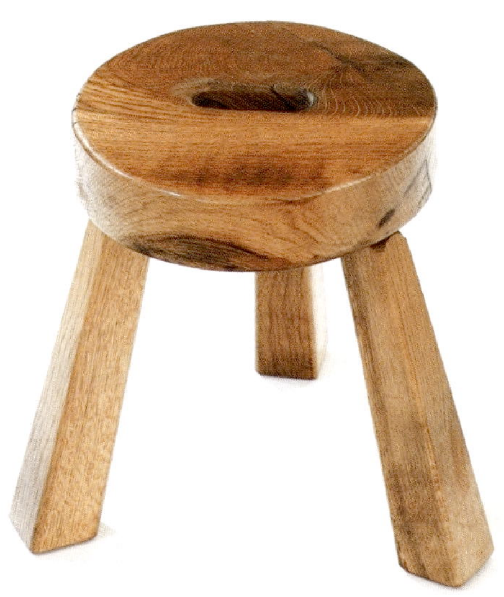

far left: High back stool, oak
left: Traditional milking stool, oak and elm

The quirky guitar-shaped stool, is made using a Fender Jaguar guitar as a rough template, the seat is elm and the legs are oak. Most guitars shapes can be used to make interesting stools or even small tables. On this design, I have set the legs at the extremes of the shape to give stability and functionality.

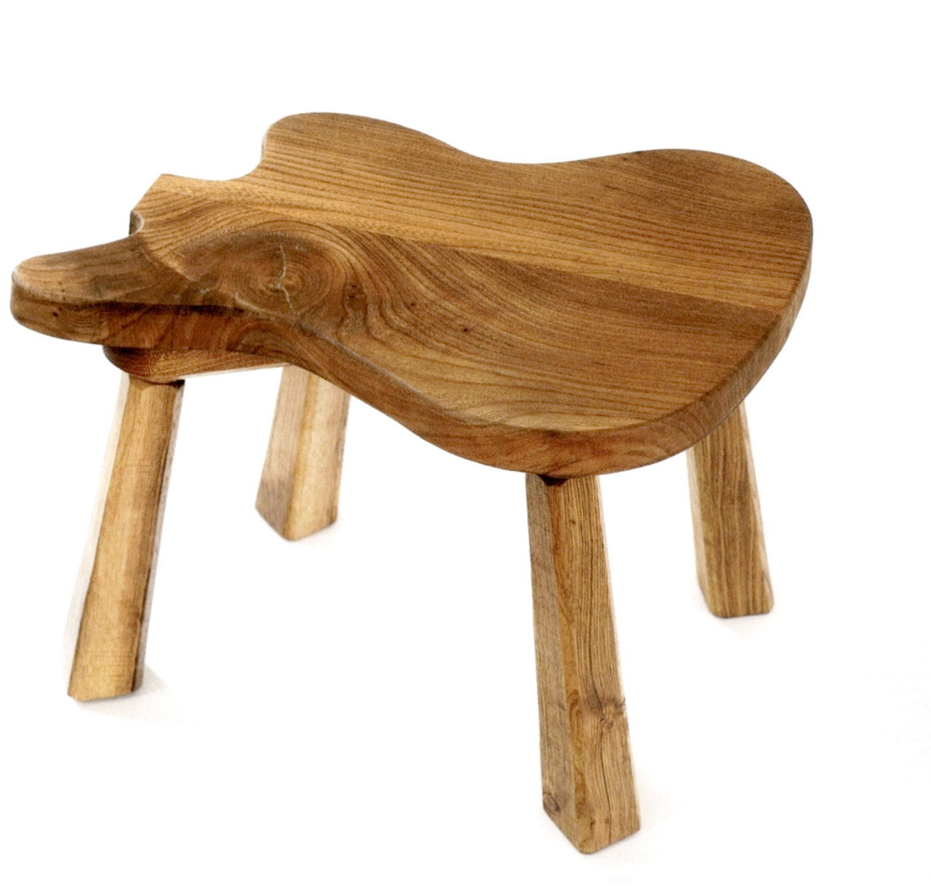

Guitar shaped stool, elm and oak

EAMON QUINN

The first stool I made was for my daughter. As I knew it was going to be used as a standing stool as much as a seat it had to be stable. That same stool has found a permanent place in our living room and despite its small size is probably the most used piece of furniture in the room. It is certainly the most versatile.

I still make these stools in small batches of four or five, each time varying them slightly, sometimes longer sometimes shorter or with a shelf under the seat.

Oak stool

This is a longer version of the first stool that I made. It is made in oak and held together by mortice and tenon joinery which is both decorative and strong. The sides are splayed and extend beyond the top making it completely stable.

Crotch oak stool

Some time ago I was in my local sawmill and the owner handed me this beautiful piece of crotch oak. This is where the trunk of the tree divides or branches resulting in some very interesting grain patterns. It had been knocking about my shed since then waiting for the right opportunity. The simplest of treatments along the lines of a Shaker peg-leg stool and a few dovetail keys seemed the best way to highlight the beautiful figure in this piece of wood.

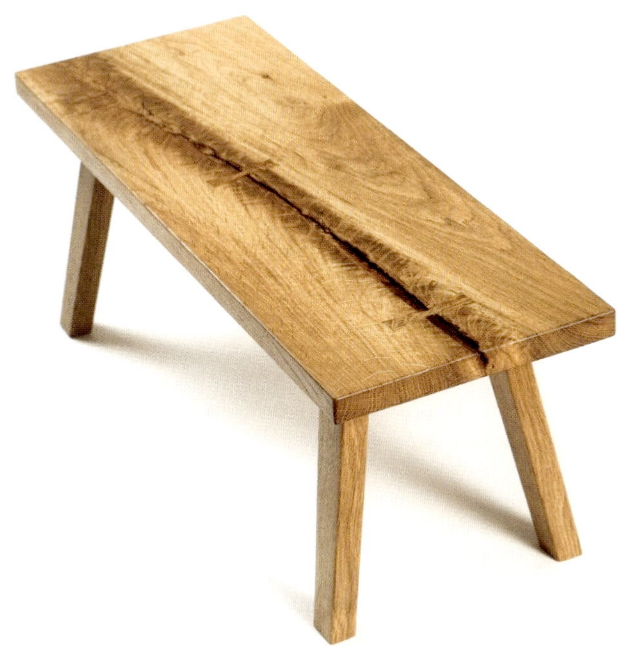

Crotch oak stool

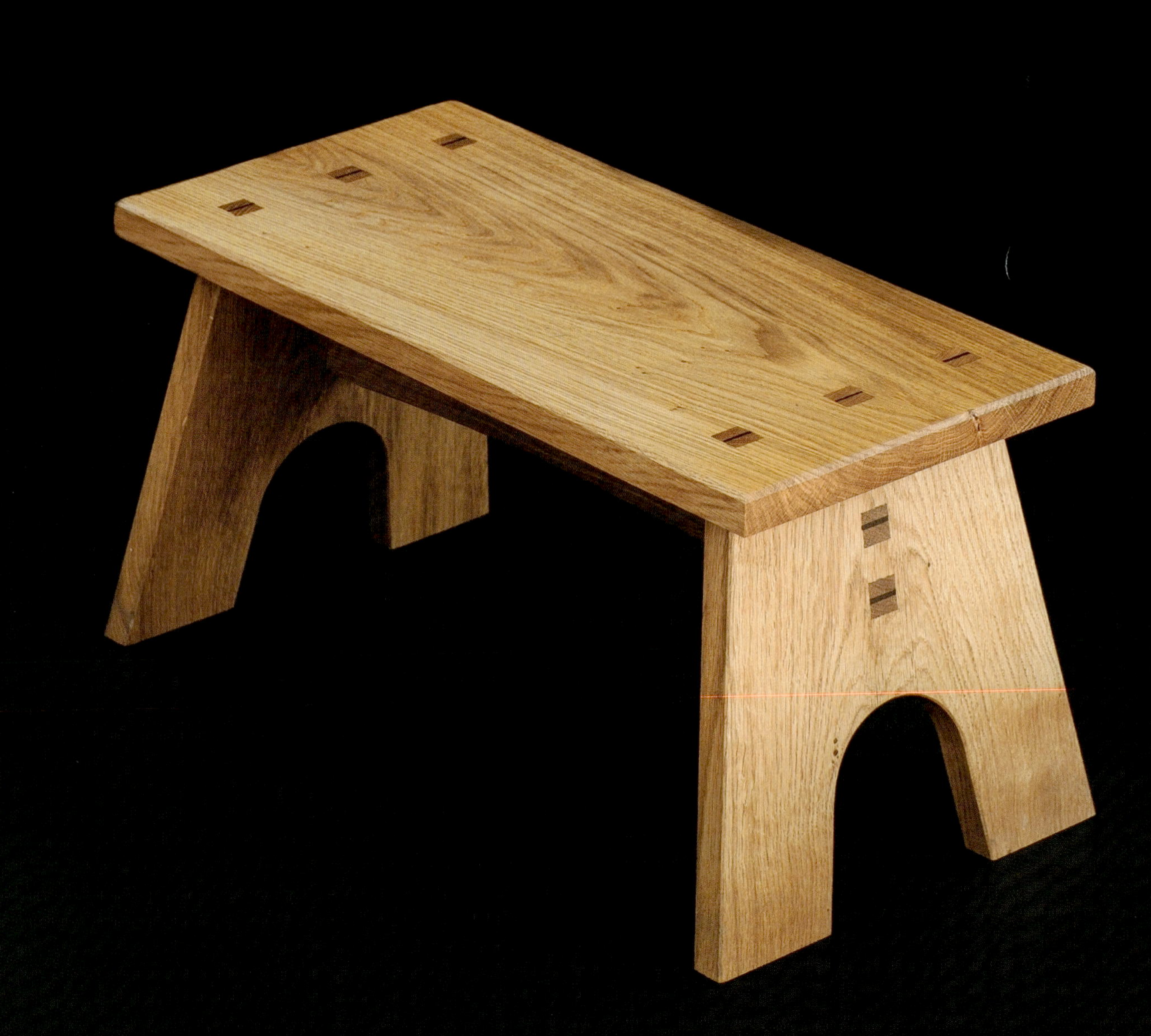

Ash trees, depending on their age and the soil in which they grow, sometimes develop dark and varied coloring in the centre of the log. This is commonly known as olive ash. One of the joys of woodworking is to play around with the patterns in the wood. The olive pattern in this piece of ash seems to flow over the edge of the stool.

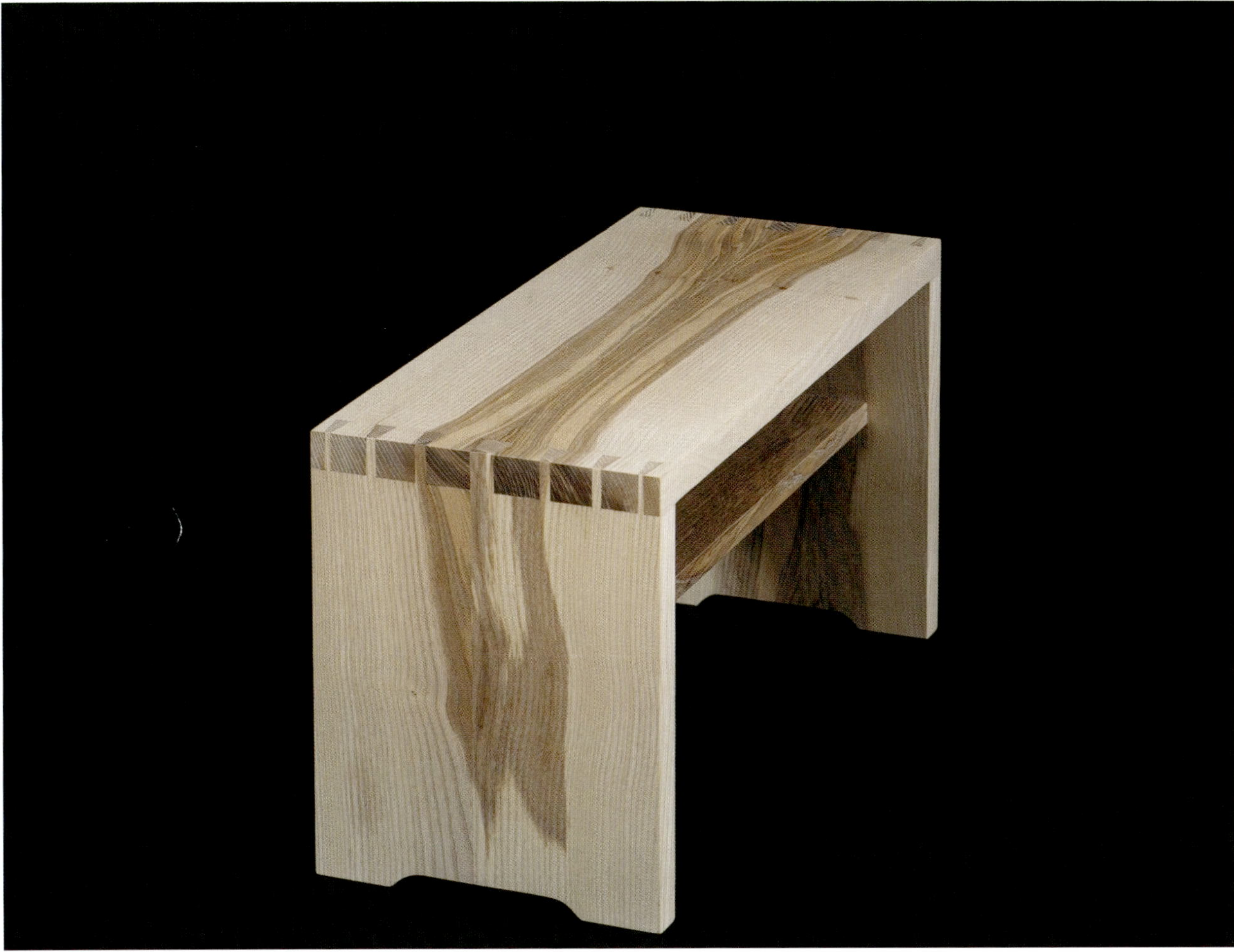

left: Oak stool
above: Olive ash stool with dovetail joinery

135

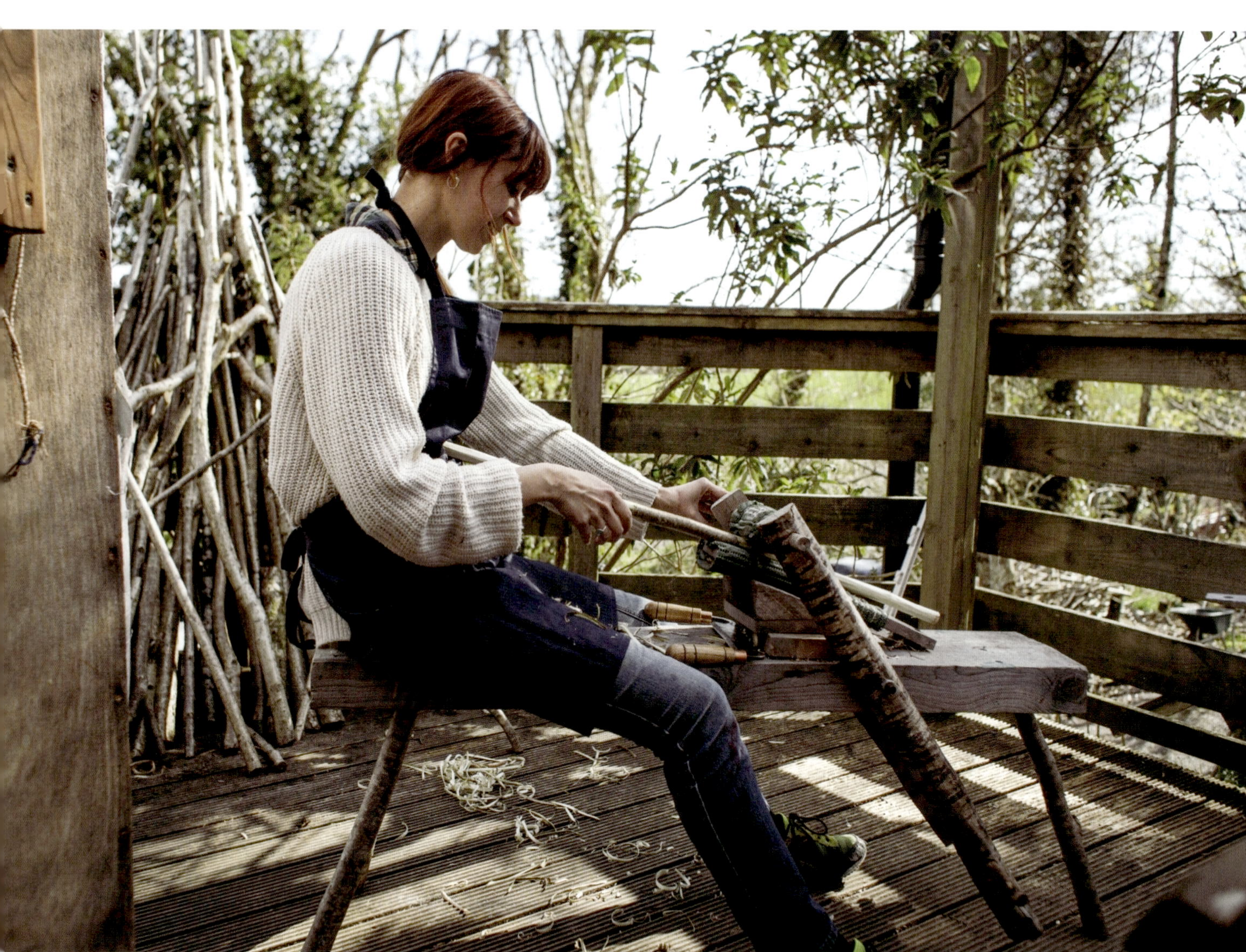

Ana using the shaving horse

CHAPTER FIFTEEN
CONCLUSIONS

When I began planning this book, I thought I was going to write something like *Tao and The Art of Green Wood Chair Making* but somehow the 'stools' thing kept cropping up and would not be ignored. It soon became clear that *Green Wood Stools* was a more realistic project and although my focus changed, I continue to find that Taoist theory runs parallel with many of my green wood observations and experiences.

According to the Taoists, yin and yang, light and shadow, useful and useless are all different aspects of the whole, and when we choose one side and disregard the other, we upset nature's balance. This philosophy informs every choice I make when green woodworking.

The search for harmony and balance influences my decisions, whether I am selecting suitable sticks, deciding on a finish, or choosing how to space the components, I take my time and trust my intuition. Despite my intent, the process is largely intuitive.

My purpose in writing this book is to share what I have learned and to show what is possible. I also hope to inspire others to have a go at making their own stools. The green wood approach is so accessible, people see it and immediately think "I could do that". It is gratifying to know that folk are working away in their back gardens, designing and making their own furniture because they have seen it in a book. They get it and believe they can do it too. That is empowerment!

Now, having reached the end of this process and looking back at what I have written, I wonder how this book differs from my first book *Green Wood Chairs*? What is new? What have I learned and discovered since 2009? The answers to those questions are so diverse that I decided to simply itemise them.

- Of all the activities that I undertake in life, I am at my best mentally, physically and spiritually when making stools and chairs. It is almost a meditation.

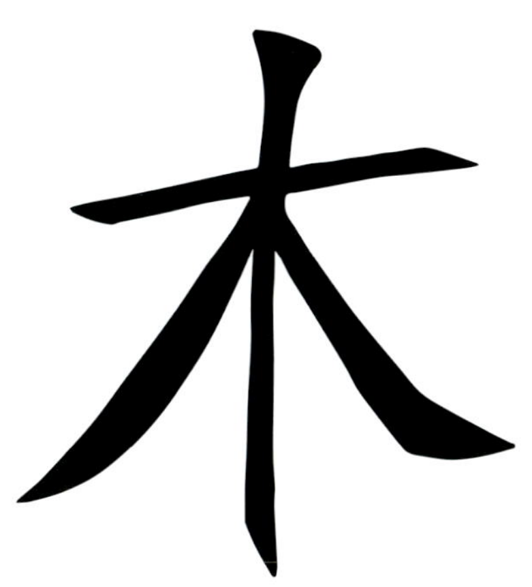

Chinese character for tree

Chinese character for hazel

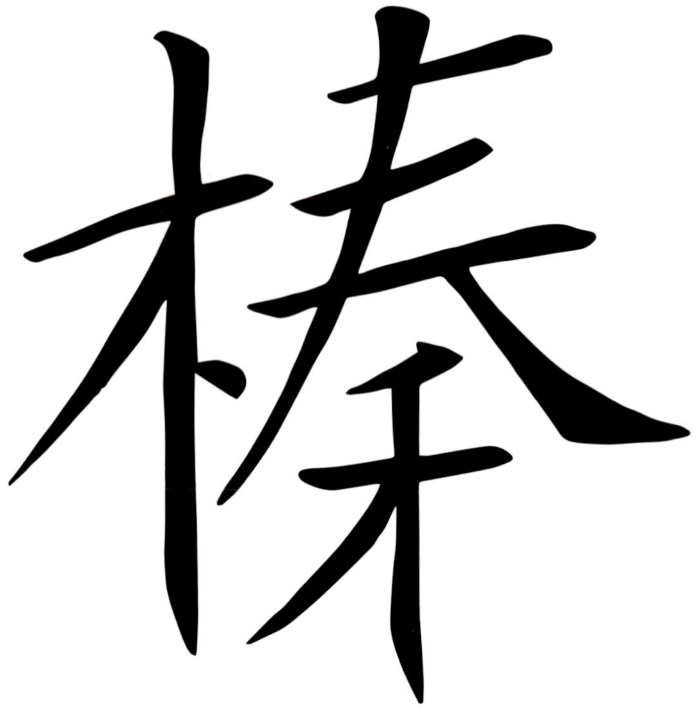

- 'The way' of the green wood chairmaker is a process which unites the energies of both the tree and the chairmaker, a relationship which combines spirit, vitality, knowledge and expertise.

- Green wood chair and stool making is a process of self-expression which absorbs all your attention and engages the subconscious mind. It is a calming and meditative activity, it could be said to have therapeutic or healing qualities.

- The making process is both collaboration and struggle, our energies combine. I often have to persuade components into place. When I push in one direction, the stick resists and pushes back. I can feel its energy and I work with it. That energy, or tension, is the force which holds green wood structures together and makes them strong.

- The selection of components is what defines the stool or chair and connects it to its maker. This is why everybody's work is different, even if they use the same design, dimensions and material. How or why we choose a particular stick is a mystery. I usually know exactly the stick I want and when I see it, I recognise it, it is as if the stick is beckoning me.

- Even when makers use the same construction techniques but use material from other trees such as blackthorn, sycamore or alder, they will make totally different stools — different person, different tree, different stools. Everyone makes a stool that reflects their personality!

* When I finish making a piece, whether it is a chair or a stool, I walk away from it, then turn round and look at it anew. This is the reveal, the moment where I see, for the first time, what I have made. I am never sure exactly what to expect, it is always a surprise. I turn it round and step away again until I have viewed it from all sides.

* When I view a finished piece, I am not looking at the sticks it is made of but the spaces between the sticks. I judge the success of the piece by the shape and size of its spaces.

* I have discovered new uses for Veritas tenon cutters — it is a revelation to discover they can be employed to make tenons at angles. Until now, I endeavoured to make tenons as straight as possible but I discovered their versatility quite by accident.

* Stools with splayed legs are more attractive and more stable than stools with straight legs.

* It is possible to drill mortices in the stool top at 90 degrees, splay the legs out and keep them in position by using longer rails. You do not have to drill mortice holes at angles!

* The use of sheepskin and fabric not only adds colour and texture to seating but transforms its appearance and introduces a new dynamic. Natural materials complement each other.

* Stools are incredibly versatile pieces of furniture with a vast number of uses.

* Making green wood stools makes people smile.

Making things by hand, using natural materials is a great pleasure and supremely satisfying.

A part of us goes into everything we make, the stools and chairs I make are imbued with my spirit. It can't be helped, that is the way.

These days, our homes are filled with mass-produced, characterless furniture made from artificial, sometimes toxic materials. We do not really know what the things that surround us are made of or where they were made and we certainly do not know who made them!

Green wood stools very clearly bear the marks of the human hand. There may be traces left by the drawknife, perhaps someone chose to keep the moss and lichen in place, others may have left twigs and knots protruding, but whatever the design, it is clear that that stool was made by a particular person, using particular sticks for a particular purpose.

Surrounding ourselves with items we have made by hand from wood, sheepskin, wool and other natural materials, lifts our spirits and brings us joy. Using the things we have made, makes us proud and happy.

It is a simple thing to do — make a chair, make a stool — be happy!

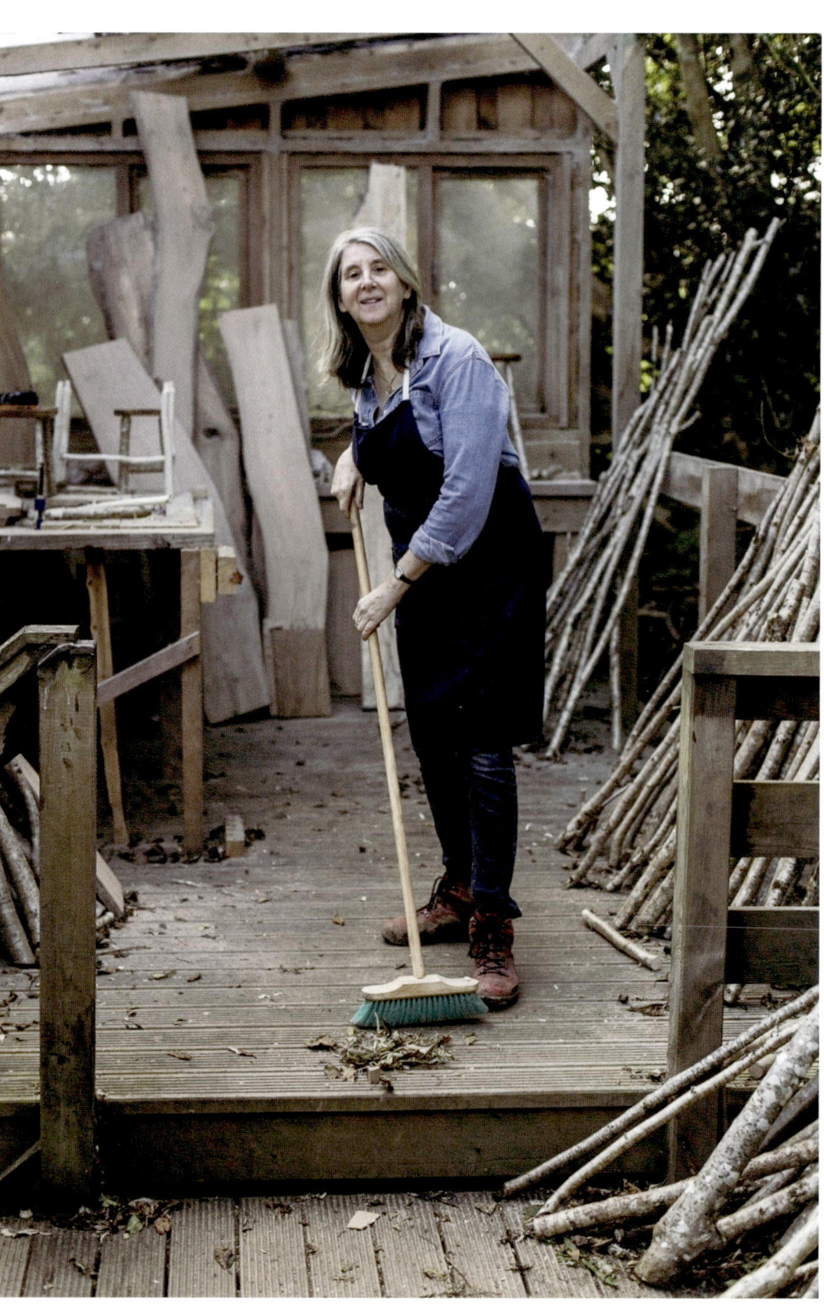

APPENDIX

Contact details for artists and craftspeople

Thomas Kay
Kay Art Design
Coomkeen, Durrus,
Bntry, Co.Cork
Ireland

phone/fax: +353 (0)27 - 61048
thomas@kayartdesign.com
www.kayartdesign.com

James Carroll
Chapel Lane
Glenealy
Co Wicklow

mob: +353 (0)86 846 4515
James@stickman.ie
www.stickman.ie

Charlie of Charlie's Chairs
Charlie Huffer:
a.k.a. Charlie's Chairs can be found at his stall on Skibbeeen Market
every Saturday

mob +353 (0)85 198 8118 email:
zumazumasmith3@gmail.com

Eamon Quinn
Kilcoe
Skibbereen
Co Cork

mob. +353 (0)87 299 8218
phone +353 (0)28 38946

Chapter 4
Benefits of walking in woods
(www.lifehack.org /7 amazing health benefits of a walk in the woods)

Chapter 6
Rush suppliers
www.seatweavingsupplies.com

Chapter 13
Contact details of local artists

Jim Turner
Rossmore Pottery, Rossmore, Clonakilty, Co Cork

phone +353 (0)23 883 8875
potterywithjim@gmail.com

Etain Hickey
Rossmore Pottery, Rossmore, Clonakilty, Co Cork

phone +353 (0)23 883 8875
etainhickey@eircom.net

Pat Connor
Cooradarrigan, Schull, Co Cork

phone +353 (0)28 28068
patconnorschull@gmail.com

Upholstery suppliers

Heritage Upholstery Scunthorpe
info@heritageupholsterysupplies.co.uk

BIBLIOGRAPHY

Coaldrake, William H.1995. *The Way of the Carpenter: Tools and Japanese Architecture* Weatherhill Inc., 1st edition

Eisenhauer, Paul D. 2010. *Wharton Esherick Studio & Collection* Schiffer Publishing, 1st edition

Hill, Jack. 1995. *Country Woodworker* Mitchell Beazley, Executive Editor Judith More, 1st edition

Kinmonth, Claudia. 1995. *Irish County Furniture 1700-1950* Yale University Press, 1st edition

Memory Paterson, Jacqueline. 1996. *Tree Wisdom: The definitive guidebook to the myth, folklore and healing power of Trees* Thorsons, 1st edition

Nakashima, George. 1988. *The Soul of a Tree: A Master Woodworkers Reflections* Kodansha International Ltd., 1st paperback edition

Penn, Robert. 2015. *The Man who made things out of Trees* Particular Books, 1st edition

Rieman, Timothy D. and Burks, Jean M. 1993. *Complete Book of Shaker Furniture* Harry N Abrams Inc., 1st edition